THE POST-CRISIS IRISH VOTER

Manchester University Press

The post-crisis Irish voter

Voting behaviour in the Irish 2016 general election

*Edited by Michael Marsh, David M. Farrell
and Theresa Reidy*

MANCHESTER UNIVERSITY PRESS

Published by Manchester University Press
Altrincham Street, Manchester M1 7JA
www.manchesteruniversitypress.co.uk

British Library Cataloguing-in-Publication Data
A catalogue record for this book is available from the British Library

Library of Congress Cataloging-in-Publication Data applied for

ISBN 978 1 5261 2264 3 hardback

First published 2018

Typeset by
Deanta Global Publishing Services, Dublin, Ireland
Printed in Great Britain
by TJ International Ltd, Padstow

Contents

List of figures and tables

Figures

Tables

Appendix tables

Notes on contributors

David Barrett is Researcher at the Geary Institute in University College Dublin. He undertook his PhD research at Trinity College Dublin, where he examined infighting within political parties. He has a long-standing interest in political parties, electoral behaviour and public opinion and has written on Irish and Greek politics.

Rory Costello is Lecturer in Politics at the University of Limerick. His research focuses on EU politics, Irish politics, political parties and democratic representation. He has (co)-authored articles in journals such as *Party Politics*, *West European Politics*, *Electoral Studies*, *Journal of European Public Policy*, *European Union Politics* and *American Journal of Political Science*.

Michael Courtney is Postdoctoral Researcher in the School of Law and Government at Dublin City University. He currently works on VOX-POL, a European Union Framework Programme 7 (FP7)-funded network of excellence, studying violent online political extremism. He has published on political parties in the *Journal of Legislative Studies* and *Irish Political Studies*, and will release a co-authored book on political communications in Irish elections with Manchester University Press in 2018 with Michael Breen, Iain McMenamin, Eoin O'Malley and Kevin Rafter.

Kevin Cunningham is Lecturer in Statistics at Dublin Institute of Technology. He has published a number of book chapters and peer-reviewed journal articles on public policy, political parties, elections and campaigns. Kevin has worked for a number of political parties in Ireland, the United Kingdom, Australia and France. He runs his own research company and his work has been published in all major Irish newspapers and broadcasters.

Johan A. Elkink is Associate Professor in Politics at the School of Politics and International Relations at University College Dublin. He specializes in quantitative methods in political science, particularly spatial econometrics and their applications in democratization and voting behaviour. He has co-authored reports on voting behaviour in the Irish referendums on the Lisbon Treaty and co-edited *The Act of Voting* (Routledge). His work has appeared in the *Journal of Politics, Comparative Political Studies, European Journal of Political Research* and *Electoral Studies*.

David M. Farrell, MRIA, is Head of Politics and International Relations at University College Dublin. A specialist in the study of representation, elections and parties, his most recent books include *Political Parties and Democratic Linkage* (co-authored, Oxford University Press, 2011) and *A Conservative Revolution? Electoral Change in Twenty-First Century Ireland* (co-edited, Oxford University Press, 2017). His current work is focused on constitutional deliberation, and in that capacity he is the research leader of the ongoing Irish Citizens' Assembly.

Michael Gallagher, MRIA, is Head of the Department of Political Science and Professor of Comparative Politics at Trinity College, University of Dublin. He is co-editor of *Politics in the Republic of Ireland* (6th edn, Abingdon, 2018), *Representative Government in Modern Europe* (5th edn, New York, 2011), *The Politics of Electoral Systems* (Oxford, 2008), *Days of Blue Loyalty: The Politics of Membership of the Fine Gael Party* (Dublin, 2002) and a number of books in the *How Ireland Voted* series. In 1989, he devised the least squares index, the standard measure of electoral system disproportionality.

John Garry is Professor of Political Behaviour in the School of History, Anthropology, Philosophy and Politics at Queen's University Belfast. He has published widely on the themes of elections, public opinion and parties. His latest book is *Consociation and Voting in Northern Ireland: Party Competition and Electoral Behaviour*, published in 2016 by University of Pennsylvania Press. He was also a co-author of the prize-winning book *The Irish Voter*, published in 2008 by Manchester University Press.

Michael Marsh, MRIA, is Emeritus Professor of Political Science at Trinity College Dublin. The author of a wide variety of articles on parties and electoral behaviour, he has co-edited each of the last five books in the *How Ireland Voted* series, and has been a principal investigator for the Irish National Election Study since its foundation. He was co-author of the first book arising out of those studies, *The Irish Voter* (Manchester, 2008), and co-edited the next one, *A Conservative Revolution?* (Oxford, 2017).

Gail McElroy is Professor in Political Science at Trinity College, Dublin. Recent published work explores party competition in the Republic of Ireland, voting behaviour in preferential voting systems and political group cohesion in the European Parliament.

Eoin O'Malley is Associate Professor at the School of Law and Government, Dublin City University. His research interests broadly relate to Irish politics including cabinet government, policy-making and leadership. He is author of over forty peer-reviewed publications, and co-editor of *One Party Dominance: Fianna Fáil and Irish Politics 1926–2016* (Routledge, 2017).

Stephen Quinlan is Senior Researcher at the GESIS Leibniz Institute for the Social Sciences, Mannheim and Project Manager of the Comparative Study of Electoral Systems (CSES), a study that explores electoral behaviour in over forty states globally. His research focuses on comparative electoral behaviour and public opinion including turnout, elections, referendums and social media's impact on politics. His research has been published in *Information Communication and Society*, *Electoral Studies*, and *Irish Political Studies*.

Theresa Reidy is Lecturer in the Department of Government and Politics at University College Cork. Her research interests lie in the areas of political institutions and electoral behaviour and her recent work has been published in *Electoral Studies*, *Parliamentary Affairs* and *Politics*. She is leading a European Commission-funded project on voter facilitation and engagement practices and is a co-convenor of the PSAI specialist group Voters, Parties and Elections.

Jane Suiter is Associate Professor in the School of Communications at Dublin City University. She is an expert on communication, deliberation and participation and is co-principal investigator on the Irish Citizen Assembly, having also worked on other deliberative events such as the Constitutional Convention and We the Citizens. She is communications director of a COST project on populist political communication. She is also co-convener of the PSAI specialist group Voters, Parties and Elections, with an interest in direct democracy and referendums.

Liam Weeks is Lecturer in Politics in the Department of Government, and Politics University College Cork, and an Honorary Senior Research Fellow at the Department of Modern History, Politics and International Relations, Macquarie University, Sydney. His research interests include elections and electoral systems. He is author of *Independents in Irish Party Democracy* (Manchester, 2017), co-editor of *Radical or Redundant? Minor Parties in Irish Political Life* (Dublin, 2012) and co-author of *All Politics is Local: A Guide to Local Elections in Ireland* (Cork, 2009). His next book (co-edited), *The Treaty. Establishing Ireland's Independence* will be published by Irish Academic Press in 2018.

Editors' preface

The Irish National Election Study (INES) of 2016 is the fourth such study of an Irish election since 2002. As we set out in the following pages, it is hard to imagine a more significant election to study – Ireland's first post-crisis election.

This book is very much a joint endeavour. Under the helpful auspices of the Political Studies Association of Ireland (PSAI), we organized a workshop in parallel with the 2016 conference of the association held in Belfast. The workshop was funded by the Irish Research Council New Foundations scheme. We are very grateful to our chapter authors for having produced draft chapters on time and to order, for their speedy responses to our requests for redrafts, and for redrafts of redrafts in the months that followed.

We provide full details of the INES surveys in chapter 1 and the appendix to this volume, but here we wish to acknowledge the financial help that enabled them to happen. Unfortunately – as in 2011 – we were unable to secure research council funding to conduct the 2016 election study. But we were determined that an election study should proceed and therefore sought assistance from a wide range of sources to enable us to co-sponsor with RTÉ (the national broadcaster) the Behaviour and Attitudes/RTÉ exit poll, and to commission two separate (but related) telephone polls, carried out by RED C soon after the election. We are grateful to the following for making all of this possible: the School of Politics and International Relations at University College Dublin; the Department of Political Science at Trinity College Dublin; the Department of Government at University College Cork; the School of Politics, International Studies and Philosophy at Queen's University Belfast; the School of Law and Government at Dublin City University; the Oireachtas (Irish parliament); and the Department of Justice and Equality.

Without these generous sources of funding, there would not have been an INES 2016. But, frankly, this model of putting out the begging bowl far and wide to support academic research of Irish elections is not sustainable. It is our fervent hope that by the time of the next Irish elections, the academic community will have secured sufficient resources to enable a properly-funded election study to be implemented once again, and that – as in most other democracies today – this becomes the norm in Ireland.

Finally, we are grateful to Tony Mason of Manchester University Press for his support and advice (and patience) at every stage of this process.

1

Ireland's post-crisis election

Michael Marsh, David M. Farrell and Theresa Reidy

The 2016 general election in the Republic of Ireland was dramatic. It delivered the worst electoral outcome for the established parties in the history of the state, the most fractionalized party system in the history of the state, the greatest number of Independent (non-party) TDs (MPs) elected to parliament in the history of the state, several new political parties and groups, and was one of the most volatile elections with among the lowest of election turnouts in the state's history. These outcomes follow a pattern seen across a number of Western Europe's established democracies in which the 'deep crisis' of the Great Recession has wreaked havoc on party systems (e.g. Hernández and Kriesi, 2015). The objective of this book is to assess this most extraordinary of Irish elections both in its Irish and wider cross-national context. With contributions from leading scholars on Irish elections and parties, and using a unique dataset – the Irish National Election Study (INES) 2016 – this volume explores voting patterns at Ireland's first post-crisis election and considers the implications for the electoral landscape and politics in Ireland.

This chapter sets the scene for the chapters that follow. We start by presenting a short background to the 2016 election, before describing the features of the 2016 INES. We then outline the key themes addressed in the book. This is followed by an overview of each of the chapters.

Background to the 2016 election

The general election was held on 26 February 2016. There were a number of legislative and political developments during the 2011–2016 Dáil (Irish parliament) term which shaped the dynamics of competition at the election. The number of seats to be filled in the thirty-second Dáil was reduced to 158 following the passage of the Electoral (Amendment) (Dáil Constituencies) Act, 2013. A commitment to reduce the number of TDs had been included in the programme for government as part of the political reform plans of the government elected in 2011. The reduction in numbers contributed to an intensification of competition for the available seats and was generally viewed to have harmed the government more than other groups (Gallagher and Marsh, 2016).

Legislative gender quotas were introduced through the Electoral (Amendment) (Political Funding) Act, 2012. The new legislation made a large proportion of state funding for political parties contingent on their running a minimum of 30 per cent of candidates of both sexes. In practice, of course, this worked as a quota for female candidates, and Fianna Fáil and Fine Gael experienced some internal tensions in their efforts to meet this obligation. Finally, new party formation was a feature of the 2011–2016 Dáil with Renua emerging as a splinter group from Fine Gael, the Social Democrats forming out of a new alignment of Independent TDs and, similarly, Independents 4 Change emerging from an alignment of former party TDs and Independent TDs, although the latter would continue to organize as a loose coalition and did not adopt the features of a political party (for more on all this see Gallagher and Marsh, 2016; Marsh, Farrell and McElroy, 2017). Independents have long been a feature of the political system and in 2016 some of this group also adapted their operating principles, with several sitting TDs and senators

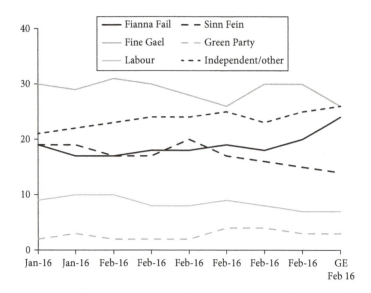

Figure 1.1 Party support levels during January and February 2016 and election result.

Source: RED C Marketing and Research (http://www.redcresearch.ie/).

Note: Dates used in Figure 1.1 do not relate to poll dates – they are time points for illustration.

forming loose alliances, most notably the Independent Alliance. In sum, the election, when it was announced, was for a smaller Dáil, with more women candidates contesting than ever before and with several new party entrants to electoral competition.

Despite speculation during the late summer of 2015 that an early election was imminent, the thirty-first Dáil saw out its full term. The Dáil was dissolved on 3 February 2016 by the Taoiseach (prime minister) Enda Kenny and the short campaign which followed was generally deemed dull and uninteresting by the attending media. Protestations of boredom aside, the campaign did matter and as can be seen from Figure 1.1, there were notable changes in the support levels for the main parties and groups during that time. Fianna Fáil and Independents trended up while Fine Gael and Sinn Féin trended down. The decline in support for Fine Gael ran contrary to a narrative in advance of the campaign that once voters engaged with important economic issues, the fortunes of the government parties would revive. The polls captured the fragmented landscape quite well and it was apparent from early in the campaign that the thirty-second Dáil would be more diverse and fragmented than ever before.

The final outcome of the election is recorded in Table 1.1. Turnout was 64.5 per cent. There are a number of striking features which emerge, two of which in particular are worth noting. The combined vote share of the long-standing largest parties, Fianna Fáil and Fine Gael, dropped below 50 per cent for the first time. There was a sharp rise in the vote share for Independents and small parties, resulting in a fragmented electoral landscape. How and why voters delivered these outcomes is addressed throughout the chapters in this book.

Table 1.1 Results of the 2016 general election

Party	% Vote Share	Dáil Seats
Fine Gael	25.5	50
Fianna Fáil	24.3	44
Sinn Féin	13.8	23
Labour	6.6	7
AAA-PBP	3.9	6
Social Democrats	3.0	3
Greens	2.7	2
Other	20.2	23

Source: Department of Housing, Planning and Local Government.

AAA-PBP = Anti-Austerity Alliance – People Before Profit.

The 2016 INES

All of the analyses in this volume make extensive use of the 2016 INES. This is the fourth such study (the output of the earlier studies is presented in Marsh et al., 2008; Marsh, Farrell and McElroy, 2017). Budget limitations required a somewhat different approach to the earlier studies; accordingly, on this occasion, the INES consisted of three discrete surveys (full details of these are provided in the appendix to this volume).[1] First, there was a nationwide exit poll of 4,283 voters as they left the polling station (done in conjunction with the national broadcaster, RTÉ, it was implemented by the Behaviour & Attitudes market research company). Because the exit poll was face to face, it facilitated the inclusion of a mock ballot, a crucial element in the study of voting behaviour in this most 'candidate-centred' of electoral systems: the single transferable vote (Farrell and McAllister, 2006). Respondents were provided with a facsimile of the ballot they had just completed moments earlier and asked to mark it as they had done. This provides us with information on the voter's ranking of both candidates and parties. It was supplemented by questions asking voters to rate the parties, such as the standard items tapping affective orientations to parties, and questions asking respondents to rate the candidates. This provides a dataset, as with previous waves of INES, that is unusually (perhaps uniquely so) rich in terms of tapping respondents' rating and ranking of the elements of electoral choice.

By its nature, an exit poll is time delimited to no more than about 10 minutes, which restricts how many questions can be asked. To maximize the number of questions we could ask, the respondents – all of whom had first completed the mock ballot and answered a series of core questions – were divided into three subsamples, each of which were given a different set of questions.

In order to broaden our analysis of voting behaviour in this election, we also commissioned two separate telephone polls of representative samples of Irish voters. These surveys were implemented by RED C. One of the polls applied a battery of questions from the latest wave of the influential Comparative Study of Electoral Systems (CSES) project (www.cses.org), which in this election round was focused on the theme of populism – a prominent theme in much of the analysis in this book.

In the next section, we set out the key themes of this election (some of which are particular to this election, others the culmination of tendencies that started earlier) that guide the analysis to follow in the remaining chapters.

Key themes

The objective of the book is to provide a comprehensive understanding of voter decision making in Ireland while also assessing some of the theoretical propositions that currently dominate debates on elections in established democracies. From an Irish perspective, six propositions drawn from the international literature are particularly pertinent: changing partisan identities, issue mobilization, new ideological dimensions of politics, party system change, populism and generational effects. Structuring the analysis along these lines facilitates both a deep analysis of the 2016 election and the location of the Irish experience in a cross-national perspective.

Changing partisan identities: Partisanship has long been low in Ireland by international standards, yet elections have tended to produce relatively stable outcomes over many decades. The year 2016 was an especially volatile election and the final result raises interesting questions about party attachment. As we have noted, several new parties emerged between 2011 and 2016; their capacity to establish enduring partisan ties will be important for their long-term prospects. The reversal of Fianna Fáil's decline and the consolidation of Sinn Féin support hint at changing partisan identities, certainly in the latter case. The relationship between voters and parties is addressed across chapters 2, 5, 7, 9 and 10.

Issue mobilization: A number of controversial policies were introduced during the 2011–2016 parliamentary term, most notably water charges, which prompted huge protests across the state and a widespread refusal to pay (leading to a decision by the government elected in 2016 to abolish the charges). The high-profile marriage equality referendum in 2015 led to a surge in voter registration and turnout jumped sharply from previous referendums (Elkink et al., 2017). Taken in the round, it is clear that issues have the capacity to mobilize voters, and how these types of issues manifested at the 2016 election will be considered across chapters 3, 5, 7, 8 and 10.

Ideological dimensions: Voters in many established democracies are increasingly distrustful of, and indeed angry at, politicians and political parties. This situation is sometimes attributed to economic uncertainty and vulnerability caused by hyper-globalization, the idea being that globalization has created a different set of economic winners and losers and so has activated a new and enduring political cleavage. A social dimension has also been mooted, one that suggests voter attitudes can increasingly be interpreted along a localist-internationalist spectrum. Ireland, like so many small open economies, does not fit easily into these lines of analysis. Despite the deep economic crisis from 2008, globalization has brought many improvements, most especially increased employment. But not all parts of the country have benefitted equally – Dublin, the engine of the national economy, has powered ahead, leaving a strong perception of regional imbalance in the economic recovery. When we intersect the long-standing localist disposition of Irish voters with the complexity of twenty-first-century economics, we may find that the tectonic plates of politics are shifting. Left and right, never especially powerful in underpinning voter preferences, and conservative and liberal, may be evolving into new dimensions; the question of the precise substance and shape of these dimensions and how likely they are to endure will be considered across chapters 3, 4, 5, 6 and 10.

Party system change – hollowing of the centre: The party-political landscape in Ireland has certainly changed. The vote share of the traditional parties shrank below 50 per cent for the first time in 2016 and new parties gained ground. Candidate gender quotas were introduced in 2012 and required all parties to offer voters a greater choice. Chapters 5, 7, 9 and 11 will develop this analysis across the book and emphasize the implications of 2016 voter behaviour for the party system.

Populism: Many countries have seen a surge in anti-establishment sentiment and consequent growth in support for populist political parties. Distrust of politicians and political parties is high in Ireland, but this feature of anti-politics is moderated by localist considerations and candidate-centred aspects of competition. The introduction of water charges begot a large protest movement which was subsequently integrated into, in part, a coalition of parties on the left. Chapters 3, 7 and 10 will investigate this development, paying particular attention to what populism means in an Irish context and proceeding to evaluate the support base of new parties contesting elections for the first time in 2016 and of Independents.

Generational effects: There is plenty of international evidence of the impact of generational change on voting behaviour. It is unlikely that Ireland will be immune from this. We can anticipate generational differences in a number of respects, including differing values and attitudes towards politics, perhaps a greater focus on national policy questions (over localist, particularist concerns) and variations in degree and forms of political involvement (e.g. greater use of social media). In addition, the differential impact of the recession across the generations could also feed into variations in voting behaviour. This issue features most in chapters 2, 5, 8 and 10.

The ten chapters that follow track the behaviour of the post-crisis Irish voter in this 2016 election in the light of these themes. In the next section, we briefly review the focus of each of the chapters.

Overview of chapters

The single transferable vote (STV) electoral system used for elections in Ireland provides a valuable data resource for political scientists. Because it invites voters to rank order as many (or as few) candidates as they like on the ballot paper, it provides important information on voting patterns beyond the first preference expressed on the ballot paper. In chapter 2, Kevin Cunningham makes use of mock-ballot data gathered as part of the exit poll (INES1) of voters as they were leaving the polling station. This allows him to examine the stability in first preference voting behaviour in 2016 and how this has changed since before the financial crisis. The chapter also explores the patterns of lower preferences and what they might mean for the party system. Finally, Cunningham addresses whether preferences mattered in terms of the number of seats a party won in 2016.

Cunningham's main findings are twofold. First, he notes that the erosion of party allegiances that was so evident in the 2011 election (Marsh, Farrell and McElroy, 2017) has continued. Even though the worst of the financial crisis had abated, large numbers of voters continued to switch votes from one party to another in 2016. Second, there is the intriguing finding of the emergence of two parallel party systems in terms of the transfer of voter preferences, with voters on the right transferring votes between the main established parties while those on the left transferred between non-established parties (principally Sinn Féin and AAA-PBP). This latter trend has important implications for Sinn Féin, which in the past tended to be 'transfer toxic', but perhaps is no longer so, at least to supporters of parties of the left.

The evidence of change in party allegiances raises important questions about the ideological positioning of parties in 2016, which is the focus of chapter 3. One of the classic features of party politics in Ireland – that helps to mark it out as 'unique' (Whyte, 1974; Carty, 1981) – is the lack of ideological distinction between the parties, particularly relating to the two main established parties, Fianna Fáil and Fine Gael. In this chapter, Kevin Cunningham and Johan A Elkink evaluate the extent to which ideology may now matter more than before. They do so by analysing the relationship between the ideological positions of parties and vote choice, and by developing a dimensional mapping of ideological space based on rankings in the mock-ballots. Their principal conclusion is that while it may still be the case that ideology does not play a lead role in Irish politics, perhaps now, in their words, it might be seen at least as 'a supporting actor'. It remains the case that ideological positioning does not separate the two largest Irish parties, Fine Gael and Fianna Fáil; however, ideology does determine whether someone might vote for either or neither of these parties. On average, Irish voters select parties that are ideologically close to them on a left–right scale, most prominently so for voters on the left of the spectrum where left versus right does matter in their choice between parties. Cunningham and Elkink's analysis reveals a significant overlap between socio-moral, economic left and right and globalization issues, but there is evidence that populism is offering a new cross-cutting dimension defining political competition. Overall, from a comparative perspective, the Irish case may appear more conventional in terms of left–right competition than typically assumed; it also has an undercurrent of anti-globalization that is similar to that found in other European states.

In chapter 4, John Garry delves more deeply into the social and ideological bases of voting behaviour in 2016. Referring to the classic debates in the comparative literature on political cleavages (Lipset and Rokkan, 1967) and earlier empirical investigations of the Irish case (notably by Marsh et al., 2008), the core question he seeks to answer is whether there may be a strong link between voters' socio-demographic traits, their broad policy beliefs and their party choice in this election. Building upon a similar study of the 2011 election, which found evidence of the emergence of class-based politics (Tilley and Garry, 2017), the analysis on this occasion reveals some interesting trends, particularly relating to Sinn Féin. Its steady rise in electoral support over time has seen it emerge as a major player in Irish party politics, with important implications for how we might view the ideological basis of voting behaviour in Ireland. Garry's analysis finds that Sinn Féin's strong socio-demographic profile (working class, left-wing and in favour of Irish unity) sets it apart from the other major parties, differentiating it in terms that would be familiar in a political cleavage-based analysis.

When voters form attachments to political parties, this can colour their perceptions of candidates, policies and events. As Campbell et al. (1960) put it, 'Identification with a party raises a perceptual screen through which the individual tends to see what is favourable to his partisan orientation.' Party attachments therefore tend to be immune to all but the most seismic political shocks (Green et al., 2004). The economic crisis that engulfed Ireland in 2008 may represent such a shock, leading as it did to a period of unprecedented electoral volatility. In chapter 5, Rory Costello presents the first dedicated study of party attachment in Ireland in the wake of the economic crisis. Previous research shows that party identification has historically been an important factor in Irish voting behaviour (Carty, 1981). Partisanship began to decline from the 1980s onwards, but Marsh et al. (2008) were still able to report that the majority of voters had some degree of party attachment at the beginning of the millennium. This chapter examines how party attachment has evolved in recent elections. The core question Costello seeks to answer is whether the electoral turbulence in 2011 and 2016 was simply a symptom of a fundamentally dealigned electorate, or whether we are witnessing a realignment in Irish politics. In other words, has the number of floating voters increased in the wake of the crisis, or have people begun to form new party attachments that are likely to shape elections in the future? The analysis shows that while party attachments were ruptured in 2011 (most notably so in the case of Fianna Fáil), in 2016, by contrast, partisanship increased, and there were some interesting trends among young voters in particular, with many of them beginning to form new allegiances.

In chapter 6 Michael Marsh seeks to explain a significant puzzle of the 2016 election. There is now a very extensive literature linking economic performance with the electoral performance of government parties, with the relationship being a positive one. The 2016 election was an unusual illustration of a government being punished despite being able to point to a record of very significant economic growth and rapidly falling unemployment as Ireland's recovery from the economic crash and bailout made it such a good example of the success of 'austerity' policies. Drawing on many studies that argue for certain contingencies in the relationship, this chapter explores a number of ways in which the 'good economy-government returned to office' relationship went wrong. A key finding, contrary to general tendencies in the literature on economic voting, is that 'pocketbook' considerations were very significant in determining how voters felt about the government parties. The chapter offers some reasons why the Irish case is unusual and also questions the theoretical bases on which 'pocketbook' voting is downplayed in the economic voting literature.

In chapter 7, the focus turns to the significance of candidates in Irish elections. The act of voting is often judged to be party-centred (Elkink and Farrell, 2016), but in Ireland it is generally seen as taking place through the prism of candidates: parties select their candidates with care to take account of that; candidate-centred behaviour is also shown by the large and growing number of Independents elected in recent Irish elections – in record numbers in 2016. The importance of party versus candidate has been examined in previous studies (Marsh, 2007; Marsh et al., 2008). In this chapter, Michael Courtney and Liam Weeks bring the discussion up to date for 2016. The financial crisis had a number of political impacts, and one was to increase the importance of party vis-à-vis candidate in 2011 (Marsh, Farrell and McElroy, 2017). This was because national issues, which parties are more capable of dealing with than individual candidates, became of greater importance. With the gradual recovery of the Irish economy in the latter half of the tenure of the Fine Gael–Labour coalition, Courtney and Weeks consider whether the dynamics of party and candidate were altered. Their analysis shows that voters have returned to the more familiar habit of candidate-centred ballot choices, though significant party-centred behaviour persists.

Chapter 8 concentrates on when voters make their voting decisions, paying particular attention to the campaign period. Theresa Reidy and Jane Suiter argue that knowing when decisions are made is a vital part of understanding how elections work. The evidence presented demonstrates that a growing proportion of voters report making their final voting choice during election campaigns. Modern election campaigns, with their manifesto launches, party leader debates and intense scrutiny of opinion polls, matter a great deal. These campaigns work by raising awareness of new parties and candidates and providing vital information on the policy positions of competing actors. Reidy and Suiter's analysis reveals that they are decisive in shaping voter decisions. Young people, women and urban voters are more likely to arrive at their final vote choice during the campaign period and, importantly, voters who decide during the campaign are also more likely to have changed their preference from the previous election. These findings have important implications for the political system. They provide further evidence of the challenges parties face in building long-term allegiance with their voters. Furthermore, it is clear that election results may become more unpredictable as larger proportions of voters arrive at their final decision close to election day, making early campaign opinion polls more problematic as predictors of final outcomes.

In 2016, Ireland joined over fifty countries worldwide in the adoption of candidate gender quotas, and it became the first case of a country doing so under the STV electoral system. Its impact was evident from the dramatic rise in the number of women candidates fielded in this election – 163, as compared with 86 in 2011. In chapter 9, Gail McElroy builds on her previous research of the Irish case (McElroy and Marsh, 2010; 2011) to assess whether the use of gender quotas had any impact on voters' attitudes towards women candidates. Her analyses of INES data in previous elections found no evidence of voter prejudice against female candidates. There could be reason to expect that this might change in the light of gender quotas. As McElroy observes, the introduction of the quota in 2016 was a significant 'shock' to the system: parties were forced to find a large number of women candidates very quickly, so the recruitment pool was likely to have more 'average' women in it. This allows her to test for true bias among the Irish electorate. Her analysis reveals little evidence of this on the whole, apart from the slight exception of Fianna Fáil, whose supporters revealed some male bias. Apart from that partial exception, the findings generally are consistent with previous studies: what matters most is how well the candidate is known, and therefore it is incumbency that is the main factor, not the sex of the candidate.

In chapter 10, David Farrell, Michael Gallagher and David Barrett assess how the record-breaking levels of electoral flux in 2016 may have impacted on attitudes towards representative politics in Ireland. The chapter addresses three themes. First, they examine voter attitudes to the role of TDs in 2016. The Irish tradition of high degrees of localism in representative politics is based on the strong attachment of Irish voters to a constituency orientation from their politicians (Gallagher and Suiter, 2017; Gallagher and Komito, 2018). While there may be grounds for expecting that the high levels of electoral change in recent elections may have had some impact on this, the analysis in this chapter shows that a desire for a constituency orientation remains as strong as ever. There are, however, some changes in how voters make contact with their elected representatives – the second theme dealt with in this chapter. The intensity (or degree) of contact is resilient, but its form is shifting to more impersonal or virtual means of contact (especially among younger voters): the days of the 'weekly clinic' – that classic mainstay of representative politics in Ireland – may be numbered. Finally, the chapter examines what Irish voters think of their politicians overall – this latter theme referencing ongoing international debates about the emergence of populist attitudes (which were central to this round of CSES questions, asked in the INES 2016). The evidence from the Irish case is quite positive, with many voters indicating a favourable disposition towards their politicians. This is not universal, however; supporters of Sinn Féin and AAA-PBP are somewhat more critical of politicians.

The final chapter (chapter 11) addresses the importance of leadership effects in 2016. Stephen Quinlan and Eoin O'Malley assess the impact of the leaders of the four main parties in influencing the vote for their parties. Overall, they find some evidence that party leadership mattered in this election, but not a lot. The Fianna Fáil leader, Micheál Martin, was the most popular of the leaders yet this did not translate into significant additional votes for his party. By contrast, the leaders of Fine Gael (Enda Kenny) and Sinn Féin (Gerry Adams), though less popular, were better at influencing the turnout of their base of supporters.

Conclusion

Late in the evening of the election count on 27 February 2016, as it became apparent that the result was one in which no party could claim a success (Gallagher and Marsh, 2016), one of the hosts on the RTÉ election results programme speculated whether Ireland was about to enter a period of Borgen-style government – referencing the popular Danish political drama about a prime minister who, against all the party-political odds, managed to cobble together a minority coalition government. It was a prescient observation. Government formation was to take several months and the final deal, when agreed, returned Fine Gael to power in a minority administration with the involvement of a number of Independent TDs, including some Independents from the Independent Alliance group. The government is reliant on a confidence-and-supply agreement with Fianna Fáil which commits that party to abstaining on key legislation, and the deal covers three budget years.

The speculation from the beginning of this government has been that it will not be long-lasting, with many expecting that the next election will be no later than 2019. But so far, the government has endured. At the time of writing (late autumn 2017), the government has successfully passed its second budget and the Fine Gael party has changed leader, resulting in the election by the Dáil of Leo Varadkar as Taoiseach. All of this has the familiar feel of political life as normal. In short, while there was much that was extraordinary about this election and its outcome, there is also much that remains the same about Irish politics.

Note

1 The INES 2016 received funding from the following sources: the School of Politics and International Relations at University College Dublin; the Department of Political Science

at Trinity College Dublin; the Department of Government at University College Cork; the School of Politics, International Studies and Philosophy at Queen's University Belfast; the School of Law and Government at Dublin City University; the Oireachtas (Irish parliament); and the Department of Justice and Equality.

References

Campbell, Angus, Philip E. Converse, Warren E. Miller and Donald E. Stokes. 1960. *The American Voter*. New York: John Wiley and Son.

Carty, R. Kenneth. 1981. *Electoral Politics in Ireland: Party and Parish Pump*. Cork: Brandon.

Elkink, Johan, and David Farrell (eds). 2016. *The Act of Voting: Identities, Institutions, and Locale*. London: Routledge.

Elkink, Johan, David Farrell, Theresa Reidy and Jane Suiter. 2017. 'Understanding the 2015 marriage equality referendum in Ireland: Context, campaign and conservative Ireland', *Irish Political Studies*. 32: 361–81.

Farrell, David, and Ian McAllister. 2006. *Australia's Electoral Systems: Origins, Variations and Consequences*. Sydney: University of New South Wales Press.

Gallagher, Michael, and Jane Suiter. 2017. 'Pathological parochialism or a valuable service? Attitudes to the constituency role of Irish parliamentarians', in Michael Marsh, David Farrell and Gail McElroy (eds), *A Conservative Revolution? Electoral Change in Twenty-First Century Ireland*. Oxford: Oxford University Press, pp. 143–71.

Gallagher, Michael, and Lee Komito. 2018. 'The constituency role of Dáil deputies', in John Coakley and Michael Gallagher (eds), *Politics in the Republic of Ireland*. 6th edition, London: Routledge, pp. 191–215.

Gallagher, Michael, and Michael Marsh (eds). 2016. *How Ireland Voted, 2016: The Election that Nobody Won*. London: Palgrave Macmillan.

Green, Donald P., Bradley Palmquist and Eric Schickler. 2004. *Partisan Hearts and Minds: Political Parties and the Social Identities of Voters*. New Haven, CT: Yale University Press.

Hernández, Enrique, and Hanspeter Kriesi. 2015. 'The electoral consequences of the financial and economic crisis in Europe', *European Journal of Political Research* (published online, 2015; accessed 28 April 2016).

Lipset, Seymour M., and Stein Rokkan. 1967. *Party Systems and Voter Alignments: Cross-National Perspectives*. New York: Free Press.

Marsh, Michael. 2007. 'Candidates or parties? Objects of electoral choice in Ireland', *Party Politics*. 13: 500–27.

Marsh, Michael, David M. Farrell and Gail McElroy (eds), 2017. *A Conservative Revolution? Electoral Change in Twenty-First-Century Ireland*. Oxford: Oxford University Press.

Marsh, Michael, Richard Sinnott, John Garry and Fiachra Kennedy. 2008. *The Irish Voter: The Nature of Electoral Competition in the Republic of Ireland*. Manchester: Manchester University Press.

McElroy, Gail, and Michael Marsh. 2010. 'Candidate gender and voter choice: Analysis from a multimember preferential voting system', *Political Research Quarterly*. 63: 822–33.

McElroy, Gail, and Michael Marsh. 2011. 'Electing women to the Dáil: Gender cues and the Irish voter', *Irish Political Studies*. 26: 521–34.

Tilley, John, and John Garry. 2017. 'Class politics in Ireland: How economic catastrophe realigned Irish politics along economic divisions', in Michael Marsh, David Farrell and Gail McElroy (eds), *A Conservative Revolution? Electoral Change in Twenty-First Century Ireland*. Oxford: Oxford University Press, pp. 11–27.

Whyte, John, 1974. 'Ireland: Politics without social bases', in Richard Rose (ed.), *Electoral Behaviour: A Comparative Handbook*. New York: The Free Press, pp. 619–51.

2

Mining the ballot: Preferences and transfers in the 2016 election

Kevin Cunningham

Introduction

The purpose of this book is to explain Irish voting behaviour (why people in Ireland vote the way that they do) after the crisis. The 2016 general election was the first since the 'earthquake' election of 2011, which saw a historic change in the Irish party system. While the 2009 and 2014 European elections pointed to a shift in voting patterns, the second-order effects apparent in those elections (see Marsh, 1998; Hix and Marsh, 2011) would blur our understanding of developments since 2008. Thus, the 2016 general election is the first test of permanency of a shift in voting behaviour since the economic crisis that began in 2008.

To understand the post-crisis voter, this chapter analyses first preference votes cast for each political party, and the stability of those preferences over time and across parties. The chapter explores the additional data produced by Ireland's distinctive electoral system – the single transferable vote (STV). Voters are invited to rank candidates on the ballot paper, marking a '1' beside the candidate they most prefer, a '2' beside their second most preferred candidate, a '3' beside their third most preferred candidate and so on. Voters can rank any number of candidates, from just one candidate to all candidates. The count proceeds in rounds eliminating the candidates with the fewest votes and redistributing their votes according to lower preferences. Candidates are certain to be elected if they achieve a quota of votes as determined by the number of votes cast and the number of candidates to be elected (although when the count is concluded, some will be declared elected simply because they have more support than any other remaining candidate). Lower preferences are thus an important part of a voter's considerations and therefore information about these lower preferences gives us a greater insight into the thought processes underlying voting behaviour.

A number of different rubrics may drive the pattern of preferences on the ballot. It may be that the voter considers the political parties they like while avoiding political parties they explicitly do not like. They may favour governing parties or opposition parties, parties of the left or, equivalently, of the right. Voters may favour specific candidates due to local or personal factors. Other thought processes such as convenience might dictate a significant number of preferences, with voters favouring candidates higher up on the ballot paper.

This chapter discusses the post-crisis Irish voter, first by looking at the instability in first preference voting behaviour and how this has changed since before the crisis. It also explores trends among the lower preferences – how many parties voters are voting for, and the patterns of lower preferences – and what it might mean for the party system. Finally, we explore whether preferences mattered in terms of the number of seats the party won.

Stability of preferences

Until 2011, the Irish political system was known for its somewhat unusual stability. While support for the individual parties changed quite significantly from one election to the next, the party system did not change very much. Between 1927 and 2007 the average absolute change in the Fianna Fáil and Fine Gael vote from one election to the next was 4 per cent. However, as Figure 2.1 shows, support levels tended to oscillate in a range that left intact the basic structure of the party system: in eighteen post-war elections, the order and relative sizes of the three largest parties remained the same. Fianna Fáil was consistently the largest party, typically receiving between 39 and 52 per cent of the vote; Fine Gael was the second largest with support ranging between 19 and 39 per cent; and the Labour Party was third (in all but one election), with support ranging between 6 and 19 per cent of the vote.

As Figure 2.1 also shows, the 2007 election was the last election to be characterized by this pattern of stability. Since the economic crisis, the party system has entered a period of instability or at least realignment. The average change in vote share increased from 3.7 per cent to 14.1 per cent in 2011 and 10.1 per cent in 2016. The 2011 election is ranked as the third most volatile election in long-established European democracies since 1945 and as the most volatile without the presence of a significant new party (Mair, 2011: 287–88). While the 2016 election saw less change than 2011, it was still the second most volatile of all Irish elections. The 2011 election was characterized by a dramatic collapse in support for the government, and 2016 was no different. Despite considerable economic gains over the previous five years, support for the two governing parties fell by 23 per cent in total. The 2016 election was thus ranked as the eighth most volatile of all elections in Western Europe since 1945 (Farrell and Suiter, 2016: 279–83).

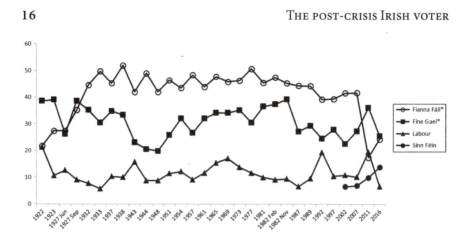

Figure 2.1 First preference vote shares since 1922.

*Note that Figures Fine Gael relate to Pro-Treaty Sinn Féin in 1922 and Cumann na nGaedheal from
1923 to 1933. Fianna Fáil relates to Anti-Treaty Sinn Féin in 1922 and Republican Sinn Féin in 1923.

Source: 'ElectionsIreland', http://www.electionsireland.org 1998–2017, Christopher Took and Seán
Donnelly.

To understand this post-crisis voter, the analysis begins by looking at trends
in individual voting behaviour between 2011 and 2016. Firstly, respondents in
INES1[1] were asked whether they voted in the previous election and, if they did
vote, which party they supported. Using this information and what we know
about the overall vote shares of the 2011 and 2016 general elections we can
estimate the matrix in Table 2.1 of where voters came from and who they voted
for in the 2016 election.

From Table 2.1 we can summarize the number of people switching,
the number of people staying and proportions of non-voters across the two
elections. Approximately 29 per cent switched from one party (including
Independents as one group) to another (including Independents) while almost
the same proportion, 28 per cent, stayed with their party of choice (or remained
with Independents) between the two elections. This is a dramatic change since
before the crisis. We contrast this with data from the 1997–2002 electoral cycle
(studied by Marsh et al., 2008), when a larger 34 per cent remained with their
party of choice, while just 11 per cent switched from one party to another. This
represents a decline from three out of four of those who did vote staying with
their party of choice down to one in two.

While volatility in the post-crisis era consisted of people switching between
parties, in the pre-crisis era many more voters appear to make more deliberate
decisions as to whether they would vote or not. Between 2011 and 2016,
23 per cent stayed at home on both occasions, whereas 20 per cent voted in only
one election. In the period 1997–2002, while a similar proportion (22 per cent)

Table 2.1 Voting and non-voting in 2016, by voting and non-voting in 2011

	2011 Vote								
2016 Vote	Fine Gael	Fianna Fáil	Sinn Féin	Labour	Green	Independent	Other	Did not vote	Total
Fine Gael	11.5	0.5	0.2	1.7	0.1	0.6	0.2	1.8	16.6
Fianna Fáil	3.4	7.2	0.3	1.4	0.1	1.0	0.7	1.6	15.8
Sinn Féin	1.0	0.5	3.5	1.6	0.1	0.5	0.2	1.6	9.0
Labour	0.9	0.2	0.0	2.2	0.0	0.4	0.1	0.5	4.3
AAA-PBP	0.4	0.0	0.0	0.8	0.2	0.0	0.6	0.7	2.6
Social Democrats	0.2	0.1	0.0	1.0	0.1	0.3	0.0	0.2	2.0
Green	0.2	0.0	0.0	0.7	0.3	0.1	0.0	0.5	1.8
Independent	2.1	1.2	0.6	2.5	0.0	3.6	0.2	1.0	11.3
Other	0.6	0.2	0.2	0.5	0.1	0.3	0.0	0.1	1.9
Did not vote	4.5	2.1	2.2	1.0	0.5	1.4	0.0	23.3	34.9
Total	25.2	12.2	6.9	13.6	1.3	8.5	2.1	30.1	100.0

Note: Author's analysis of INES3 and 2016 election results, N=1000. Data in the table are iteratively adjusted to ensure that the margins correctly reflect the results in 2011 and 2016. AAA-PBP = Anti-Austerity Alliance – People Before Profit.

stayed at home on both occasions, a much larger proportion (33 per cent) voted in only one election.

This analysis is reliant on two electoral cycles and the ability of a respondent to recall who they voted for. It is also subject to recall bias, where respondents may be more likely to recall past preferences in line with current preferences. This does mean that the proportion of respondents changing from one party to another may be even greater than the 29 per cent reported here (see Cunningham and Marsh, 2018). The panel design of the Irish National Election Study covering the period 2002–2007 asked respondents about their vote in 2002 and again in 2007 and so did not have to rely on the memory of the respondent. Sixty-three per cent of the sample had the same preference (party or Independent) at the start and end of the period (author's analysis of data from the INES 2002–2007). Given what we know about recall bias, this is more in line with the self-reported three in four voters staying with their party of choice between 1997 and 2002, rather than the self-reported one in two between 2011 and 2016.

Table 2.2 breaks this down by party of choice and, in contrast with the 1997–2002 period, it shows that the rise in the number of people switching to another party, or 'defecting', was consistent across all parties and Independents, whether they were rising or falling in terms of their support levels between 2011 and 2016. Naturally, as a party experiencing vote loss, the Labour Party had the largest increase in defectors (up from 25 per cent between 1997 and 2002 to 77 per cent between 2011 and 2016). Of the 2011 Labour Party supporters, few stayed at home in 2016, meaning that the effect of the fall in support for the Labour Party was to be more dramatic than otherwise in the constituencies

Table 2.2 The proportion of voters switching from their party of choice, staying with their party and not voting from one election cycle to the next, 2011–2016 and 1997–2002 (per cent)

	2011–2016			1997–2002		
	Stayed with party	Voted for another party	Did not vote	Stayed with party	Voted for another party	Did not vote
Fine Gael	47	35	18	54	18	28
Fianna Fáil	59	23	18	62	12	26
Sinn Féin	51	19	31	81	13	6
Labour	16	77	7	44	25	31
Independent	44	39	16	46	33	21
Did not vote	-	22	78	-	43	57

Source: Author's analysis of data: 1997–2002 from Marsh et al. (2008) and 2011–2016 from INES3.

Note: Shading used highlights higher values.

in which it ran candidates. However, what is perhaps more surprising is that the proportions of defectors from Sinn Féin and Fianna Fáil were also greater in 2016 despite both parties increasing their support levels between 2011 and 2016. This is even more remarkable considering the low ebb Fianna Fáil found itself in in 2011.

While decisions about party preferences have become more volatile, decisions over whether or not to vote seem to have become more consistent. Seventy-eight per cent of those who did not vote in 2011 remained non-voters in 2016. This compares with the 57 per cent who stayed at home on both occasions between 1997 and 2002. The greater consistency of non-voters in 2011–2016 is even more remarkable considering that the fall in turnout was considerably larger between the 1997 and 2002 elections (76.5 per cent to 62.6 per cent) than between the 2011 and 2016 elections (69.9 per cent to 65.1 per cent), as one would expect a greater proportion of those who did not vote in 1997 not to have voted in 2002, given that many more people did not vote in 2002.[2]

To understand more about the pattern of voting one can look at the pattern of first, second and lower preferences in 2016. Extensive research on Irish voting behaviour has used aggregate material at a constituency level available from official results (see Gallagher, 1978; 1992; 1999; 2003; Sinnott, 1995; Sinnott and McBride, 2011; O'Kelly, 2016; Elkink and Farrell, 2016). This analysis tells us how many votes typically transfer from one candidate to another but is limited to the situations where a candidate is eliminated or when a candidate has a surplus. It therefore obscures our understanding of what is intended by voters when they cast their vote. In this instance, our analysis draws on mock-ballot data. The RTÉ/INES exit poll (INES1), like previous rounds of the INES, asked voters to replicate the preferences indicated on their ballot and we can use these data to infer the exact nature of the preferences.

Choice options and number of preferences

The number of different parties that voters express a preference for gives us an idea of the nature of any diffusion of party preferences. This is particularly relevant in the context of a significant increase in the number of political parties achieving representation. Table 2.3 shows the number of parties voters express preferences for. This is compared with the number of different parties standing in the voter's constituency and against the voter's first preference vote.

In some cases, supporters of political parties express preferences for only one party. This custom, sometimes known as 'plumping', is practised by the most loyal of supporters, for whom no other party is worthwhile voting for. Fianna Fáil voters, followed by Sinn Féin and Fine Gael voters, are most likely to plump for their chosen party. Just 15 per cent gave a preference to just one party; the remainder expressed further preferences for other parties. This is

Table 2.3 Number of different parties voted for by number of options (per cent) and first preference choice

| | Number of different parties voted for | | | | | | | Party first preference | | | | | | | |
| | Number of different parties/groupings standing | | | | | | | | | | | | | | |
	5	6	7	8	9	10	11	FF	FG	SF	Lab	GP	Ind	AA	All
1	24	20	22	18	11	15	12	23	17	18	6	3	13	9	15
2	28	48	36	33	28	30	26	33	33	33	27	14	32	24	31
3	27	22	27	31	36	32	30	29	28	32	38	35	32	35	32
4	6	4	10	10	13	11	15	8	10	9	16	25	12	17	12
5	14	2	2	4	5	5	7	3	4	5	6	10	4	6	5
6	-	3	1	1	2	3	5	1	2	2	1	4	2	3	2
7	-	-	4	1	1	1	1	2	2	0	1	2	2	0	1
8	-	-	-	3	0	1	1	0	1	0	1	2	1	0	1
9	-	-	-	-	4	0	0	1	2	0	2	2	1	2	1
10	-	-	-	-	-	3	1	0	1	0	0	2	0	1	1
11	-	-	-	-	-	-	2	-	0	0	0	1	0	0	0
Total	100	100	100	100	100	100	100	100	100	100	100	100	100	100	100
Avg.	2.6	2.3	2.5	2.7	3.1	2.9	3.2	2.5	2.9	2.6	3.2	3.9	2.9	3.2	2.9
N	78	94	820	520	1309	910	552	905	1064	686	304	153	656	201	4283

Source: INES1 2016.

Note: Shading used highlights higher values. Ind = Independent; FF = Fianna Fáil; FG = Fine Gael; GP = Green Party; Lab = Labour; SF = Sinn Féin.

lower than previously, but only marginally so (it compares with 18 per cent in 2002). In 2002, 52 per cent indicated a preference for one or two different parties whereas now this figure is down – again marginally so – to 46 per cent.

While the number of parties achieving representation in the Dáil has increased, the number of parties voters express a preference for has only marginally increased. In all constituencies, voters had a minimum choice of four parties or groupings as Fianna Fáil, Fine Gael, Sinn Féin and the Green Party stood candidates in all constituencies. Yet, just 7 per cent of those that could mark a preference for more than five parties did so. In total, the average number of parties that voters express a preference for has increased marginally from 2.8 to 2.9.

The data also show the extent to which tactical considerations play an important role in a voter's considerations. Table 2.3 reveals considerable differences in the number of preferences expressed by supporters of different parties. While 23 per cent of Fianna Fáil supporters plumped for Fianna Fáil, just 3 per cent of Green Party supporters voted only for the Green Party. These figures are not influenced by the numbers of parties on offer as both parties stood in every constituency. Looking across all parties, there is some indication that voters are strategic in terms of the number of preferences that they express. Green, Labour and Anti-Austerity Alliance-People Before Profit (AAA-PBP) supporters tend to indicate more preferences, perhaps in recognition of the relatively greater likelihood that their candidate would be eliminated and their vote might be more likely to transfer to another party. These parties also ran fewer candidates meaning that whereas a voter could express preferences for two or three Fianna Fáil or Fine Gael candidates, they would not have been able to do so for, say, the Green Party, which ran a single candidate in all constituencies. In comparison to those supporting Fianna Fáil and Sinn Féin, Fine Gael voters tended to express preferences for a larger number of other parties. This is perhaps explained by public encouragement between Fine Gael and Labour politicians to express second preferences for one another as coalition partners.

Polarization of lower preferences

Lower preferences tell us not just about the parties that voters like but also about the parties that voters actively dislike. These characteristics are not necessarily the inverse of one another, as some parties polarize opinion (e.g. Sinn Féin) more than others (e.g. the Green Party). Table 2.4 shows the proportion of cases where each party is awarded a voter's first, second, third, fourth, fifth, sixth, lower or no preference, excluding constituencies where the parties do not field a candidate. Broadly speaking, second and third preferences follow the aggregate pattern of first preferences; however, some parties such as Labour

Table 2.4 Distribution of successive party preferences excluding cases where the parties did not stand

	Fine Gael	Fianna Fáil	Sinn Féin	Labour	AAA-PBP
First preference party	25	21	16	8	7
Second preference party	12	9	6	8	7
Third/fourth preference party	10	11	6	15	6
Fifth/sixth preference party	2	3	1	3	2
Lower preference party	1	2	3	2	3
No preference	50	54	68	64	75

Source: INES1 2016.

Note: Shading used highlights higher values. Note that in 13 per cent of cases Labour did not stand a candidate and in 29 per cent of cases the AAA-PBP did not stand a candidate. Sample size: 4,283. AAA-PBP = Anti-Austerity Alliance – People Before Profit.

attract relatively more second, third and fourth preferences than, say, Sinn Féin, which incidentally attracts twice the number of first preference votes.

One may conclude that Sinn Féin and the AAA-PBP are more *disliked* by voters. Both are awarded lower and no preferences (71 per cent, 78 per cent) more often than Fianna Fáil (56 per cent), Fine Gael (51 per cent) and Labour (66 per cent). As this figure is related to the overall support levels of the parties, we may exclude first preference votes to get a clearer picture of which parties are disliked most. Of those that do not express a first preference for Sinn Féin, 81 per cent do not give any preference to the party. Similarly, for the AAA-PBP, of those that do not give the party a first preference vote, 81 per cent do not give the party a lower preference. This contrasts with figures of 67 per cent, 68 per cent and 70 per cent respectively for Fianna Fáil, Fine Gael and Labour.

These figures reflect the considerable change in voting behaviour between the pre-crisis voter and the post-crisis voter. Pre-crisis, most voters expressed a preference for each of the main parties and a minority left these parties entirely off the ballot. In 2002, just 28 per cent did not express a preference for Fianna Fáil. In 2016, 54 per cent left Fianna Fáil entirely off their ballot. While the party is much less popular than it was in 2002, the decline is remarkable even considering the scale of its vote collapse in 2011. This 54 per cent is not too dissimilar from the 59 per cent that did not express a preference for the Labour Party in 2002, which was a much smaller party with only 13 per cent of the vote. For Fine Gael, in 2016, 47 per cent did not issue a preference for the party. Despite increasing its vote share since 2002, fewer people in 2016 expressed a preference for the party. In 2002 the main parties were more popular and had a much greater share of first preference votes. Clearly, parties with lower first preference votes will attract fewer lower preferences.

When we exclude first preferences for each party, the difference between the pre-crisis and post-crisis voter is still observable. Among those that did not express a first preference vote for Fianna Fáil, just 47 per cent expressed no lower preference in 2002 compared with 67 per cent in 2016. For Fine Gael in 2002, 60 per cent of those that did not vote for the party first did not express any preference for the party. In 2016 this rose to 68 per cent. Among non-Labour voters, 66 per cent left the party entirely off the ballot in 2002, a figure that rose to 70 per cent in 2016. With respect to Sinn Féin, however, the electorate has softened marginally. In 2002, 85 per cent of those whose first preference vote was not Sinn Féin left the party entirely off the ballot. In 2016 this fell to 68 per cent.

While voters selected marginally more parties on the ballot, the main parties were left entirely off the ballot considerably more often. A common theme is that mainstream parties have lost their total dominance of the party system. This is something we also observed from an increase in switching between parties and the decline in selective turnout. Our analysis thus far points to the emergence of a divided party system.

First and second preferences

To further understand the changes taking place we examine the relationship between a respondent's first preference and his or her second preference. While this gives us an idea about party 'solidarity', or the extent to which parties matter over individual candidates (see also chapter 7), it also informs us about the nature of this hollowing of the centre.

In terms of party solidarity, a voter may express their first and second preferences along party lines or be influenced by specific candidates. Clearly, in some cases, a voter may choose the sole Labour Party candidate followed by the sole Green Party candidate and still maintain that they are voting along party lines. However, for the larger parties, we can see more clearly whether the party label appears to matter. Table 2.5 gives the distribution of second preferences among voters that had an opportunity to express a second preference for another candidate from the same party as their first preference. We can see that they give a second preference for the same party in roughly 62 per cent of cases, rising to 68 per cent in the case of supporters of Sinn Féin. The loyalty of Sinn Féin voters may be somewhat inflated as there are few constituencies where Sinn Féin ran more than one candidate and these areas were particularly favourable to the party. However, considerable party solidarity remains among current supporters of the larger parties.

Table 2.5 also shows that many voters express a significant number of second preferences for parties that are similar in outlook. For example, voters giving a first preference to Fine Gael tend to give their next party preference to a

Table 2.5 Distribution of first and second preferences of voters with an option to give a second preference to the same party

Second preference	First preference		
	Fine Gael	*Fianna Fáil*	*Sinn Féin*
Fine Gael	60	12	3
Fianna Fáil	10	61	4
Sinn Féin	1	6	68
Labour	12	3	1
AAA-PBP	1	1	8
Independent	8	10	10
Other	5	4	6
No other party	3	3	3
Sample size	991	650	241

Source: INES1 2016.

AAA-PBP = Anti-Austerity Alliance – People Before Profit.

candidate of its coalition partner, Labour. Voters who express a first preference for Sinn Féin tend to identify candidates of the similarly left-leaning AAA-PBP after they have selected Sinn Féin candidates. To understand the structure more broadly, we must examine all votes while focusing on the pattern of first party preference and the next preferred party preference – their second party preference. Table 2.6 tells us to what extent supporters of one party are willing to support other parties.

The larger parties generally receive more second party preferences than smaller parties. This is unsurprising when we consider the fact that that the larger parties are generally more popular and stand more candidates for which non-partisan rubrics – personal and local factors (see chapter 7) – also apply when choosing to support one candidate over another. That said, their share of second party preferences is generally smaller than their first preference vote share.

The relationship between first and second party preferences reveals how the post-crisis voter interprets the party system. There is a close connection between Fine Gael and Labour in the minds of many voters: 33 per cent of voters who gave their first preference to Fine Gael gave their next preference to Labour while 50 per cent of voters who gave their first preferences to Labour gave their next preference to Fine Gael. Similarly, there is a close connection between Sinn Féin and the AAA-PBP: 18 per cent of voters who gave their first preference to Sinn Féin gave their next preference to the AAA-PBP while 31 per cent of voters who gave their first preferences to the AAA-PBP gave their next preference to Sinn Féin. Sinn Féin broadly attracted considerable anti-establishment support.

Table 2.6 Patterns of party choice: Proportion of first preferences for each party going to each possible second next preferred party

First preference party	None	Next preferred party									
		Fine Gael	Fianna Fáil	Sinn Féin	Labour Party	AAA-PBP	Green Party	Social Democrats	Renua Ireland	Independent	Other
Fine Gael	18	0	19	2	33	1	5	3	4	14	1
Fianna Fáil	23	20	0	11	8	3	4	4	6	20	1
Sinn Féin	18	7	10	0	3	18	4	4	2	28	5
Labour	7	50	14	4	0	3	6	5	1	11	0
AAA-PBP	10	5	4	31	6	0	11	5	3	21	2
Green	4	17	10	5	18	12	0	7	3	22	3
Social Democrats	5	21	15	12	10	4	13	0	3	14	4
Renua	1	28	22	5	4	3	8	4	0	25	1
Independent	14	18	17	13	7	6	3	3	4	14	2
Other parties	4	5	11	24	4	11	7	4	5	25	0
Total	16	14	12	8	13	5	5	4	3	17	2

Source: INES1 2016.

Note: Shading used highlights higher values. Sample size: 4,283. AAA-PBP = Anti-Austerity Alliance – People Before Profit.

Twenty-four per cent of voters who gave their first preference to other parties gave their next preference to Sinn Féin. Independents tended to receive a large number of next preferences from all supporters, particularly Sinn Féin (28 per cent) and the AAA-PBP (21 per cent), while Independent supporters tended to give their next preference to parties according to the overall distribution of first preference votes: in other words, Independent voters look like a cross section of voters for parties. There are thus two 'systems' of transfers: some voters voting and transferring their vote between one set of parties, and a second set of voters voting and transferring their vote between another set of parties. This explains the rise in the number of parties being represented without a significant rise in the number of parties that voters are issuing preferences for. The first system of preferences is between Fine Gael, Labour and Fianna Fáil – the established parties towards the right of the left–right spectrum – and the second system is between Sinn Féin and the AAA-PBP towards the left of the left–right spectrum (for more detail, see chapter 3).

Some parties receive a much greater proportion or a much lower proportion of next and lower preferences than their first preference share. The Labour Party, for example, had almost twice as many second party preferences as Sinn Féin despite having almost half as many first preferences. Similarly, the Green Party received considerably more second preferences than Renua, despite achieving a similar first preference vote share. These are clear indications of which parties are liked, if not loved, by many (Labour and the Greens) and which parties are loved by some but also disliked by many (Sinn Féin and Renua).

The value of transfers

After discussing the information that lower preferences and the ballot offer us, we must also address the overall value of lower preferences. Just 14 per cent of those elected and 4 per cent of all candidates are elected on the basis of their first preference votes, meaning that the remainder, at least in theory, need to attract lower preferences in order to be elected. Arguably, those that polarize opinion may be disadvantaged and do worse in terms of the number of candidates that they get elected given their first preference vote share than, say, those parties that are everyone's *second favourite*.

The relationship between second preferences and electoral success is conditional on the fact that second and lower preferences from other candidates only matter if preferences actually transfer from one party to another. First preferences only transfer where a candidate is eliminated before the final count or where he or she is elected with a surplus. On the basis of election data from 2016, we can calculate that just 31 per cent of first preference votes were transferred to another candidate. The remaining 69 per cent stayed with the voter's first preference, who was either elected or eliminated in the final round of counting.

Table 2.7 Party first preference vote shares, percentage of votes transferred from each party and their overall contribution to the share of all transferred votes as taken from the results of the 2016 election (2016 Electoral Data)

	First preference vote share	% of party's first preference vote transferred	Share of all transferred votes
Fine Gael	26	13	10
Fianna Fáil	24	20	15
Sinn Féin	14	28	12
Labour	7	48	10
AAA-PBP	4	50	6
Green Party	3	85	7
Social Democrats	3	46	4
Renua Ireland	2	86	6
Independent	17	48	26
Other parties	1	96	2

Note: Shading used highlights higher values. AAA-PBP = Anti-Austerity Alliance – People Before Profit.

Table 2.7 shows that a much greater share of the first preference votes of candidates of smaller parties was transferred. While the first preference vote shares of the two largest parties make up half of all first preferences, they only make up a quarter of all transferred votes. By contrast, support for Independent candidates transferred more than that for Fine Gael and Fianna Fáil combined, as the former were much more likely to be eliminated. Furthermore, many of the votes that did transfer from the larger parties transferred internally to other candidates on the party ticket. As such, the value of being the next preferred party among Fine Gael or Fianna Fáil voters was small relative to the size of those parties' first preference vote. Indeed, in the explicit 'transfer pact' between Labour and Fine Gael, the lower preferences from the Labour Party were probably much more valuable than the lower preferences from Fine Gael, despite the former being almost four times the size of the latter.

In relation to the aforementioned two systems of transfers, the anti-establishment left-wing one is far more viable than it might initially appear. Although Sinn Féin and the AAA-PBP are more toxic than other parties, they are not significantly disadvantaged. Sinn Féin's problem of attracting few transfers from Fine Gael is ameliorated by the party's ability to attract significant transfers from the AAA-PBP, the Social Democrats and other parties that tend to get eliminated and who together account for 12 per cent of all transfers.

The impact of attracting lower preferences can be estimated from the relationship between the number of first preferences a candidate receives and whether he or she is elected or not. The reason why this is a probabilistic, rather than deterministic, relationship is due to the impact of lower preferences. A candidate with a given vote share may or may not be elected due to his or her ability to attract a greater or smaller number of lower preference votes and the ability of the party to 'manage' the vote between the candidates it is running in a given constituency. For example, at one extreme, Catherine Ardagh of Fianna Fáil failed to get elected in Dublin South Central on 63 per cent of the quota, while at the other end of the spectrum, Independent candidate Katherine Zappone was elected in Dublin South West on 40 per cent of a quota. In the case of Catherine Ardagh, she was overtaken by Bríd Smith of the AAA-PBP who attracted enough transfers from eliminated candidates from Sinn Féin and the Social Democrats. On the other hand, Katherine Zappone was able to overcome a 2,000-vote gap between herself and the Fine Gael candidate by winning sufficient numbers of transfers from eliminated Independent, Green, Labour Party and AAA-PBP candidates.

We can approximate the marginal effect of lower preference votes by looking at aberrations in the otherwise assumed relationship between first preference votes and whether the candidate is elected or not. While other factors pertaining to the composition of candidates running in a given constituency will also impact on a candidate's fortunes, we can assume that these factors will be broadly random from one constituency to the next. Any residual differences between the predicted seats and actual seat count we can attribute to transfers and the internal party management of candidate first preference votes. To estimate the relationship, one must account for differences in the district magnitude (or number of members elected) of constituencies. Constituencies with three, four and five seats require different shares of the vote (the quota) for a candidate to get elected. We therefore estimate the candidate's first preference totals in terms of the quota that would ensure election. To account for the non-linear nature of this relationship in 2016 we employ a non-linear model using the square and the cube of the proportion of the quota received, 'PQ'. This gives us the following formula, which is graphically displayed in Figure 2.2:

$$\text{Probability of winning} = \text{logit}^{-1} (-28.6 + 131.6PQ - 212.6PQ^2 + 125.6PQ^3)$$

where PQ is the proportion of the quota won in terms of first preference votes.

We use this model to estimate how many seats each party would expect to win based on the first preference performance of its individual TDs. We first estimate the probability that each candidate will win a seat. For example, Catherine Ardagh had an 86 per cent chance of winning a seat based on this model while Katherine Zappone had a 13 per cent chance of winning. We

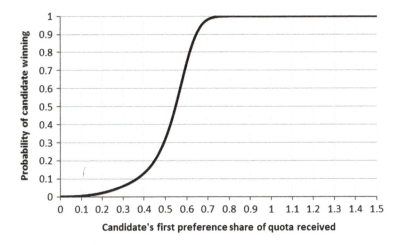

Figure 2.2 The estimated relationship between the quota received and the probability of winning a seat.

Source: 'ElectionsIreland', http://www.electionsireland.org 1998–2017, Christopher Took and Seán Donnelly.

can then estimate how many seats the party should expect to win in order to understand the impact of transfers on overall seat numbers. Table 2.8 compares the number of seats won by each party with the estimated number of seats the party would have won if transfers had been distributed according to the model.

What Table 2.8 shows is that the effect of transfers in 2016 was minimal. Only a few seats were affected positively or negatively by lower preferences. The toxicity of Sinn Féin cost the party one seat, whereas the transfer-friendliness of the Greens produced a single additional seat over what would otherwise have been expected. Independent and AAA-PBP candidates also performed better than what would have been otherwise expected, perhaps on account of significant numbers of lower preferences transferring between them.

Conclusion

Our analysis of ballots (first preferences and lower preferences) reveals several important features of the post-crisis Irish voter. Firstly, the unprecedented changes in first preference voting have been underpinned by enormous amounts of party switching rather than by selective turnout – a behavioural trait which appears to have declined in the aftermath of the crisis. This change reflects the erosion of long-term party allegiances. In previous elections, party allegiances may have remained strong where loyalists stayed at home rather than voted for another party. Post-crisis, as this comparison suggests, larger numbers of

Table 2.8 Number of seats won, number of occasions the party would have won without any additional counting, modelled estimates of expected seats and effective seat bonus due to vote management and transfers

Party	Actual seats	First preference rank wins	Model expected seats	Rounded model seat bonus
Fine Gael	49	51	50.6	−2
Fianna Fáil	44	46	44.2	0
Sinn Féin	23	23	23.8	−1
Labour	7	6	7.6	−1
AAA-PBP	6	5	5.3	1
Social Democrats	3	3	3.5	0
Green	2	1	1.1	1
Renua	0	0	1.1	−1
Independent, Others	23	22	19.8	3

Note: Based on election count data from the 2016 general election. AAA-PBP = Anti-Austerity Alliance – People Before Profit.

people are actively switching rather than staying at home. Finally, those that stay at home are becoming more consistent in that form of voting behaviour.

Secondly, there is significant evidence of some hollowing of the centre ground in Irish politics or, in other terms, of the emergence of an anti-establishment left wing in Sinn Féin and the AAA-PBP. While a number of new parties have emerged, the number of party preferences expressed by voters has barely changed. This is the result of the emergence of two separate party systems with preferences transferring between establishment parties towards the right of the left–right spectrum and preferences transferring between non-established parties towards the left of the left–right spectrum. While the group of non-established parties have little appeal among voters of established parties, they are not disadvantaged as they benefit from the relatively larger amount of lower preferences available from the elimination of smaller non-established candidates and parties. This means that in spite of attracting a relatively low number of first preferences, non-established parties are barely penalized by the fact that the electoral system also gives weight to lower preferences. After two elections it is as of yet unclear what direction the Irish political system is likely to take. The party system could very well revert to type, with Sinn Féin coming in from the cold attracting and relying on transfers from the established parties, or a bipolar system could emerge around Sinn Féin and Fine Gael. Either way, at this point it seems unlikely that the level of volatility in the two most recent elections can be sustained.

Notes

1 Note that those who could not remember how they voted were excluded from the analysis. The data are fitted iteratively so that the table marginals reflect 1997 and 2002 results. The shade of each cell relates to the relative magnitude of the data, with higher values highlighted in a darker colour.
2 One caveat in respect of applying an analysis of reported turnout is the quality of the electoral register, which is larger than the number of valid electors on account of a significant numbers of duplicates and deceased people that remain on the register.

References

Cunningham, Kevin, and Michael Marsh. 2018. 'Voting behaviour', in John Coakley and Michael Gallagher (eds), *Politics in the Republic of Ireland*. 6th edition. London: Routledge, pp. 137–63.

Elkink, Johan A., and David M. Farrell (eds). 2016. *The Act of Voting: Identities, Institutions and Locale*. London: Routledge.

Farrell, David M., and Jane Suiter. 2016. 'The election in context', in Michael Gallagher and Michael Marsh (eds), *How Ireland Voted 2016: The Election that Nobody Won*. Basingstoke: Palgrave Macmillan, pp. 277–92.

Gallagher, Michael. 1978. 'Party solidarity, exclusivity and inter-party relationships 1922–1977: The evidence of transfers', *Economic and Social Review*. 10(1): 1.

Gallagher, Michael. 1992. 'The election of the 27th Dáil', in Michael Gallagher and Michael Laver (eds), *How Ireland Voted 1992*, Dublin: Folens/PSAI Press, pp. 57–78.

Gallagher, Michael. 1999. 'The results analysed', in Michael Marsh and Paul Mitchell (eds), *How Ireland Voted 1997*, Boulder: Westview Press, pp. 121–50.

Gallagher, Michael. 2003. 'Stability and turmoil: Analysis of the results', in Michael Gallagher, Michael Marsh and Paul Mitchell (eds), *How Ireland Voted 2002*. London: Palgrave, pp. 88–118.

Hix, Simon, and Michael Marsh. 2011. 'Second-order effects plus pan-European political swings: An analysis of European Parliament elections across time', *Electoral Studies*. 30: 4–15.

Mair, Peter. 2011. 'The election in context', in Michael Gallagher and Michael Marsh (eds), *How Ireland Voted 2011*. London: Palgrave Macmillan, pp. 283–97.

Marsh, Michael. 1998. 'Testing the second-order election model after four European elections', *British Journal of Political Science*. 28: 591–607.

Marsh, Michael, Richard Sinnott, John Garry and Fiachra Kennedy. 2008. *The Irish Voter: The Nature of Electoral Competition in the Republic of Ireland*. Manchester: Manchester University Press.

O'Kelly, Michael. 2016. 'Locality in Irish voter preferences', in Johan Elkink and David Farrell (eds), *The Act of Voting: Identities, Institutions and Locale.* London: Routledge, pp. 137–60.

Sinnott, Richard. 1995. *Irish Voters Decide: Voting Behaviour in Elections and Referendums since 1918.* Manchester: Manchester University Press.

Sinnott, Richard, and James McBride. 2011. 'Preference voting under PR-STV, 1948–2011', in Michael Gallagher and Michael Marsh (eds), *How Ireland Voted 2011.* London: Palgrave Macmillan, pp. 205–21.

3

Ideological dimensions in the 2016 elections

Kevin Cunningham and Johan A. Elkink

Introduction

This chapter explores the emergence of new and old ideological dimensions in the context of a changing party system. The Irish voter is characterized as non-ideological: prone to issuing voting preferences based on locality (Chubb, 1957; Carty, 1981; Marsh, 2007) and family traditions (Carty, 1981; Sinnott, 1995; Gallagher and Marsh, 2002). The political system has thus been accurately marked as *sui generis* (Whyte, 1974), an 'exception' (Carty, 1981), and even a 'problem child' (Urwin and Eliassen, 1975) as it eschews the traditional left–right basis of political competition in Western European politics. This has been most clearly illustrated by the weak influence of social class and of left-wing politics. It is manifested in the dominance of two ideologically indistinguishable catch-all parties: Fianna Fáil and Fine Gael (Benoit and Laver, 2003; Lutz, 2003) and the persistent weak levels of support for the Labour Party, the long-term flag-bearer of the left or, more precisely, centre-left.

Irish society has been changing quite dramatically. Party identities have declined, the Irish political system entered a period of very considerable volatility following the global financial crisis in the early 2010s and new dimensions of political competition defined by globalization seem to be all but replacing traditional economic left and right in Western Europe. In this context, this chapter re-examines the ideological nature of political competition in Ireland. We first discuss how and why ideology may have a greater role in defining party competition both historically and in the immediate context of post-crisis Ireland. Second, we discuss the key dimensions of ideology, new and old, before exploring the extent to which attitudinal questions underpinning those dimensions reflect the preferences of voters. This helps us to answer questions such as whether ideology is a significant component of party choice and whether voting behaviour in Ireland ties in with the thesis that contemporary European politics revolves around a new cleavage of 'winners' and 'losers' of globalization as well as other cleavages around left-wing populism potentially more relevant to the post-crisis voter and the politics of austerity.

The evidence suggests that classic left–right self-placement is a significant predictor of vote choice dividing Fine Gael and Fianna Fáil from Sinn Féin and Labour. We find that this is related to two underlying dimensions: economic left–right issues divide Fine Gael from Sinn Féin, and socio-moral issues divide Fianna Fáil from Labour. We understand that these two features explain left and right. A second dimension relating to populism, the importance of local issues and evaluations of the economy in the past five years, divides Fine Gael and Labour from Fianna Fáil and Sinn Féin. Due to the significant impact of left and right, we explore this in detail to find that voters position themselves close to the ideological positions of their chosen party. Voters position Fianna Fáil and Fine Gael on the right, Labour in the middle and Sinn Féin on the left. Finally, we use the sequence of preferences on replicated ballots from the RTÉ/INES exit poll (INES1) to understand the dimensions of political competition as derived from actual voting behaviour. This dimensional analysis suggests that preferential ordering reflects the aforementioned dimensions with elements of economic left–right, socio-moral left–right, populist versus elitist and government versus opposition underpinning the relative positions of political parties in the two-dimensional space. Typical issues relating to globalization more specifically are not yet a feature of Irish politics but it is clear that there is some overlap between left–right and the populist-elitist dimensions in this regard.

Decline of environmental constraints

Lipset and Rokkan's (1967) analysis of party systems suggests that Ireland's apparent uniqueness is due to fundamental differences between Ireland and other Western European countries. The political system that emerged in 1922 inevitably reflected the divisions of the deeply divisive civil war between radical nationalists and moderate nationalists. Only these two groups had the organizational capacity to establish a viable political organization and both parties sought to inherit the political capital of their ancestor party Sinn Féin.

Environmental factors also inhibited the emergence of a classic left–right divide, notably an agrarian economy and a dominant Catholic Church. Little challenged by a cautious Labour Party (Gallagher, 1985: 92), Fianna Fáil filled much of the political space that would otherwise be held by a party defined on the left: the populist stances of Fianna Fáil and its capacity to appeal to rank-and-file trade union members further undermined any significant support base for the left. In the intervening period, as European democracies moved from manufacturing-oriented economies to service-oriented economies, Ireland moved from its agrarian-oriented economy to a service-oriented economy. The role of the Catholic Church in political life has subsided considerably and the status of Northern Ireland following the Good Friday Agreement served to de-politicize the historical fault line between the two civil war parties. These changes mean that political debates in Ireland increasingly reflect typical debates in other European countries.

Evidence of statistically significant differences between party supporters emerged from the 1980s onwards: on left–right positions, religious-moral outlook, nationalism and environmentalism (Mair, 1986; Laver, Mair and Sinnott, 1987; Breen and Whelan, 1994; Farrell, 1999; Benoit and Laver, 2003). In highly politicized referendums on abortion and divorce, Fianna Fáil adopted the more socially conservative position, opposing the introduction of divorce and supporting stricter legislation in relation to abortion; Labour typically adopted the more liberal stance.

Expert studies suggest that the Irish political system could be characterized in terms of two dimensions: social policy and tax-spend policy, with the two larger parties in one corner representing the economically right and socially conservative positions and Labour and all the smaller left-leaning parties in the opposite corner (Laver, 1992). However, although statistically significant, the substantive impact of this has been weak (Marsh et al., 2008). Ideology on the socio-moral axis may significantly influence support for the Labour Party, but the party system and the relative levels of party support have barely changed. Only a small subset of voters had perhaps interpreted these differences as a basis for determining which party they would vote for. This is mainly due to the persistent dominance of – and insignificant differences between – Fianna Fáil and Fine Gael. For ideological dimensions to explain party support, Fianna Fáil and Fine Gael would need to lose a significant amount of their vote.

It is not so remarkable that the two parties would dominate political competition in the nascent state, but what is remarkable is that the same dynamic would persist many years after the aforementioned unique environmental conditions had subsided. As party identification – required to sustain this order – declined steadily from the 1980s (Marsh, 2006), a change event such as the post-2008 economic crisis was necessary for a significant redistribution of party preferences outside of the two larger parties. The elections of 2011 and 2016 were among the most volatile of all elections in Western Europe since 1945, the 2011 election earning the title of the most volatile election without a significant new entrant (Mair, 2011). The two parties averaged a total of 79 per cent of the vote in the 1980s, 65 per cent in the 1990s and 66 per cent in the 2000s. Following the economic crisis, support for the two parties declined further to a 52 per cent average in the 2010s with left and left-of-centre parties averaging a total of 32 per cent.

Ideological dimensions

Left and right

The 2008 global financial crisis had a profound and devastating impact on the Irish economy and much of the blame was placed on Fianna Fáil. In the 'earthquake' election of 2011, support for Fianna Fáil collapsed. For the first time since 1927 it was not the largest party and for the first time ever it was the third largest party. It was this collapse that precipitated some belief that a new left–right cleavage might emerge in Irish politics (for discussion, see Marsh, Farrell and McElroy, 2017).

The party system had, in Fine Gael, a classic centre-right party with significant support, but it required the emergence of something from the left to develop a classic left–right basis of political competition. In 2011 the left performed better than in any previous election, winning 31 per cent of the vote. For the second time, the Labour party had won 19 per cent of the vote. However, the party's decision to go into government in coalition with Fine Gael greatly undermined the development of a left–right basis of political competition (Marsh and Cunningham, 2011) as, following a longstanding pattern, in the 2016 election support for the minor coalition partner, Labour, collapsed. The 2016 election saw the party system take another turn with the partial recovery of Fianna Fáil and the continuing growth of Sinn Féin. Today's main left-wing opposition is Sinn Féin, and while the party's roots look more like the civil war politics of old with a strong association with Northern Ireland and constitutional nationalism, the party's support is much more clearly defined in terms of a working-class social base than perhaps any other party before it (see chapter 4). The rise of Sinn Féin in addition to the Labour Party, and a multitude of smaller left-leaning forces (including the Anti-Austerity Alliance, People Before Profit (AAA-PBP), Social Democrats, Socialist Party and Workers' Party) meant that support for the left in total remained high in 2016 at 29 per cent.

Data from the 2016 general election would suggest that ideology was important for some voters and unimportant for others. In the post-election survey (INES3) voters were asked on a scale of 0 to 10 how important it was that the candidate they chose had the same political viewpoint as the voters had themselves. The average score for this question was 6.3, with 39 per cent of Irish voters recording 5 or less on the scale. To understand the magnitude of this we can compare it with other factors that might be considered important, such as their chosen candidate having the same age, the same gender, the same level of educational attainment, the same social class, or being from the same area as the voter. Political viewpoint is the most important consideration but it does not dominate. In 31 per cent of cases the candidate's political viewpoint was the most important consideration and in a further 22 per cent it was at least as important as the next most important factor. However, for 47 per cent of voters a factor other than political viewpoint was more important. In 29 per cent of cases, having the same level of education was of higher importance. In 26 per cent of cases, where the candidate lived was more important than political viewpoint and in 20 per cent of cases the candidate being from the same social class was more important. A theme emerges where, for a significant number of voters, the local and personal relationships they have with candidates are deemed to be more important than their ideological positions (see chapter 10 for a more extended discussion).

On their own admission, ideology only matters much for roughly half of all voters and there is a pattern to this. When we compare this result against the person's left–right position a clear trend appears. Among 'left-leaning' voters (those that place themselves as 4 or lower on a left–right scale), 42 per cent rate a candidate's political viewpoint as more important than any other issue and, for 23 per cent of them, it was at least as important as the next most important factor. Among the most left-leaning voters (defining themselves as 2 or lower on the left–right scale), 77 per cent regard the candidate's ideological viewpoint as at least as important as any other consideration. By contrast, on the right-hand end of the spectrum, there is no such sharp focus on political viewpoint. It is notable that political viewpoint is considerably less important for supporters of Fianna Fáil (for just 29 per cent it was the most important) and Independent candidates (for 26 per cent it was the most important). This compared with supporters of Labour (35 per cent), the AAA-PBP (51 per cent) and the Green Party (58 per cent). Clearly, ideology is important, but seemingly it is more important for left-leaning voters intending to vote for left-wing parties.

Local factors

Structural factors also complicate the development of a clear left–right divide in Irish politics. One outcome of Ireland's single transferable vote (STV) electoral system is that it allows support for Independent candidates based on local values and patronage rather than left or right ideologies. These candidates benefitted enormously from the collapse of Fianna Fáil as they were uniquely positioned to capture some of the anti-system populist vote that might in other jurisdictions be captured by a left-wing political party (Carty, 1981; Komito and Gallagher, 2010; Marsh, 2007; Bowler and Farrell, 2017) (see chapter 7 for more details). The exit poll (INES1) asked respondents whether the party or the candidate was more important. Excluding those that did not know, 46 per cent stated that the party was more important than the candidate whereas 54 per cent stated that the candidate was more important than the party. Arguably, as candidates can be supported on policy grounds, it is almost certainly the case that national policy claims made by candidates are not definitive. Furthermore, when we ask if they would still vote for the same candidate if they ran for another party, 40 per cent say they would, and 17 per cent state that it would depend on which party.

Globalization

The local-national division is reflected in new dimensions of political competition. Across Europe, party choice is typically structured by a single left–right ideological dimension (e.g. Oppenhuis, 1995; Van der Eijk and Franklin, 1996). However, this is deemed to be insufficient in the context of the pressures of increasing globalization (Kriesi et al., 2006; 2008). Globalization has yielded winners and losers as increasing international integration and the role of market forces on economies have reduced government influence on local economies. As a result, solutions designed in terms of traditional left-wing or right-wing political responses have become much less effective. This has resulted in support for populist parties that have attempted to address rising frustration and distrust of politicians with support for protectionist solutions seeking to reverse globalization.

The behaviour of political parties is now defined by a socio-economic as well as a socio-cultural dimension. Cross-cutting traditional economic left–right divisions and the conservative-liberal dimension are sometimes explained in terms of the 'winners' and 'losers' of globalization (Kriesi et al., 2006; 2008), or, equivalently, in terms of those that see themselves as 'anywhere' as opposed to those that have rooted themselves 'somewhere' (Goodhardt, 2017; Jennings and Stoker, 2017). The 'winners' or 'anywheres' may be characterized as having higher levels of education, being economically mobile and valuing openness and autonomy. They consist of a combination of middle-class left-wing voters with cosmopolitan values and liberal right-wing voters favouring international liberalization and free trade. The 'losers' or 'somewheres' are more often rooted, particularly in towns and rural areas; they value their local identity, group attachments, community and familiarity. They combine working-class voters with traditional left-wing values and those resorting to a stronger anti-immigration, more right-wing perspective (Teney, Lacewell and De Wilde, 2014). This dimension relates closely to the expected impact of globalization on low-skilled and high-skilled workers, based on economic theory around factor endowments, which predicts that in rich countries, lower-skilled workers will suffer more negative competition from immigration (Mayda and Rodrik, 2005; O'Rourke and Sinnott, 2006).

In many cases, this globalization dimension is underpinned by a populist dimension that juxtaposes 'the pure people' against 'the corrupt elite' (Mudde, 2004). This is most evident in Ireland in relation to the emergence of the anti-water charges protests, in line with what Meyer and Tarrow (1998) termed 'movement societies' where political protest has become an integral part of Western European countries' political life, employed with greater frequency by more diverse constituencies to represent a wider range of claims than ever before. We arrive at several competing or complementary dimensions of voting behaviour: economic left–right, socio-moral left–right, globalization, populism, the value of the local candidate and the constitutional status of Northern Ireland.

Analysis of ideological dimensions

We explore each ideological dimension by first seeking to understand the extent to which it relates to party preferences. For parsimony, we identified specific attitudinal questions that represented the dimensions most closely. With respect to the traditional economic left and right, we look at both tax and spend and income inequality attitudes. In relation to the socio-moral dimension we use the respondents' attitudes towards abortion. Respondents record their own position on abortion from a total ban on abortion, 0, to a complete liberalization, 10. Those that give themselves a score between 0 and 3 are classified as being 'pro-life', those that give themselves a score between 7 and 10 are classified as being 'pro-choice' and the remainder are classified as being 'unsure'. Respondents are also asked about their position on a 'left–right scale'. Those with a score between 0 and 3 are classified as being 'left', those with a score between 7 and 10 are classified as 'right' and those in between are classified as being of the 'centre'. We explore the new globalization dimension via responses to an attitudinal question on immigration. The role of constitutional nationalism in terms of the status of Northern Ireland ties in with this. In relation to populism, we looked at attitudes towards the people and elites. The role of a TD in terms of providing a local service relates to the populist and globalization dimensions.

Because many of these dimensions overlap we estimated the relationship between these attitudes and vote choice independently. Specifically, we modelled the relationship between each attitudinal variable and each respondent's party choice using a multi-level regression model, having reformatted the data so that each case represented a respondent-party choice. Each model enabled us to estimate each party's support in each category. The mean support of the party and the support within the subgroup of each set of attitudes are given in Figures 3.1a to 3.1d.

The respondent's position on the left–right scale is significant with respect to the Fianna Fáil, Fine Gael, Sinn Féin and AAA-PBP votes. The Fine Gael vote rose from 24 per cent to 38 per cent among those who defined themselves as being on the right. Similarly, the Fianna Fáil vote increased from 21 per cent to 33 per cent. In relation to the left, Sinn Féin's support increased from 17 per cent to 36 per cent whereas AAA-PBP increased their vote from 5 per cent to 13 per cent among those that identified themselves as left. In the case of Fine Gael, this appears to be related to significant (if not substantially) right-wing positions on economic and socio-moral grounds. The party performs 5 per cent better among those who disagree with increases in tax and spend policies, 4 per cent better among those who would not like the state to act to reduce income inequality and 3 per cent better among those who adopt a position that might be classified as being 'pro-life'. The factors that underpin Fianna Fáil as a right-wing party reflect socio-moral themes more than economic themes. Fianna Fáil support increases by 4 per cent to 25 per cent among those that identify themselves as 'pro-life'. Continuing with the socio-moral themes, the Labour Party performs 2 per cent better among those that are pro-choice.

Globalization issues seem to map closely onto the socio-moral dimension, but weakly so. Both Fine Gael and Fianna Fáil perform 2 per cent better among those who would like to see greater limits on non-EU immigration; the Green Party performs 5 per cent better among those who would disagree with this. Immigration has a limited impact on Irish politics: nationalist sentiment is more commonly reflected in relation to Northern Ireland, for which Fine Gael and Fianna Fáil hold a much less nationalist position than Sinn Féin, who perform 10 per cent better among those who would like to see Northern Ireland unite with the Republic of Ireland. The issue of Northern Ireland appears to be a core belief for Sinn Féin supporters rather than a defining feature of the political system.

The populism dimension is better defined. Fine Gael performs 7 per cent better among those who would disagree that 'people, rather than politicians should make decisions'. Fianna Fáil and Sinn Féin are more likely to agree with the alternative, more populist view of people rather than politicians making decisions as both parties perform 2 per cent better among those who agree. Equivalently, Fianna Fáil and Independents attract 3 and 4 per cent more support, respectively, among those who agree that TDs should provide a local service, whereas Fine Gael and Labour perform 4 and 5 per cent better among those who would disagree with the idea that TDs should provide a local service.

We may characterize the party system as being defined as right versus left, in economic terms dividing Fine Gael from Sinn Féin and in socio-moral terms dividing Fianna Fáil from Labour. Another dimension cuts across this, dividing the more populist and localist Fianna Fáil and Sinn Féin from Fine Gael and Labour. Immigration and the role of Northern Ireland are much weaker. Even if statistically significant in some cases, the marginal impact of these variables renders them somewhat irrelevant.

To explore this in greater detail we examine the extent to which each ideological dimension relates to support for each party while accounting for other ideological dimensions. We conduct a series of separate regression analyses looking at the relationship between attitudinal responses and the extent to which respondents 'like' each party. This allows us to understand the relationship between dimensions – whether some dimensions add explanatory power and whether others are merely related to one another. Note that we must rely on a single dataset (INES2) for this form of analysis, limiting the range of dimensions that we can assess. We therefore rely on the dataset that has adequate measures of left and right, socio-moral left–right (through religion),

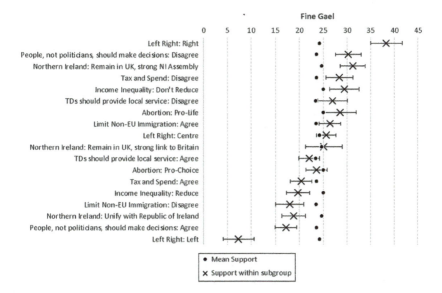

Figure 3.1a Mean support for Fine Gael and predicted support for Fine Gael within attitudinal categories.

Source: INES1 2016, INES2 2016 and INES3 2016.

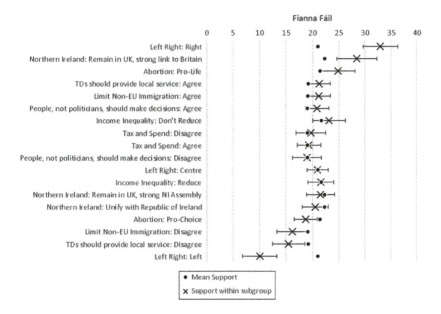

Figure 3.1b Mean support for Fianna Fáil and predicted support for Fianna Fáil within attitudinal categories.

Source: INES1 2016, INES2 2016 and INES3 2016.

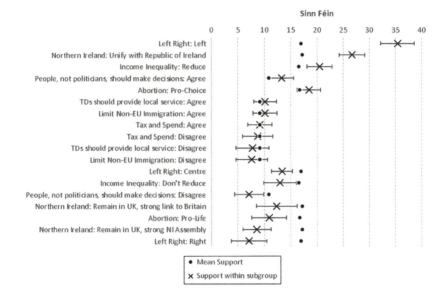

Figure 3.1c Mean support for Sinn Féin and predicted support for Sinn Féin within attitudinal categories.

Source: INES1 2016, INES2 2016 and INES3 2016.

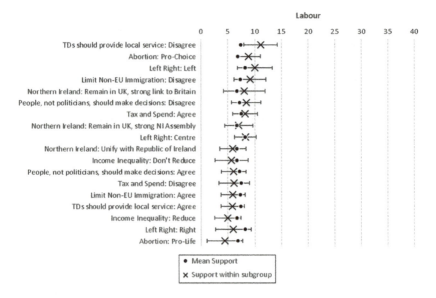

Figure 3.1d Mean support for Labour and predicted support for Labour within attitudinal categories.

Source: INES1 2016, INES2 2016 and INES3 2016.

economic left–right (through tax and spend attitudes), populism (through attitudes towards people or politicians making decisions) and globalization (through attitudes towards immigrants). We do not have an adequate measure to replicate the Northern Ireland dimension and in relation to socio-moral issues, we rely on membership of a religion. Although this is not the question on abortion, we do know that these are strongly related to one another. As per INES1, 50 per cent of those that are atheist, agnostic or spiritual advocated a very pro-choice position compared with just 23 per cent of those who had a religion. Seventy-seven per cent of those that were atheist, agnostic or spiritual adopted a pro-choice position compared with 50 per cent of those with a religion.

We also control for demographic variables and perceptions of the economy which relate to support for parties in this specific election. We control for age, gender, social class, education, work status and the type of area voters live in. We also control for their perception of the performance of the economy – whether it got worse, stayed the same or got better (see also chapter 6 in this volume). This is an important control for there may very well be significant numbers that momentarily dislike their typical party of choice due to their perceptions of the economy. The results of the regressions are given in Table 3.1.

Our first observation is that a person's left–right position is a highly significant predictor of which parties a voter is likely to favour. Those that are more left-wing are also more likely to like Sinn Féin, whereas those that are more right-wing are more likely to like Fine Gael or Fianna Fáil. The second most prominent feature is the populist dimension, that is, the extent to which people, not politicians, should make decisions. Those that like Fine Gael and Labour are much less likely to adhere to this view whereas those that tend to like Sinn Féin are more likely to agree with it. This appears to be more prominent once the respondent's left–right position is accounted for.

We also sought to determine the true difference between supporting Fianna Fáil over Fine Gael as estimated by subtracting the self-reported extent to which voters liked Fianna Fáil from the self-reported extent to which they liked Fine Gael. Those that tend to like Fianna Fáil more than Fine Gael are also more likely to adopt the more populist perspective. This corroborates earlier evidence supporting a populist dimension with Labour and Fine Gael towards the elitist end and Fianna Fáil and Sinn Féin towards the populist end. The regression suggests that Fianna Fáil supporters are more likely to be in favour of tax and spend policies. One should bear in mind that these effects are estimated while already accounting for the party's left–right position. The party is perhaps perceived as being right wing on the basis of its socio-moral position rather than economic issues. Certainly, those that like Fianna Fáil are significantly more likely to adhere to a religion while those that like Labour are significantly less likely. Our analysis of this variable supports earlier evidence

Table 3.1 Regression analysis estimating the extent to which a respondent likes Fine Gael, Fianna Fáil, Sinn Féin, Labour, and the difference in the extent to which they like Fianna Fáil over Fine Gael

	Fine Gael		Fianna Fáil		Sinn Féin		Labour		Fianna Fáil–Fine Gael	
	Estimate	P-Value	Estimate	P-Value	Estimate	P-Value	Estimate	P-Value	Estimate	P-Value
Intercept	0.171	0.718	0.257	0.000 ***	0.259	0.000 ***	0.560	0.000 ***	-0.290	0.000 ***
Left	-0.521	0.017 *	-0.090	0.001 ***	0.121	0.000 ***	-0.028	0.245	0.026	0.470
Right	0.380	0.022 *	0.062	0.003 **	-0.086	0.000 ***	-0.023	0.224	-0.025	0.377
Agree people should make decisions	-0.290	0.069 .	-0.019	0.355	0.091	0.000 ***	-0.056	0.002 **	0.048	0.078 .
Unsure people should make decisions	-0.014	0.963	-0.093	0.013 *	-0.019	0.637	-0.016	0.632	-0.083	0.095 .
In favour of tax and spend	0.041	0.890	0.124	0.001 ***	-0.009	0.811	0.056	0.088 .	0.120	0.016 *
Unsure of tax and spend	0.071	0.816	0.096	0.013 *	-0.050	0.224	0.028	0.406	0.084	0.102
Have religion	0.172	0.394	0.134	0.000 ***	0.048	0.083 .	-0.068	0.003 **	0.092	0.008 **
Agree culture harmed by immigrants	0.107	0.611	0.021	0.430	-0.008	0.785	-0.047	0.044 *	0.001	0.982
Unsure culture harmed by immigrants	0.087	0.730	0.046	0.152	0.008	0.826	-0.004	0.891	0.027	0.529

	B	p		B	p		B	p		B	p		B	p	
Economy was same	−0.769	0.000	***	0.002	0.919		0.071	0.004	**	−0.131	0.000	***	0.181	0.000	***
Economy got worse	−1.444	0.000	***	−0.059	0.150		0.103	0.018	*	−0.238	0.000	***	0.254	0.000	***
University degree	0.153	0.354		0.051	0.016	*	−0.051	0.022	*	0.023	0.219		0.017	0.531	
Working class – C2DE	−0.287	0.114		−0.044	0.055	.	0.103	0.000	***	−0.076	0.000	***	0.021	0.490	
Farmers	0.331	0.322		0.000	0.996		−0.089	0.042	*	−0.018	0.615		−0.072	0.186	
Female	0.229	0.159		−0.039	0.057	.	−0.102	0.000	***	0.080	0.000	***	−0.090	0.001	**
Homemaker	−0.102	0.745		0.006	0.879		0.020	0.638		−0.027	0.431		0.024	0.644	
Part-time	−0.034	0.883		0.002	0.936		0.002	0.938		−0.023	0.379		0.012	0.765	
Retired	0.329	0.309		0.007	0.870		−0.013	0.766		0.061	0.094	.	−0.067	0.213	
Student	−0.139	0.729		−0.048	0.339		0.042	0.435		−0.025	0.576		−0.015	0.819	
Unemployed	−0.480	0.151		−0.086	0.037	*	0.007	0.867		0.006	0.869		0.013	0.804	
Large town or city	−0.072	0.713		0.026	0.290		0.056	0.037	*	0.004	0.870		0.043	0.193	
Rural	0.199	0.340		0.066	0.012	*	0.012	0.668		0.002	0.931		0.022	0.527	
Small town	0.099	0.719		0.043	0.216		0.067	0.073	.	−0.006	0.839		0.019	0.678	
Age 25–34	0.077	0.823		0.001	0.988		0.016	0.736		−0.074	0.058	.	−0.018	0.755	
Age 35–44	−0.179	0.606		0.018	0.681		−0.018	0.701		−0.081	0.038	*	0.057	0.322	
Age 45–54	−0.155	0.662		0.006	0.901		−0.046	0.340		−0.048	0.231		0.040	0.501	
Age 55–64	−0.146	0.696		0.022	0.645		−0.057	0.257		−0.087	0.037	*	0.054	0.384	
Age 65+	−0.160	0.713		0.082	0.134		−0.092	0.116		−0.102	0.037	*	0.119	0.101	

Source: INES2 2016.

indicating that the socio-moral dimension was one which had Labour at one end and Fianna Fáil at the other. The controls account for perceptions of economic performance, with significant differences between those that support the government (Fine Gael and Labour) over the opposition (Fianna Fáil and Sinn Féin), and demographics, with Sinn Féin supporters in particular more likely to be working-class, male and without a university degree.

Left and right in Ireland

Our analysis of ideology leads to a recognition of the importance of understanding what left and right means to voters in Ireland. Policies that define the left or right can vary over time and across countries. Although voters may very well identify themselves as being on the left or the right it is not immediately clear what this means. The left and right may be characterized in terms of economic policy (for income redistribution or tax and spend policies) or social policy, reflecting the established position of the church set against more liberal social values, or indeed newer dimensions around globalization.

Using a regression analysis, we can estimate the left and right positions of voters in terms of attitudinal responses to key issues, while controlling for demography and economic voting behaviour. On the basis of the results of this regression analysis, given in Table 3.1, we observe that left–right is related to traditional economic and socio-moral issues. Although left–right does not appear to be significantly related to the populist dimension, it is strongly related to both economic tax and spend policies as well as to the socio-moral agenda. Those that are more right-wing are significantly less likely to be in favour of increases in tax and spend policies. In terms of the socio-moral agenda, those that pronounce that they are atheist, agnostic or labelled as someone without a religion tend to be more likely to position themselves on the left, but only marginally so. Those that are more likely to believe that Ireland's culture is harmed by immigrants are also marginally more likely to position themselves towards the right. The model explains 15 per cent of the variance in left–right position. Although these figures remain relatively low, they represent an increase from 4 per cent for the pre-crisis voter (Marsh, 2007).

To understand left and right further in an Irish context we use the voters' interpretations of where each party sits on the left and right scale. If there were no left or right in Irish politics, we would expect the party system to be clustered in the centre of the political space. Figure 3.2a is a set of box plots depicting where Irish voters placed Irish parties. For the purposes of comparison, Figure 3.2b is a set of box plots of where British voters placed British parties (using data from the 2015 British Election Study). The two plots help us to compare the parties within the Irish system and against a classic left–right political system as in British politics.

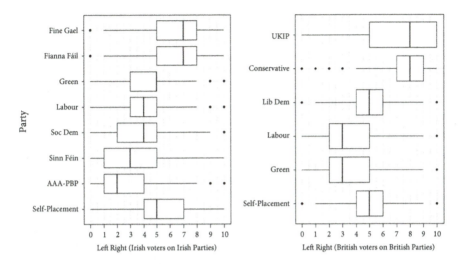

Figure 3.2a and 3.2b Irish and UK voter's self-placement and placement of political parties.
Source: INES2 2016, BES2015.

Firstly, there is little overlap between Fianna Fáil-Fine Gael and the parties on the left: Labour, Social Democrats, Sinn Féin and AAA-PBP. Coupled with the fact that these latter parties make up almost 30 per cent of the vote, it is clear that the voters understand the positions of the parties in terms of left and right. Fianna Fáil and Fine Gael occupy much of the centre-right where, unlike the British voter, most Irish voters are positioned.

Our comparison between the Irish party system and the British party system reveals that there are only subtle differences. The Irish voter is a little to the right of the British voter and the Irish party system is a little to the left of the British party system, if a little more concentrated. Fianna Fáil and Fine Gael are both much closer to the centre of the scale than the Conservatives and UKIP. Irish Labour, the Irish Green Party and the Social Democrats are to the left of the Liberal Democrats. Finally, Sinn Féin and the AAA-PBP are marginally to the left of the British Labour Party and the British Greens. The difference between Sinn Féin and Fine Gael is comparable to the difference between the British Labour Party and the Conservatives.

To further understand how far left and right influences party choice we analyse the relationship between the self-placements of voters and placements of their chosen party. As Table 3.2 shows, the self-placement of supporters is close not only to their assessment of their chosen party but also to the assessment of their chosen party by non-supporters. It is noticeable that, aside from supporters of Sinn Féin, supporters of parties tended to position their

Table 3.2 Regression analysis of estimated left–right position

	Estimate	P-value	
Intercept	5.116	0.000	***
Agree people should make decisions	−0.197	0.191	
Unsure people should make decisions	−0.311	0.259	
In favour of tax and spend	−1.027	0.000	***
Unsure of tax and spend	−0.784	0.006	**
Have religion	1.264	0.000	***
Agree culture harmed by immigrants	0.444	0.022	*
Unsure culture harmed by immigrants	0.559	0.018	*
Economy was same	−0.424	0.012	*
Economy got worse	−0.345	0.250	
University degree	0.029	0.850	
Working class – C2DE	0.029	0.863	
Farmers	0.561	0.065	.
Female	−0.255	0.094	.
Homemaker	−0.096	0.741	
Part-time	−0.240	0.265	
Retired	0.026	0.931	
Student	0.077	0.837	
Unemployed	0.019	0.950	
Large town or city	−0.140	0.446	
Rural	−0.065	0.737	
Small town	0.071	0.783	
Age 25–34	0.257	0.426	
Age 35–44	0.390	0.228	
Age 45–54	0.468	0.156	
Age 55–64	0.594	0.088	.
Age 65+	1.137	0.005	**

Source: INES2 2016.

party further away from the centre of political competition than they placed themselves. For example, the average Fine Gael supporter places him or herself at 6.3, and his or her party at 7.2, and non-supporters place Fine Gael at 6.5. This suggests that voters place their chosen party at a position more extreme than their own position, in line with the policy discounting model advocated by Grofman (1985). It is also interesting to note that supporters of established, mainstream parties – Fianna Fáil, Fine Gael, Labour and the Green Party – tended to place these parties further from the centre than non-supporters of each of these parties. However, supporters of non-established parties – Sinn Féin and AAA-PBP – tended to place those parties closer to the centre than non-supporters of these parties.

Table 3.3 Average assessments of supporters, non-supporters and the average position of supporters themselves

Party	Supporter's average assessment	Non-supporter's average assessment	Supporter's average left–right self-placement
Fine Gael	7.2	6.5	6.3
Fianna Fáil	6.8	6.4	6.3
Sinn Féin	4.7	2.7	4.4
Labour	4.1	4.3	5.1
Green Party	4.0	4.5	4.4
Social Democrats	3.9	3.8	4.3
AAA-PBP	2.8	2.3	3.8

Source: INES2 2016.

AAA-PBP = Anti-Austerity Alliance – People Before Profit.

To evaluate whether voters select the party closest to them, we conduct a regression analysis comparing the proximity of a voter to each party with whether they voted for that party. We include two additional control variables. In the first model, we include each party as some parties will, for reasons other than left–right position, receive more support. For example, their relative strength might also be attributed to their historical support levels, likelihood to enter government or other ideological and non-ideological reasons. In the second model, we also add the party's relative extremism. From the literature on policy discounting (Grofman, 1985), voters may believe a party's ability to pursue its agenda will be diluted to some degree and so they may counter this by supporting a party with a more extreme position than their ideal policy position (Kedar, 2005). Thus, we include a variable to account for the party's relative extremism, measured as the party's absolute deviation from the mid-point of five.

The regression analysis reveals a strong relationship between where the respondents located themselves relative to other parties and their choice, suggesting that parties located to within one point of their personal left–right placement were significantly more likely to be chosen as the first preference. Figure 3.3 depicts the relationship between the voter's party proximity (the absolute difference between the voter's position and that of a party) and his or her likelihood to support that party. It suggests that almost half of all respondents choose a party within one point of their own position on the left–right scale. The results of this regression analysis are given in Table A3.1 in the Appendix. We also find that voters do tend to vote for parties with more extreme positions than their own, rather than the parties closest to them.

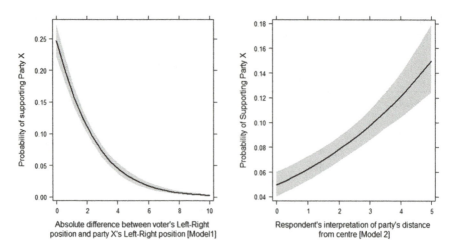

Figure 3.3 Effect plots explaining the effect of [1] voter-party proximity and of [2] party extremism on vote choice.
Source: INES2 2016.

A dimensional analysis of preference rankings

The purpose of this chapter is to investigate the extent to which ideological positioning affects vote choice. One can also reverse the question, and ask whether vote choice can be used to estimate ideological positioning. This is particularly useful as the analysis above does assume that we properly capture the ideological positioning of the respondent with the few attitudinal questions asked in the survey. Perhaps respondents do vote purely for ideological reasons, but their ideology is expressed on different dimensions, or the key dimensions are not accurately measured by the relevant survey questions. Given some assumptions, we can derive a possible ideological positioning of political parties from the relationship between parties in terms of vote transfers. All else being equal, if parties are ideologically close to each other, we expect voters to use their preference votes to support both parties, while if they are ideologically distant, defining major fault lines in political competition, then fewer voters would vote for both parties. We make use not only of the reported first preference vote, but the full preference ordering reported on the ballot in the exit poll.[1] This preference ordering is acquired using a mock-ballot paper, which is handed to the respondent at the start of the RTÉ/INES exit poll (INES1) interview. This interview takes place only minutes after the actual voting by the respondent, so that it is likely that the respondent still has a reasonably good recollection of how the real ballot paper was filled out. Table 3.3 gives an overview of the relationship between first and second preference votes. Specifically, we estimate each party's share of transfers from each other party. We also compare this figure with the party's first preference vote share to see whether a party is attracting more, or fewer, transfers than it might if there were no relationship between parties.

We can see, for example, that Sinn Féin attracts 36 per cent of its second preferences from AAA-PBP. If second preferences went according to first preference shares, in terms of the Sinn Féin's first preference popularity that figure is 2.3 times the number that might be expected. This is indicative of the close relationship between the two parties. In return, AAA-PBP receives a proportion of second preferences from Sinn Féin that is 4.9 times greater than we might expect from the former's first preference vote share. From our earlier analysis, we know that both parties are most closely defined in terms of left wing, favouring redistribution. Labour and Fine Gael form another grouping, with Fine Gael receiving 2.1 times its vote share in terms of the proportion of second preferences it receives from the Labour Party. In return, the Labour Party receives 4.9 times its first preference share in terms of the share of second preferences from Fine Gael. The two parties stood together in government and are united by a similar level of opposition towards populism.

We continue along those lines, but instead of looking at only the first and second preference, we consider the full ballot paper, and use dimensional analysis to provide a visualization of the results. For this analysis we look at the highest preference ranking given by a respondent to each of the parties. For example, if a respondent gives a first preference to a Fine Gael candidate, a second preference to a Labour candidate, a third preference to another Fine Gael candidate and a fourth preference to a Fianna Fáil candidate, then this respondent will score a one for Fine Gael, a two for Labour and a four for Fianna Fáil.[2] This leaves, of course, a lot of parties not scored for that particular respondent, since not all parties stand in all constituencies, and most respondents do not rank all candidates on the ballot (for more on this see chapter 2).[3] Since the algorithm used only takes ranking into account, not the distance between those rankings, we assign the lowest possible ranking in the dataset – the longest ballot paper has 22 candidates – to all rankings where that particular party did not receive any vote from that particular respondent, whether because it did not stand in the constituency or because the voter decided not to give a vote.

Based on these preference scores for each respondent and each party, we can construct a distance matrix between parties. If many respondents give high or low preference rankings to the same pair of parties, those parties have a short distance, and vice versa; when many voters give high preference to one party but low preference to the other, those parties will have a large distance. Such a distance matrix therefore provides a description of the ideological space in which Irish party competition takes place. Parties that are close to each other are competing closely for the same voters, while parties that are further away from each other appeal to very different segments of the voters. To a large extent, we can assume this to be driven by ideological factors – for example, left-wing parties can be

Table 3.4 Party second preference share of party first preferences

		Second preference								
First preference	Fine Gael	Fianna Fáil	Sinn Féin	Labour Party	AAA-PBP	Green Party	Social Democrats	Independent	Other Right	Other Left
Fine Gael	-	26 [1.2]	3 [0.2]	35 [4.9]	2 [0.3]	5 [1.3]	4 [1.2]	19 [1.4]	5 [1.6]	2 [1.0]
Fianna Fáil	29 [1.1]	-	17 [1.1]	10 [1.4]	5 [1.2]	4 [1.1]	6 [1.5]	21 [1.5]	7 [2.3]	1 [0.5]
Sinn Féin	8 [0.3]	13 [0.6]	-	4 [0.5]	23 [4.9]	5 [1.5]	4 [1.1]	31 [2.3]	7 [2.1]	4 [2.1]
Labour Party	54 [2.1]	16 [0.7]	4 [0.3]	-	3 [0.6]	6 [1.8]	5 [1.4]	10 [0.7]	1 [0.3]	1 [0.4]
AAA-PBP	6 [0.2]	6 [0.3]	36 [2.3]	7 [1.0]	-	12 [3.4]	6 [1.7]	18 [1.3]	4 [1.3]	6 [2.9]
Green Party	18 [0.7]	11 [0.5]	5 [0.4]	18 [2.6]	13 [2.7]	-	7 [1.8]	18 [1.3]	5 [1.5]	5 [2.5]
Social Democrats	22 [0.9]	15 [0.7]	13 [0.8]	10 [1.4]	5 [1.0]	13 [3.7]	-	14 [1.0]	5 [1.4]	3 [1.4]
Independent	26 [1.0]	23 [1.1]	17 [1.1]	9 [1.3]	6 [1.3]	4 [1.0]	4 [1.1]	-	7 [2.2]	4 [1.9]
Other right	25 [1.0]	22 [1.0]	9 [0.6]	3 [0.4]	5 [1.2]	9 [2.4]	4 [1.1]	21 [1.5]	-	2 [1.2]
Other left	7 [0.3]	6 [0.3]	16 [1.1]	12 [1.7]	13 [2.8]	9 [2.5]	1 [0.4]	30 [2.2]	4 [1.4]	-

Percentage of first preference voters for party in the row who give a second preference for party in the column (e.g. 26 per cent of those who voted Fine Gael gave Fianna Fáil as their second preference). In square brackets, the ratio of second preferences compared with the party's first preference vote share (e.g. The Labour Party's second preferences from Fine Gael are 4.9 times greater than the Labour Party's first-preference vote share in this survey).

Source: INES1 2016.

AAA-PBP = Anti-Austerity Alliance – People Before Profit.

expected to compete for voters primarily with other left-wing parties. The most expressive technique to interpret such a distance matrix would be to take the spatial analogy further and produce a map, a graphical visualization of the distances. Multidimensional scaling is a statistical technique to reduce such a distance matrix to a two-dimensional representation, such that the relative distances between the different parties are preserved to the greatest extent possible.[4] We are thus able to visualize this two-dimensional figure and interpret the visualization as a map of the ideological space in which Irish voting takes place.

Figure 3.4 provides this visualization when including the traditional Irish parties and a few that were prominent in the lead-up to the elections, some of which were founded in response to the global financial crisis.[5] The first dimension (the dashed diagonal line) clearly aligns with the left–right economic-based ordering of political parties in Ireland. As with a real geographical map, we are free to rotate the map as we see fit, and therefore are free to interpret the diagonal as opposed to the horizontal axis. Indeed, when we look at the self-placement on a left–right scale by the respondents and rank the parties by average self-placement of their (first-preference) voters, we obtain a reasonably similar ordering: from right to left, we would have Fine Gael, Fianna Fáil,

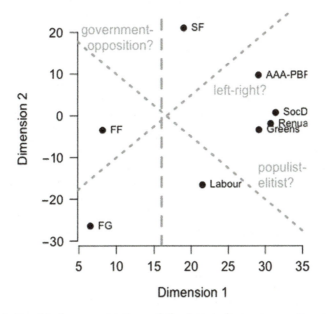

Figure 3.4 Graphical representation of the latent dimensions estimated by the multidimensional scaling algorithm, summarizing distances between parties based on the highest preference for each party assigned by each respondent.
Source: INES1 2016.

Renua, Social Democrats, Labour, Greens, Sinn Féin and AAA-PBP.[6] All the larger parties are classified by their left–right positioning, although smaller parties such the Greens, Renua and the Social Democrats are somewhat to the left of expectations. Results for the smaller parties have to be taken with a grain of salt, however, as the absolute numbers of transfers between these parties among the respondents in the survey are very low indeed. An alternative interpretation of the horizontal axis would be the populist dimension dividing establishment Labour and Fine Gael from anti-establishment Fianna Fáil and Sinn Féin. On the right are the larger, established parties, and on the left, the newer, small parties. Voters may signal an anti-establishment attitude by voting for a number of different parties, ranging from left-wing AAA-PBP to right-wing Renua, simply to indicate dissatisfaction with the establishment parties.

This dimensional space is the result of both ideology and other factors that separate voters, including retrospective evaluation of government performance. The second dimension in the figure appears primarily to depict a government-opposition dimension, with Labour and Fine Gael close to each other and to the party closest to the governing coalition, Fianna Fáil, while Sinn Féin is the most pronounced opposition party. Somewhat related to the government-opposition dimension is a more ideological dimension based on a populist worldview separating the ordinary people from the elite. As discussed earlier in the chapter, Sinn Féin and Fianna Fáil can be taken as significantly more populist than Labour and Fine Gael, which would be a potential alternative, more ideological explanation of the second axis, in this case perpendicular to the left–right axis in Figure 3.4.

To validate our interpretation of the multidimensional scaling results would be to correlate the two resulting dimensions, the two axes of the plot, with demographic and attitudinal variables available on the survey. For the sake of brevity, we leave out the details of the regression analysis.[7] The first dimension (the x-axis) correlates weakly with left–right self-placement and more strongly with whether respondents identify as Catholic and their level of church attendance. The second dimension (the y-axis) correlates instead with the left–right self-placement of the respondents. These correlations are particularly weak, however, with various demographics and ideological questions in the surveys only explaining about two per cent or less of the variation in the axes.

A new globalization dimension

Given the current attention to the phenomenon of populism and anti-globalization, especially since the election of Donald Trump to the US presidency, the question remains why there is no clear anti-globalization party in Ireland. Elsewhere, this has led to anti-establishment and typically anti-immigration parties on the right, such as the United Kingdom Independent Party, the Front

Nationale (National Front), the Alternative für Deutschland (Alternative for Germany) or the Partij voor de Vrijheid (Party for the Freedom), or anti-globalization parties on the left, such as Podemos or Syriza. While most of these parties are populist in nature, emphasizing the contrast between policies implemented by the elites and policy preferences of much of the population (Mudde and Kaltwasser, 2017), the ideologically more important commonality is the anti-globalization position, resulting in resistance primarily to liberal immigration policies and to European integration and free trade. Increased international integration is seen as harmful to the local labour market and local culture. De Vries (2017) investigates the relative importance of the economic and cultural components of this cosmopolitan-parochial divide, finding that, at least in the Netherlands, this divide is primarily driven by the relative economic insecurity of individual voters as a consequence of globalization.

Given the recent global financial crisis, we could expect Ireland to be fertile ground for such a political party. Some of this electoral space is occupied by Sinn Féin, as quite clearly their supporters do favour some of these policy approaches. While left-wing, it has a clear anti-globalization stance, similar to how the Socialistische Partij (Socialist Party) in the Netherlands is a key competitor to the Partij voor de Vrijheid, or similar to left-wing populist parties such as Podemos and Syriza, although this does not translate into an anti-immigration attitude for Sinn Féin. Indeed, O'Malley (2008) shows that anti-immigration attitudes correlate with increased support for Sinn Féin, despite the pro-immigration stance of the party, suggesting that the party captures to some extent this anti-globalization segment of the population. Whether as a result of a lack of campaigning by Sinn Féin or otherwise, immigration positioning is a very weak predictor of voting behaviour in comparison with other dimensions. The electoral system also affects the party's ability to manoeuvre. Given the country's history of emigration and limited immigration, any stance on immigration would almost certainly be divisive. The requirement to win transfers from other parties means that such a divisive issue may damage the party's electoral prospects. Furthermore, the party must also adopt a coherent stance north and south of the border where it operates. Given that Irish people have for several centuries migrated to Britain, such a position would also be somewhat incoherent. That no other parties or political entrepreneurs emerged is also interesting. It is perhaps in part related to the lack of ideology in the party system in the first place. If the parties are sufficiently pragmatic and populist to adjust to changes in public opinion regarding socio-economic or cultural policies, then there are fewer objectionable policies that anti-establishment parties will react against.

Drawing on the regression analysis reported above to determine support for specific parties, we evaluate party support against basic demographics. Sinn Féin is the party of the working class; it is also the party of the less well-educated. Support for Fianna Fáil is also significant in this demographic group. By contrast,

Fine Gael and Labour perform significantly better among those with university education and from higher social grades. The groups that are identified by Kriesi et al. (2006) as more vulnerable to international integration and apparently more likely to support more parochial parties are therefore more likely to support the two more nationalist parties, while they are less likely to support Labour or Fine Gael. Using a battery of questions that measure populism more specifically we construct an index based on these questions, and a multinomial regression analysis explaining vote choice confirms this result. Controlling for demographics, left–right position and religiosity, more populist voters are significantly more likely to vote Sinn Féin or Independent, and significantly less likely to vote Fine Gael, than to vote Fianna Fáil. In the dimensional analysis of the full preference ranking on the ballot paper, we also find suggestive evidence of a populist ideological dimension, juxtaposing Sinn Féin and Fianna Fáil to Fine Gael and Labour. Notably, Fine Gael and Labour have indeed significantly different views to Sinn Féin in respect of immigration and one of the key significant differences between Fianna Fáil and Fine Gael relates to immigration.

Conclusion

Although ideology may not play the lead in Irish politics, it is at the very least a supporting actor. Crucial to this assertion is the rise of left-wing parties in the aftermath of the financial crisis. In Ireland, the mean electoral support for 'class left' parties between the 1950s and 1980s was 13 per cent. This compared with 42 per cent across 14 Western European democracies (Gallagher, Laver and Mair, 1992). In the immediate aftermath of the financial crisis, support for left and centre-left parties has risen to just under 30 per cent in total. This is widely facilitated by support for Sinn Féin – a party which is more closely defined by social class than the Labour Party. Left and right are significant predictors of party support and there appears to be a consistent relationship between the positions adopted by voters and the parties they support. Economic left–right separates Fine Gael supporters from Sinn Féin supporters while socio-moral left–right more clearly divides Fianna Fáil and the Labour Party.

Drawing similar conclusions to McElroy's (2017) analysis of the post-crisis voter, we observe that voters no longer have a difficulty in placing both themselves and political parties on a general left–right dimension. However, unlike McElroy's analysis that was based on data from 2011, we observe some increasing policy coherence to these placements with voters' preferences on economic and social issues increasingly corresponding with their own perception of their left and right. While ideological positioning may not separate the two largest parties, it does determine whether someone might vote for either or neither of those parties. On average, Irish voters select parties that are ideologically close to them on a left–right scale. This left–right dimension is also clearly dominant in the analysis of the latent ideological space of party competition, where vote transfers are used to estimate the relative ideological distances between parties. When visualizing these distances on a map, we can clearly see the parties ordered along the left–right dimension, in line with expert surveys and self-placement by voters of the parties.

Controlling for left and right, those that like Fianna Fáil tend to be more likely in favour of tax and spend policies. The notion that Fianna Fáil is somewhat left of Fine Gael on economic terms should come as little surprise. Fianna Fáil leaders have never shied away from such credentials: De Valera was quoted as saying, 'In those days I believe we could be called socialists, but not communists' (Mair, 1987: 17). In the 1980s, Fianna Fáil leader Charles Haughey denounced the 1982–1987 government's monetarist approach, referring to Keynes as the 'last economist worth his salt' (reported in the *Irish Times*, 6 February 1987). More recently Fianna Fáil Taoiseach Bertie Ahern went so far as to define himself as a 'socialist' (*Sunday Independent*, 31 October 2004). Fianna Fáil appears to be identified by voters as being on the right of the left–right scale on account of its conservative position on socio-moral issues while Fine Gael is more closely associated with economic conservativism. While arguably advocating more profligate and economically left-of-centre policies, Fianna Fáil's political positioning reflects a populist dimension more than a left-wing economic one. Yet, by contrast to Sinn Féin, the party is still widely considered to be significantly further to the right, economically. Sinn Féin has emerged as a left-wing party.

Although there is a significant overlap between socio-moral and economic left and right and globalization, populism offers a clear, second, cross-cutting dimension defining political competition. Sinn Féin and Fianna Fáil supporters are more likely to advocate more populist attitudes whereas Fine Gael and Labour supporters are more likely to advocate more elitist attitudes. Although immigration and globalization do not currently play a significant role in Irish politics, they map onto the Irish political system as somewhere between left–right and populist dimensions. One significant caveat is that this analysis reflects a period in which Fine Gael and Labour were in government. Thus, the most clearly identifiable distinction in the latent space analysis is more simply, and more idiosyncratically, the contrast between the government of the day and the opposition.

The Irish case in a comparative perspective may appear more conventional in terms of left–right competition than typically assumed; it also has an undercurrent of anti-globalization similar to that found in other European states. The flexible nature of the two catch-all parties that dominate the party system may lead to further development of this dimension. However, the stability of Irish politics suggests that movement in this direction may very well be slow. That, of course, depends on whether Irish politics has entered a period of continued instability or whether it is in a shorter phase of re-alignment.

Chapter Appendix

Table A3.1 Modelling the relationship between a respondent's party choice and the difference between where they put themselves and where they put each party on the left–right scale

Fixed effects:	Est.	SE	P-Value		Est.	SE	P-Value	
Intercept	−2.300	0.248	0.000	***	−2.868	0.264	0.000	***
Fianna Fáil	1.988	0.260	0.000	***	2.171	0.264	0.000	***
Fine Gael	2.573	0.258	0.000	***	2.705	0.261	0.000	***
Green	0.467	0.287	0.104		0.786	0.293	0.007	**
Labour	1.009	0.275	0.000	***	1.350	0.281	0.000	***
Sinn Féin	1.747	0.268	0.000	***	1.940	0.272	0.000	***
Social Democrats	0.416	0.295	0.158		0.660	0.299	0.027	*
Party-self left–right difference	−0.481	0.031	0.000	***	−0.555	0.033	0.000	***
Party distance from centre					0.244	0.034	0.000	***

Source: INES2 2016.

SE = standard error.

Notes

1 In this manner, we make use of the unique feature of STV electoral systems whereby we have relative preferences for a range of parties for each voter to perform our ideological analysis of voting behaviour. An alternative, for example, would be to use sympathy scores, measures of how much a voter likes each party or probability-to-vote questions. While these are perfectly valid alternatives, an advantage of the approach presented here is that generally in surveys, questions about behaviour – such as how a ballot was filled out – tend to be somewhat more reliable than attitude questions or hypothetical questions such as the probability to vote.
2 One weakness of this approach is that voters will base their preference on not only the party, but also the candidate (see chapter 10), which intervenes with the ideological interpretation of the party ordering.
3 Our measure thus provides a measure of the highest preference given to each party, based on the candidates ranked. An alternative approach would be to simply rank the parties, ignoring intra-party transfers. For example, in our analysis, a voter who ranks candidates from, respectively, Fine Gael, Labour, Fine Gael and Fianna Fáil would in our data obtain a lower score for Fianna Fáil than someone who ranks them as Fine Gael, Labour, Fianna Fáil and Fine Gael, while if simply parties were ranked, scores would be identical. We argue that the former voter, if ideology drives the ranking, would consider Fianna Fáil ideologically further away than the latter voter does.
4 We make use of the MDPREF algorithm which allows for multidimensional scaling with preference data, using the implementation in the 'pmr' package in R by Paul H. Lee and Philip L. H. Yu.
5 When all parties are included, all the very small parties end up in the same part of the ideological space as Renua and the Social Democrats, except for the Independent Alliance, which ends up somewhere between Sinn Féin and Fianna Fáil.
6 The rank ordering based on the 2014 data of the Chapel Hill Expert Survey also confirms this left–right ordering of Irish political parties. http://chesdata.eu/, accessed 1 August 2017.
7 Available upon request from the authors.

References

Benoit, Kenneth, and Michael Laver. 2003. 'Estimating Irish party policy positions using computer wordscoring: The 2002 election–a research note', *Irish Political Studies*. 18: 97–107.

Bowler, Shaun, and David M. Farrell. 2017. 'The lack of party system change in Ireland in 2011', in Michael Marsh, David Farrell and Gail McElroy (eds), *A Conservative Revolution? Electoral Change in Twenty-First Century Ireland*. Oxford: Oxford University Press, pp. 83–101.

Breen, Richard, and Christopher T. Whelan. 1994. 'Social class, class origins and political partisanship in the Republic of Ireland', *European Journal of Political Research*. 26: 117–33.

Carty, R. Kenneth. 1981. *Electoral Politics in Ireland: Party and Parish Pump*. Ontario: Wilfrid Laurier University Press.

Chubb, Basil. 1957. 'The independent member in Ireland', *Political Studies*. 5: 131–39.

De Vries, Catherine E. 2017. 'Benchmarking Brexit: How the British decision to leave shapes EU public opinion', *Journal of Common Market Studies*. 55: 38–53.

Farrell, David, 1999. 'Ireland: A party system transformed?', in David Broughton and Mark Donovan (eds), *Changing Party Systems in Western Europe*. London: Pinter, pp. 30–47.

Gallagher, Michael. 1985. *Political Parties in the Republic of Ireland*. Manchester: Manchester University Press.

Gallagher, Michael, and Lee Komito. 2010. 'The constituency role of Dáil deputies', in John Coakley and Michael Gallagher (eds), *Politics in the Republic of Ireland*. London: Routledge, pp. 230–62.

Gallagher, Michael, Michael Laver and Peter Mair. 1992. *Representative Government in Western Europe*. New York: McGraw Hill.

Gallagher, Michael, and Michael Marsh. 2002. *Days of Blue Loyalty: The Politics of Membership of the Fine Gael Party*. Dublin: PSAI Press.

Goodhart, David. 2017. *The Road to Somewhere: The Populist Revolt and the Future of Politics*. Oxford: Oxford University Press.

Grofman, Bernard. 1985. 'The neglected role of the status quo in models of issue voting', *Journal of Politics*. 47(1): 230–37.

Jennings, Will, and Gerry Stoker. 2017. 'Tilting towards the cosmopolitan axis? Political change in England and the 2017 General Election', *Political Quarterly*. 88(3): 359–69.

Kedar, Orit. 2005. 'When moderate voters prefer extreme parties: Policy balancing in parliamentary elections', *American Political Science Review*. 99(2): 185–99.

Kriesi, Hanspeter, Edgar Grande, Romain Lachat, Martin Dolezal, Simon Bornschier and Timotheos Frey. 2006. 'Globalisation and the transformation of the national political space: Six European countries compared', *European Journal of Political Research*. 45: 921–56.

Kriesi, Hanspeter, Edgar Grande, Romain Lachat, Martin Dolezal, Simon Bornschier and Timotheos Frey. 2008. *West European Politics in the Age of Globalisation*. Cambridge: Cambridge University Press.

Laver, Michael. 1992. 'Are Irish parties peculiar?', in John Goldthorpe and Christopher Whelan (eds), *The Development of Industrial Society in Ireland*. Oxford: Oxford University Press, pp. 359–81.

Laver, Michael, Peter Mair and Richard Sinnott (eds). 1987. *How Ireland Voted: The Irish General Election, 1987*. Dufour Editions, Dublin: Poolbeg.

Lipset, Seymour M., and Stein Rokkan. 1967. 'Cleavage structures, party systems, and voter alignments: An introduction', in Seymour M. Lipset and Stein Rokkan (eds), *Party Systems and Voter Alignments: Cross-National Perspectives*. New York: Free Press, pp. 1–64.

Lutz, Karin G. 2003. 'Irish party competition in the new millennium: Change or plus ça change?', *Irish Political Studies*. 18(2): 40–59.

Mair, Peter. 1986. 'Locating Irish political parties on a left-right dimension: An empirical enquiry', *Political Studies*. 34(3): 456–65.

Mair, Peter. 1987. *The Changing Irish Party System: Organisation, Ideology and Electoral Competition*. London: Pinter.

Mair, Peter. 2011. 'The election in context', in Michael Gallagher and Michael Marsh (eds), *How Ireland Voted 2011*. London: Palgrave Macmillan, pp. 283–97.

Marsh, Michael. 2006. 'Party identification in Ireland: An insecure anchor for a floating party system', *Electoral Studies*. 25(3): 489–508.

Marsh, Michael. 2007. 'Candidates or parties? Objects of electoral choice in Ireland', *Party Politics*. 13(4): 500–27.

Marsh, Michael, David M. Farrell and Gail McElroy (eds). 2017. *A Conservative Revolution? Electoral Change in Twenty-First Century Ireland*. Oxford: Oxford University Press.

Marsh, Michael, and Kevin Cunningham. 2011. 'A positive choice, or anyone but Fianna Fáil?', in Michael Gallagher and Michael Marsh (eds), *How Ireland Voted 2011*. London: Palgrave Macmillan, pp. 172–204.

Marsh, Michael, Richard Sinnott, John Garry and Fiachra Kennedy (eds). 2008. *The Irish Voter: The Nature of Electoral Competition in the Republic of Ireland*. Manchester: Manchester University Press.

Mayda, Anna Maria, and Dani Rodrik. 2005. 'Why are some people (and countries) more protectionist than others?', *European Economic Review*. 49(6): 1393–1430.

McElroy, Gail. 2017. 'Party competition in Ireland', in Michael Marsh, Richard Sinnott, John Garry and Fiachra Kennedy (eds), 2008. *The Irish Voter: The Nature of Electoral Competition in the Republic of Ireland*. Manchester: Manchester University Press, pp. 61–82.

Meyer, David S., and Sidney Tarrow. 1998. 'A movement society: Contentious politics for a new century', in John D. McCarthy, Clark McPhail, David S. Meyer, and Sidney Tarrow (eds), *The Social Movement Society: Contentious Politics for a New Century*. London: Rowman and Littlefield, pp. 1–28.

Mudde, Cas. 2004. 'The populist zeitgeist', *Government and Opposition*. 39(4): 542–63.

Mudde, Cas, and Cristóbal Rovira Kaltwasser. 2017. *Populism: A Very Short Introduction*. Oxford: Oxford University Press.

O'Malley, Eoin. 2008. 'Why is there no radical right party in Ireland?', *West European Politics*. 31(5): 960–77.

O'Rourke, Kevin H., and Richard Sinnott. 2006. 'The determinants of individual attitudes towards immigration', *European Journal of Political Economy*. 22(4): 838–61.

Oppenhuis, Erik. 1995. *Voting Behavior in Europe: A Comparative Analysis of Electoral Participation and Party Choice*. Amsterdam: Het Spinhuis.

Sinnott, Richard. 1995. *Irish Voters Decide: Voting Behaviour in Elections and Referendums since 1918*. Manchester: Manchester University Press.

Teney, Céline, Onawa Promise Lacewell and Pieter de Wilde. 2014. 'Winners and losers of globalization in Europe: Attitudes and ideologies', *European Political Science Review*. 6(4): 575–95.

Urwin, Derek W., and Kjell A. Eliassen. 1975. 'In search of a continent: The quest of comparative European politics', *European Journal of Political Research*. 3(1): 85–113.

Van der Eijk, Cees, and Mark N. Franklin. 1996. *Choosing Europe? The European Electorate and National Politics in the Face of Union*. Ann Arbor, MI: University of Michigan Press.

Whyte, John. 1974. 'Ireland: Politics without social bases', in Richard Rose, *Electoral Behaviour: A Comparative Handbook*. New York: The Free Press, pp. 619–51.

4

Social and ideological bases of voting

John Garry

Introduction

In contrast to our near neighbours – Northern Ireland and Britain – Ireland is often characterized as having a political system in which voting behaviour is only loosely connected to the socio-demographic and ideological traits of voters. In the British case, one academic (Pulzer, 1967: 98) famously stated that 'class is the basis of British party politics; all else is embellishment and detail'. This characterization still resonates today, with the working class, who tend to have economically left-wing beliefs, voting for Labour while the middle class, who are more likely to hold relatively pro-free-market views, tend to support the Conservative party (Evans and Tilley, 2017). In Northern Ireland, the main 'political cleavage' is even more potent. Citizens from a Catholic community background are much more likely than citizens from a Protestant community background to hold pro-United Ireland views and vote for nationalist parties, while pro-UK Protestants overwhelmingly support unionist parties (Garry, 2016).

In Ireland, there is no analogous political cleavage that allows us to easily make sense of how Irish people vote. The choice of which party to vote for at an Irish election is much less anchored in social traits and ideological beliefs linked to those traits (Marsh et al., 2008). In fact, for much of Ireland's history, the burning question for observers at election time has been: Is there any difference between the two main parties, Fianna Fáil and Fine Gael? The initial 'civil war' distinction between the parties, essentially pitting the strongly nationalist Fianna Fáil against the moderately nationalist Fine Gael, has long since faded. Furthermore, the dominance of this 'national question' at the time of the formation of the state also served to constrain the emergence of a clear economic left versus right distinction in the party system, resulting in the Labour party being unable to make strong headway as a party of the working class seeking to implement leftist beliefs (Sinnott, 1984). Whyte's much-quoted characterization of Ireland in the early 1970s as 'politics without social bases' still has significant truth (Whyte, 1974). Many analysts have examined the empirical basis of Irish voting and have found at least 'some' structure to the vote (for example, Laver's 'Politics with some social bases' (1986); see also Marsh and Sinnott, 1990; 1993; 1999; Sinnott, 1995; Garry et al., 2003; Marsh, 2007; Marsh and Cunningham, 2011). However, its limited nature is perhaps best exemplified by the finding of the first Irish National Election Study, that Labour tended to attract support more from the middle than the working class (Marsh et al., 2008).

In a recent study of the 2007–2011 election time points, Tilley and Garry (2017) did find significant evidence of a class structure to the vote, suggesting that Ireland's economic crisis, and the possible policy responses to it, may have jolted the political system towards the international norm of a choice between interventionist parties (Labour and Sinn Féin) and free-market parties (Fine Gael), leaving a defeated catch-all (Fianna Fáil) behind in the electoral rubble. Tilley and Garry found that the vote choice of Fianna Fáil defectors could be explained in class and economic policy terms: relatively middle-class and right-wing votes went to Fine Gael while the more working-class and leftist votes went to Labour and Sinn Féin. As the authors acknowledge, this class structure to the vote may have been due to the unique circumstances of that election, in which a 'catch-all' centrist party imploded due to widely perceived mismanagement of the economy. One of the aims of this chapter is to continue this examination of the role played by class and economic policy beliefs and to do so in the post-crisis context of the 2016 election.

Aside from economic matters, one cluster of issues in Ireland that *has* proved to be socially and ideologically rooted, and also highly salient politically, relates to the 'liberal versus conservative' dimension in politics – including issues such as abortion and gay rights. Highly religious voters tend to hold socially traditional views while non-religious or minimally religious voters are of a more liberal disposition. How this distinction links to voting, however, has typically been evident in the context of referendums rather than elections, with several referendums since the early 1980s on abortion and also on divorce and marriage equality, and another referendum on abortion likely in 2018. Political parties have indeed adopted positions on these issues and insofar as the liberal-conservative dimension does influence election campaigns and party competition, a relatively liberal Labour party has competed against the more conservative-minded Fianna Fáil and Fine Gael parties (Marsh et al., 2008). In order to assess whether this distinction between Labour and the two main parties still holds, the role played by socio-moral issues in structuring vote choice in 2016 will be examined in this chapter.

While these three parties – Labour, Fianna Fáil and Fine Gael – have typically dominated Irish elections, Sinn Féin can now be added as a 'major player', achieving a significant increase in vote share and seat share in 2016 and replacing Labour as the third biggest party in the state. This – seemingly sustainable – rise of Sinn Féin suggests an increased role played by social and ideological factors in the structuring of Irish voting, as the party has clearly defined positions on all three policy themes of economy, nation and socio-moral issues. Most obviously, Sinn Féin is likely to attract votes from strongly nationalist citizens, but also – given its economic leftism and social liberalism – from left-wing/working-class citizens and from those on the socially liberal side of the socio-moral debate (see discussion in Garry, 2017).

The overall aim of this chapter is to relate these broad ideological themes – economy, nation and socio-moral values – to vote choice at the 2016 election in order to paint a picture of the post-crisis Irish voter. Is there a strong link between voters' socio-demographic traits, their broad policy beliefs and their party choice?

We begin by briefly outlining some expectations regarding the social and ideological bases of party support. We then describe the data that we will use in our empirical investigation of these expectations. We report the social and ideological characteristics of the supporters of the different parties in 2016. We then focus on change over time and assess the social and ideological profile of voters who switched from the main governing party (Fine Gael) in 2016 to one or other of the rival main parties.

Expectations

A simple 'model' of voting is sketched in Figure 4.1, in which choice at election time is driven by one's everyday social experience and behaviour, and the political beliefs that are likely to flow from that experience and behaviour. On the theme of the economy, citizens are expected to vary in terms of the extent to which they are either on the free market or socialist side of the 'left versus right' debate. Citizens with leftist views, who favour a strong interventionist state to reduce inequality and fund state services, are likely to come from a working-class background, while citizens who are likely to benefit most from a more laissez-faire economic approach are likely to be middle class. Insofar as these factors influence voting, we expect the biggest differences to be between the leftist Sinn Féin and the much more economically conservative Fine Gael.

On the theme of morality, a socially conservative position is likely to be held by strongly religious citizens while social liberals are likely to come from non-religious backgrounds. We expect the traditionally conservative Fianna Fáil to be most distinct from the liberal Labour party. We suggest that both religion and education are likely to undergird beliefs on the national question, with Catholics[1] and the less educated being more likely to hold nationalist positions and, in turn, support Sinn Féin as the most clearly nationalist party. In contrast, being non-Catholic and highly educated is likely to dispose one

Theme	Social base	→	ideology	→	vote choice
Economy	*social class*		*free market vs. socialist*		
	Middle class	→	free market	→	Fine Gael
	Working class	→	socialist	→	Sinn Féin
Morality	*religiosity*		*Liberal vs. conservative*		
	Highly religious	→	conservative	→	Fianna Fáil / Fine Gael
	Not religious	→	liberal	→	Labour
Nation	*religion + education*		*strongly vs. weakly nationalist*		
	Catholic	→	strongly nationalist	→	Sinn Féin
	Not Catholic	→	weakly nationalist	→	Fine Gael
	Low educational level	→	nationalist	→	Sinn Féin
	High educational level	→	unionist	→	Fine Gael

Figure 4.1 Expectations of the social and ideological bases of vote choice.
Note: Only the strongest expectations are sketched here.

to eschew a nationalist position and hence being more inclined to support the more pluralist Fine Gael.

This model is relatively sparse as it focuses on only a small number of sociodemographic factors and hypothesizes only the strongest expected relationships regarding the social and ideological underpinnings of the vote. We additionally seek to examine the importance of factors such as age, gender and place of residence, and we also examine the Greens, AAA-PBP and Independents, but Figure 4.1 acts as a valuable heuristic guide to frame our examination of the key social and ideological expectations regarding the main parties in the system.

Measurement

All of the survey data analysed in this chapter come from one survey, namely the RTÉ/INES exit poll (INES1). The wording of the survey questions that were designed to tap citizens' stances on the three main ideological themes is reported in Figure 4.2. Two survey items are used on the economy: attitudes to taxation and spending and attitudes to equality. Abortion is used as the key issue to measure positions on the liberal–conservative continuum, and a question about the desired long-term constitutional position of Northern Ireland is asked to measure citizens' dispositions on the nationalist–unionist debate. In order to enable a simple analysis, we recode the responses of each of these four survey questions into a smaller number of categories (as detailed in Figure 4.2).

Ideally, in order to generate a high-quality measure of citizens' attitudes on a particular ideological dimension, a range of survey questions would be asked and a summary measure would be generated from this set of questions (see, for example, Evans et al. (1996) on multi-item scales measuring economic left–right and libertarian–authoritarian values). Having only

---

Socio-Moral
On a scale from 0 to 10 where 0 means you strongly believe that *there should be a total ban on abortion in Ireland*, and 10 means that you strongly believe that *Abortion should be freely available in Ireland to any woman who wants to have one*, where would you place your view?

Nation
In terms of the long term future of Northern Ireland, which would you prefer? Northern Ireland should:
Remain in the UK with a direct and strong link to Britain
Remain in the UK and have a strong Assembly and Government in Northern Ireland
Unify with the Republic of Ireland

Economy
Taxation and spending
On a scale of 0 to 10, where '0' means government should CUT TAXES A LOT and SPEND MUCH LESS on health and social services, and '10' means government should INCREASE TAXES A LOT and SPEND MUCH MORE on health and social services. Where would you place yourself in terms of this scale?

Equality
On a scale from 0 to 10 where 0 means you strongly believe that the government SHOULD ACT to reduce differences in income and wealth, and 10 means that you strongly believe that the government SHOULD NOT ACT to reduce differences in income and wealth, where would you place your view?

Note – For simplicity of analysis these variables are recoded. Socio-moral: 0-3=conservative, 5-6=centrist, 7-10=liberal. Nation: 1-2=UK, 3=Unity. Taxation and Spending: 0-3=cut taxation and spending, 4-6=centrist, 7-10=increase taxation and spending. Equality: 0-3=reduce inequality, 4-6=centrist, 7-10=not reduce inequality.

Figure 4.2 Wording of the ideology questions.

one question on the liberal-conservative theme and one question on the nationalism theme may be seen as somewhat crude in measurement terms. However, these particular single items were chosen to capture a core element of the theme that is of significant political importance. On the economic theme, we capture two distinct components of the general social democratic versus free-market approach to economic management, and these focus on equality and taxation and spending. For consistency, these are used as single item measures.

A different approach to assessing ideology and voting is to ask voters how they position themselves on a 'left' versus 'right' scale. This has the attractiveness of providing a single item overall summary of citizens' policy views. However, what we are keenly interested in examining in this chapter is the relative strength of distinct ideological dimensions (economic, nation and social/moral) in explaining vote choice. While useful in many ways, it is not possible to disentangle the distinct effects of the different ideological components of a single 'left' versus 'right' measure (see Cunningham and Elkink in chapter 3 of this volume; see also Inglehart and Klingemann, 1976; Knutsen, 1997). Furthermore, as McElroy (2017) has shown using a number of different surveys, only to a weak extent does left–right self-placement act as a proxy for policy positions for voters in Ireland.

Ideological profile of Irish voters

As illustrated in Figure 4.3, just over one third of voters favour Irish unity while almost half prefer that Northern Ireland remains in the United Kingdom (either in the form of direct rule or in the context of a functioning devolved administration). A quite high proportion of respondents do not have a clear view either way (17 per cent). Voters' responses to the question on abortion availability suggest a much greater proportion of liberals than conservatives in Ireland on this issue, with one fifth on the conservative side of the debate and almost one half on the liberal side. Irish voters emerge as quite economically left wing in terms of their responses to questions about tax and spend and equality. Over a third favour greater taxation and spending compared with only one in ten who adopts a right-wing anti-tax approach. Almost two fifths favour government action to reduce inequality compared with less than a quarter who are opposed to such government intervention. Overall, the picture emerges of Irish voters as weakly nationalist, quite strongly liberal and more likely to indicate support for interventionist than free-market economic policy options.

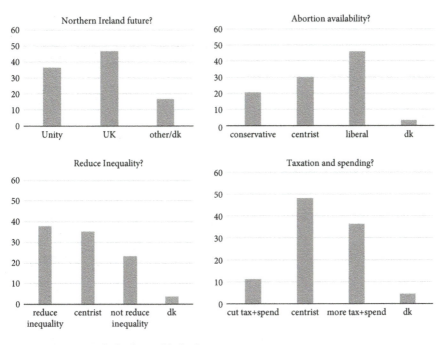

Figure 4.3 Voters' ideological beliefs.
Source: INES1 2016.

Social bases of ideological beliefs

Is there a clear social basis to these ideological beliefs? Most strikingly, in relation to economic beliefs, the answer is 'no'. As reported in Table 4.1, there are no significant social-class differences between those who favour left-wing positions on tax and equality and those who do not: 36 per cent of the middle class (ABC1) favour more tax and spend, and an almost identical figure of 37 per cent of the working class (C2DE) favour more tax and spend. The percentage difference is slightly larger for the issue of equality, but it is not statistically significant. In fact, the only social basis that emerges for the economic questions suggests that older voters and urban voters hold relatively left-wing views on taxation and spending. The picture emerging, then, is of variation among voters on economic left–right ideological issues, but the views voters hold are not rooted in, or explained by, their socio-demographic profile.

In terms of a possible social basis to views on the national question, our expectations are consistent with the data. Support for a united Ireland is less likely to come from the highly educated and is more likely to come from those with lower levels of education, and it is also more likely to come from Catholics than non-Catholics. In fact, the percentage support for unity among

Table 4.1 Social bases of ideological beliefs

	Pro-united Ireland %	Socially liberal %	More tax and spend %	Reduce Inequality %
All	**37**	**46**	**36**	**38**
Age 18–44	35	*54*	*32*	38
45+	38	*41*	*40*	38
Female	*31*	48	36	38
Male	*42*	44	37	38
ABC1	34	*52*	36	35
C2DE	40	*41*	37	40
F	32	*21*	26	44
Third-level	*32*	*54*	38	35
Not third-level	*40*	*40*	35	40
Catholic	*38*	*41*	36	39
Not Catholic	*31*	*64*	40	34
Weekly or more	35	*28*	37	36
Less/never	37	*56*	36	39
Rural	38	*35*	*29*	35
Urban	36	*52*	*40*	39

Source: INES1 2016.

Note: Figures relate to the percentage of each opinion group made up of voters with the associated socio-demographic trait. For example, 35 per cent of 18–44-year-olds favour a united Ireland and 38 per cent of 45+ year-olds favour a united Ireland. Italicized differences are statistically significant at 0.05 level or better (e.g. male respondents are statistically significantly more likely to favour a united Ireland than females [42 per cent of males compared with only 31 per cent of females]).

ABC1 = middle-class demographic; C2DE = working-class demographic; F = farmers.

low-attending Catholics (39.6 per cent) is higher than that among frequently attending Catholics (35.2 per cent), suggesting that it is the group identification as Catholic that matters rather than intensity of Catholic religious belief and engagement. A much stronger social basis for views on the liberal-conservative dimension is evident. In line with expectations, voters who regularly attend religious services (weekly or more frequently) are much less likely to be socially liberal (28 per cent) than voters who are infrequent attenders or who never attend (56 per cent). Furthermore, strong differences emerge on almost all of our social factors: liberals are likely to be younger, middle class, third-level educated, non-Catholic and urban.

In order to further tease out which particular socio-demographic characteristics are the most powerful predictors of ideological beliefs, a series of analyses were conducted which, for each ideological theme, used all the social factors simultaneously in a single model (see Table 4.2).[2] It emerges that frequent attendance at religious services is the most potent explanatory factor, while

Table 4.2 Social bases of ideological beliefs: Binary logistic regression models

	Pro-united Ireland	Socially liberal	More tax and spend	Reduce inequality
Age 18–44	0.92	1.16	0.68**	1.02
Female	0.65***	1.24	0.97	0.99
ABC1	0.92	1.24	0.89	0.83
F	0.67	0.66	0.68	1.37
Third-level	0.74*	1.23	1.19	0.87
Catholic	1.36*	0.58***	0.82	1.32
Weekly or more	0.81	0.41***	1.11	0.81
Rural	1.1	0.65***	0.65***	0.80
Constant	0.72*	1.41*	0.87	0.65**
N	1492	1492	1492	1492
Nagelkerke r-square	0.03	0.14	0.03	0.01

Source: INES1 2016.

Note: Figures reported are odds ratios (*0.05 level, **0.01 level, ***0.001 level). ABC1 = middle-class demographic; F = farmers.

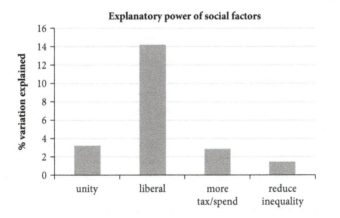

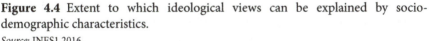

Figure 4.4 Extent to which ideological views can be explained by socio-demographic characteristics.
Source: INES1 2016.

being Catholic and living in a rural area are also strong predictors of holding conservative beliefs. As illustrated in Figure 4.4, the explanatory power of this model is quite strong, explaining 14 per cent of the variation, and importantly dwarfing the ability of social factors to explain either the nation or economy factors (which have associated explanatory power of between one and three per cent). However, while our two expected predictors of being pro-unity – being Catholic and having a low education – do emerge as significant, and consistent with Table 4.1, no class basis to economic left–right beliefs emerges, suggesting economic attitudes that are free-floating and removed from the class basis typically found in other democracies (see discussion in Evans and Tilley, 2017).

Social bases of voting

We now focus on vote choice and examine how these social and ideological variables are systematically related to opting for one particular party rather than another. We begin by providing a simple socio-demographic profiling of the type of people who vote for each party (see Figure 4.5).

In terms of the age profile, what is striking is that the three 'traditional' parties of Fianna Fáil, Fine Gael and Labour have a lower proportion of young voters than the more youth-friendly Sinn Féin, the Greens and AAA-PBP – with the Independents in between (see also chapter 5 in this volume on the Sinn Féin age profile). The social-class profile of each party's voters suggests that only about one third of Sinn Féin voters are middle class compared with almost 60 per cent of Fine Gael and Labour voters, and over 70 per cent of Green voters. AAA-PBP and Fianna Fáil share a similar proportion of middle-class voters (approx. 47 per cent), while Independents tend to have less middle-class support. The pattern of the relationship is almost identical when we look at voters with high education levels.

When we examine the Catholic and religiosity variables, both graphs (Figure 4.6a and b) show the same relationship, with the exception of Sinn Féin support. Just over four fifths of Sinn Féin voters are Catholic and this is the same proportion as for Fine Gael and Independents and only a few percentage points lower than for Fianna Fáil. Labour is significantly lower and the Greens are particularly low. But in terms of religious attendance, only one fifth of Sinn Féin voters regularly attend and the relative position of the other parties is approximately the same as the Catholic distribution. A significant proportion of Sinn Féin voters, then, are non-religious Catholics. This is consistent with the idea that Catholic identity (rather than belief or behaviour) is a driver of Sinn Féin support. In terms of place of residence, Fine Gael, Fianna Fáil and Independents have over 36 per cent of supporters who are rural dwellers, compared with only seven per cent of AAA-PBP voters.

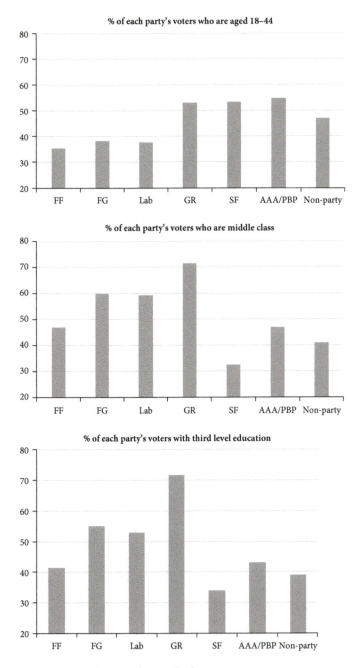

Figure 4.5 Party voters by age, class and education.
Source: INES1 2016.

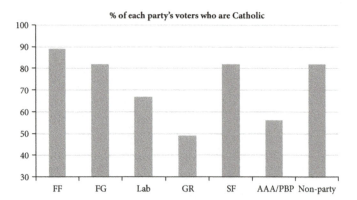

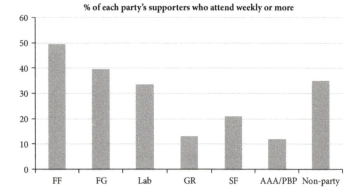

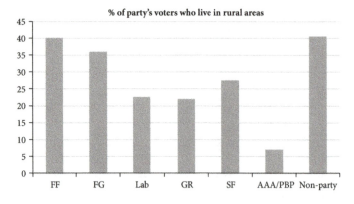

Figure 4.6 Party voters by Catholic, religiosity and residence.
Source: INES1 2016.

Ideological bases of voting

There are also some notable differences in the ideological profiles of each party's voters. Between 57 and 64 per cent of Labour, Green and AAA-PBP voters are socially liberal compared with 43 per cent or less of Fine Gael, Fianna Fáil and Independent voters. More sizeable differences are evident when one looks at the percentage of each party's voters who support a united Ireland: almost 60 per cent of Sinn Féin voters compared with between 27 and 33 per cent of Fianna Fáil, Fine Gael and Labour voters (and pro-unity Green voters are particularly rare). The pattern emerging from the two economic ideology factors is inconsistent: while Labour, the Greens and AAA-PBP voters emerge as the most left wing on taxation and spending, it is AAA-PBP and Sinn Féin whose voters tend to be left wing on the issue of equality.

Taking both demographics and ideology into account, it is worth reflecting on the extent to which the profile of the parties divides neatly into two blocks: the 'old' or traditional parties of Labour, Fine Gael and Fianna Fáil on the one hand and the 'new' or 'anti-establishment' parties on the other (Sinn Féin, AAA-PBP, Greens and Independents). Something approaching a pattern emerges in relation to age (the traditional parties have an older age profile) and religiosity (the traditional parties have a church-attending profile). Yet Sinn Féin looks more like an older party in terms of having a strongly Catholic profile and being quite rural. This possible 'two-block' interpretation is also hampered by the differences between the Greens and AAA-PBP (on education and class for example) and differences between Labour on the one hand and Fine Gael/Fianna Fáil on the other (on extent of liberal attitudes for example).

Social and ideological model of voting

In order to be more precise about the key socio-demographic and ideological predictors of vote choice, we enter the full set of variables into a series of regression models – reported in Table 4.3 – and relate our findings directly to our expectations set out in Figure 4.1. We begin by comparing Fine Gael voters with Sinn Féin voters. In line with our expectation that this comparison would be the most distinct with respect to social and ideological predictors, we find the model explains almost 40 per cent of variation (joint most predictive of the six models). In line with expectations, we find a class, education and religious attendance effect. The class effect is the strongest, with working-class voters being much more likely to support Sinn Féin than Fine Gael, and also those with third-level education and frequent religious attendance more likely to support Fine Gael than Sinn Féin. A very strong pro-unity effect emerges, with those favouring a united Ireland being much more likely to support Sinn Féin than Fine Gael, and there is also an effect of holding left-wing views on

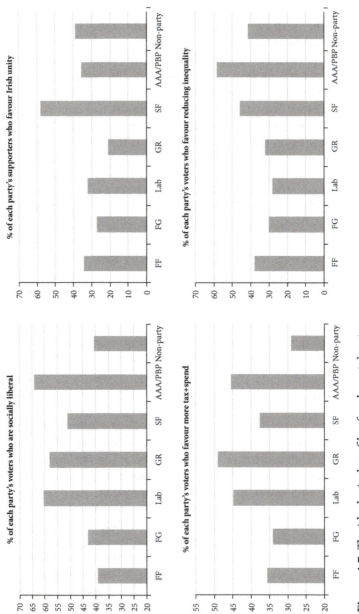

Figure 4.7 The ideological profile of each party's voters.
Source: INES1 2016.

equality relating to voting for Sinn Féin rather than Fine Gael. Overall, this may be regarded as quite a strong model of the social and ideological influence on vote choice between these two parties.

An almost identical, albeit not quite as strong, model separates Sinn Féin voters from Fianna Fáil voters (the main difference being the absence of a third-level effect and an equality effect). What is interesting, when one compares Sinn Féin voters to Labour voters, is that Sinn Féin voters are considerably more likely than Labour voters to be working class, and are more likely to be Catholic, but less likely to frequently attend religious services. Sinn Féin voters are also, unsurprisingly, much more likely than Labour voters to be pro-unity, but are also considerably more likely than Labour voters to favour a reduction in inequality.

Thus, in the comparisons between Sinn Féin and the three other main parties, quite significant social and ideological bases to voting emerge. When the three other parties – Fine Gael, Fianna Fáil and Labour – are each compared with each other, the explanatory power of the social and ideological factors is much less (between 8 and 18 per cent). The most noteworthy model is the

Table 4.3 Social and ideological bases of vote choice: Binary logistic regression models

	SF not FG	SF not FF	SF not Lab	FF not FG	Lab not FG	Lab not FF
Age 18–44	2.36***	1.99***	2.40***	1.08	0.90	0.88
Female	0.87	1.16	0.95	0.80	0.78	0.97
ABC1	0.23***	0.45***	0.18***	0.60**	1.11	2.07*
F	0.20**	0.66	1.32	0.35**	0.13	0.39
Third-level	0.46**	0.64	0.53	0.70	0.77	1.17
Catholic	1.05	0.90	2.81**	1.56	0.43**	0.31***
Weekly or more	0.47**	0.30***	0.29***	1.35	1.25	1.01
Rural	0.44***	0.50***	0.77	0.98	0.56*	0.60
Unity	3.57***	2.69***	3.73***	1.22	1.27	0.86
Liberal	1.18	1.09	0.85	0.96	1.63	1.66
More tax and spend	1.08	1.06	0.78	0.96	1.50	1.27
Reduce inequality	1.63*	1.27	2.27**	1.33	0.95	0.70
Constant	1.01	0.99	1.95	0.85	0.47	0.49
N	596	549	334	669	454	407
Nagelkerke r-square	0.38	0.28	0.38	0.08	0.11	0.18

Source: INES1 2016.
ABC1 = middle-class demographic; F = farmers.

comparison between Fianna Fáil and Labour, where Labour's middle class and non-Catholic credentials shine through. Fianna Fáil also emerges as being significantly more working class than Fine Gael.

Explaining voter dynamics: Vote choice of Fine Gael deserters

Another way to investigate the possible social and ideological bases of vote choice is to focus on over-time dynamics. Following the style of analysis of Tilley and Garry (2017), we hone in on the main governing party – Fine Gael – who lost significant support between 2011 and 2016 and we examine the vote choice of those voters who deserted the party. Hence, as reported in Table 4.4, we compare voters who voted for Fine Gael in 2011 and in 2017 and compare these 'Fine Gael stickers' to people who voted Fine Gael in 2011 but switched to either Fianna Fáil, Sinn Féin or Labour. Our rationale here is that there may be many reasons why people deserted Fine Gael, but once they do so, they must decide which of the other parties to support. While desertion may possibly be a function of disappointment with the governing performance of Fine Gael, it may be that post-desertion party choice is driven by assessing which party provides the closest socio-demographic and ideological match. Due to the low number of respondents, we simply present the results of a series of cross tabs, and only present statistically significant relationships (FG switchers to Labour, n = 70, and FG switchers to SF, n = 76).

Switchers to Labour and to Sinn Féin are the most different in terms of social class and education, with almost all switchers to Labour being middle

Table 4.4 Vote dynamics 2011 to 2016: Profiling FG stickers and switchers

		%	%	%	%	%	%	%
2011	2016	Young*	ABC1***	Third level*	Weekly*	Rural**	Unity***	Liberal**
FG	FG	32	60	55	46	37	27	38
FG	FF	33	53	53	54	34	33	39
FG	Lab	39	86	66	20	14	44	72
FG	SF	47	41	42	40	36	67	53

Source: INES1 2016.
*Statistically significant at 0.05, **0.01 and ***0.001 level.
FG/FG, n = 770; FG/FF, n = 179; FG/Lab, n = 70, FG/SF, n = 76.
ABC1 = middle-class demographic; FF = Fianna Fáil; FG = Fine Gael; Lab = Labour; SF = Sinn Féin.

class compared with only 41 per cent of switchers to Sinn Féin (and 66 per cent of switchers to Labour being third-level educated compared with only 42 per cent of switchers to Sinn Féin). The biggest ideological differences relate to being pro-unity and socially liberal. The pro-unity proportion of Fine Gael stickers is considerably lower than the pro-unity proportion of switchers to Sinn Féin. Similarly, the socially liberal proportion of Fine Gael stickers is considerably lower than the proportion of liberals among switchers to Labour.

Conclusion

The rise of Sinn Féin as a major player in Irish politics has implications for how we understand the social and ideological bases of voting. The party's strong socio-demographic profile (working class, left wing, and pro-unity) means that 'political cleavage'-based models of vote choice that work well in many other democracies begin to work reasonably well in Ireland, at least in differentiating Sinn Féin voters.

While social and ideological distinctions between Fianna Fáil, Fine Gael and Labour have traditionally been quite weak, and emerge again as quite weak in the analysis presented here, when one compares Sinn Féin voters to the voters of these three parties, clear differences emerge. Sinn Féin support is distinctly working class, pro-united Ireland and in favour of government action to reduce inequality. A similarly distinct profile of Sinn Féin supporters emerges when one focuses on those voters who switched to it from the main governing party, Fine Gael. Such switchers were significantly working class and pro-unity, in interesting contrast to Fine Gael-to-Labour switchers who were more likely to be middle class and socially liberal. So, the social and ideological distinctiveness of supporters of Irish parties is most noteworthy with respect to the role played by Sinn Féin in attracting a particular type of voter.

What the analysis in this chapter shows is that we can shed light on the determinants of ideological voting in Ireland by taking the standard dimensions that have been used internationally – relating to economy, nation and socio-morality. While it has typically been hard in prior research to identify strong differences along these dimensions between the traditional parties of Fianna Fáil, Fine Gael and Labour, this analysis demonstrates that when the emerging big player – Sinn Féin – is compared with these older parties, then political cleavages and standard ideological dimensions can help us discern significant differences in party support bases. We hence build on the analysis of the previous election by Tilley and Garry which argued in favour of the emergence of ideology in the form of class politics, but we here highlight the distinct profile of Sinn Féin.

Notes

1 Due to the traditionally small proportion of non-Catholics in Ireland, the Catholic versus non-Catholic distinction has not often been focused on in survey-based analyses of Irish voting behaviour, with religiosity (how religious are you?) rather than religion (what religion are you?) used as an explanatory variable. However, Catholics now represent only 78 per cent of the Irish population, and so this is a substantial distinction in reality (http://www.cso.ie/en/media/csoie/releasespublications/documents/population/2017/ Chapter_8_Religion.pdf). In the survey data used in this chapter, Catholics are somewhat over-represented, at 85 per cent.

2 Many of our variables are likely to be related to each other. For example, people who are young also tend to be people who have low religious attendance. Regression modelling allows us to take this into account and identify whether it is primarily age or religiosity that is the driver of opinion on moral issues. In fact (Table 4.2, column 2), it turns out that age is no longer a significant predictor when all variables are taken into account, and social class and education level also emerge as non-significant.

References

Evans, Geoffrey, and James Tilley. 2016. *The New Class Politics in Britain: The Political Exclusion of the Working Class*. Oxford: Oxford University Press.

Evans, Geoffrey, Anthony Heath and Mansur Lalljee. 1996. 'Measuring left-right and libertarian-authoritarian values in the British electorate', *The British Journal of Sociology*. 47: 93–112.

Garry, John. 2016. *Consociation and Voting in Northern Ireland: Party Competition and Electoral Behaviour*. Philadelphia: University of Pennsylvania Press.

Garry, John. 2017. 'Nationalist in the North and socialist in the South? Examining Sinn Féin's support base on both sides of the border', in Niall Ó Dochartaigh, Katy Hayward and Elizabeth Meehan (eds), *Dynamics of Political Change in Ireland: Making and Breaking a Divided Island*. London: Routledge, pp. 145–56.

Garry, John, Fiachra Kennedy, Michael Marsh and Richard Sinnott. 2003. 'What decided the election?', in Michael Gallagher, Michael Marsh and Paul Mitchell (eds), *How Ireland Voted 2002*. London: Palgrave, pp. 119–42.

Inglehart, Ronald, and Hans-Dieter Klingeman. 1976. 'Party identification, ideological preference, and the left–right dimension among Western Mass Publics', in Ian Budge, Ivor Crewe and Dennis Fairlie (eds), *Party Identification and Beyond: Representations of Voting and Party Competition*. New York: Wiley, pp. 243–73.

Knutsen, Oddbjørn. 1997. 'The partisan and value based component of left-right self-placement: A comparative study', *International Political Science Review*. 18: 191–225.

Laver, Michael. 1986. 'Ireland: Politics with some social bases: An interpretation based on survey data', *Economic and Social Review*. 17: 193–213.

Marsh, Michael. 2007. 'Explanations of party choice', in Michael Gallagher and Michael Marsh (eds), *How Ireland Voted 2007: The Full Story of Ireland's General Election*. Basingstoke: Palgrave Macmillan, pp. 105–31.

Marsh, Michael, and Kevin Cunningham. 2011. 'A positive choice, or anyone but Fianna Fáil?', in Michael Gallagher and Michael Marsh (eds), *How Ireland Voted, 2011*. Basingstoke: Palgrave Macmillan, pp. 172–204.

Marsh, Michael, and Richard Sinnott. 1990. 'How the voters decided', in Michael Gallagher and Richard Sinnott (eds), *How Ireland Voted: The Irish General Election, 1989*. Galway: Galway University Press, pp. 68–93.

Marsh, M., and R. Sinnott. 1993. 'The Voters: stability and change', in M. Gallagher and M. Laver (eds), *How Ireland Voted, 1992*. Dublin: PSAI Press, pp. 93–114.

Marsh, M., and R. Sinnott. 1999. 'The behaviour of the Irish voter', in M. Marsh and P. Mitchell (eds), *How Ireland Voted, 1997*. Boulder: Westview Press in association with the PSAI Press, pp. 151–80.

Marsh, Michael, Richard Sinnott, John Garry and Fiachra Kennedy. 2008. *The Irish Voter: The Nature of Electoral Competition in the Republic of Ireland*. Manchester: Manchester University Press.

McElroy, Gail. 2017. 'Party competition in Ireland: The emergence of a left-right dimension?', in Michael Marsh, David M. Farrell and Gail. McElroy (eds), *A Conservative Revolution? Electoral Change in Twenty-First Century Ireland*. Oxford: Oxford University Press, pp. 11–27.

Pulzer, Peter. 1967. *Political Representation and Elections in Britain*. London: Allen and Unwin.

Sinnott, Richard. 1984. 'Interpretations of the Irish party system', *European Journal of Political Research*. 12: 289–307.

Sinnott, Richard. 1995. *Irish Voters Decide: Voting Behaviour in Elections and Referendums since 1918*. Manchester: Manchester University Press.

Tilley, James, and John Garry. 2017. 'How economic catastrophe realigned Irish politics along economic divisions', in Michael Marsh, David M. Farrell and Gail McElroy (eds), *A Conservative Revolution? Electoral Change in Twenty-First Century Ireland*. Oxford: Oxford University Press, pp. 61–82.

Whyte, John. 1974. 'Ireland: Politics without social bases', in R. Rose (ed.), *Electoral Behaviour: A Comparative Handbook*. New York: Free Press, pp. 619–51.

5

Party identification in the wake of the crisis: A nascent realignment?

Rory Costello

Introduction

Many commentators have sounded the death knell for party identification. For example, Dalton claims that we are witnessing a general process of partisan dealignment and that this trend 'reflects long-term and enduring characteristics of advanced industrial societies' (Dalton, 2002: 29). Like many other countries, Ireland experienced a sustained period of political dealignment, beginning in the 1970s (or earlier) and continuing right through to the new millennium. In Eurobarometer polls taken in the late 1970s, approximately two thirds of Irish respondents described themselves as being close to a political party; this had declined to 40 per cent by the mid-1990s (Mair and Marsh, 2004: 242). As reported below, just over one quarter of respondents admitted to feeling close to a party in Irish National Election Study (INES) surveys conducted in 2002 and 2007, and this fell even further in 2011.

This is an important and, for many observers, worrying development. Partisanship is associated with political engagement, and is also seen by some as providing the stability necessary for a functioning representative democracy. As Rosenblum argues, 'Partisans are carriers of a more extended story about the party than may be told by the candidates of the moment.' Their long-term focus and attention to their party, even outside election years, acts as a 'check on short-term, arrant, political considerations' by their party, as well as providing support and sustenance to the party following electoral defeat (Rosenblum, 2010: 355). A dealigned electorate, by contrast, is usually associated with disengagement, the growth of anti-establishment populism, and, above all, political instability (Green, Palmquist and Schickler, 2004: 222; Mair, 2013: 19).

Dealignment is one potential explanation for the high levels of volatility observed in the 2011 and 2016 elections in Ireland, as argued by Marsh and McElroy (2016: 159). Not only were these the two most volatile elections in the history of the state, they also rank among the ten most volatile elections in post-war Western Europe (Farrell and Suiter, 2016). Fianna Fáil, which had been the biggest party in every general election since 1927, lost over 70 per cent of its seats in 2011; Labour lost an even larger proportion of its seats in 2016. A number of new parties emerged during this period, and a record number of voters turned away from political parties altogether and voted instead for Independent candidates. If these are symptoms of a dealigned electorate, then electoral volatility is likely to be here to stay.

Yet at other times and in other contexts, long-term declines in party identification have been reversed following a 'critical' election which disrupts the old political order and subsequent 'cementing' elections in which new political alignments become embedded (Miller and Shanks, 1996; Wattenberg, 1996: 138). The 2011 and 2016 Irish general elections could conceivably fit this pattern. As described by Burnham (1970), critical elections 'are closely associated with abnormal stress in the socioeconomic system (and) are marked by ideological polarizations and issue-distances between the major parties which are exceptionally large by normal standards'. The 2011 election in Ireland was preceded by an unprecedented level of economic stress leading to the bailout by the EU and IMF, and the economic consensus that had dominated party politics during the 2000s gave way to greater political polarization.

It is clear that the elections of 2011 and 2016 dramatically changed the Irish party system. The question that this chapter seeks to answer is whether the electoral turbulence was simply a symptom of a fundamentally dealigned electorate, or whether we are witnessing a realignment in Irish politics. In other words, has the number of floating voters increased in the wake of the crisis, or have people begun to form new party attachments that are likely to shape elections in the future? To address this question, this chapter will examine both the level and direction of party attachment in Ireland between 2002 and 2016. The chapter is organized as follows. First, the debates about the concept of party identification are introduced, and the meaning and measurement of party identification in Ireland are assessed using panel data from the Irish National Election Study (2002–2007). Next, arguments about partisan change (dealignment and realignment) are discussed, before presenting evidence on the evolution of partisanship in Ireland in the period 2002–2016, using the full set of INES studies. The chapter concludes by discussing what these findings imply for future elections in Ireland.

The meaning and measurement of party identification in Ireland

Despite its importance to generations of electoral researchers, party identification remains a highly contested concept. The traditional account, found in 'The American Voter', is that party identification is a lasting psychological attachment to a party or (according to a more recent restatement) a sense of belonging to a partisan group (Campbell et al., 1964: 67; Miller and Shanks, 1996: 120; Green, Palmquist and Schickler, 2004: 8). These attachments form relatively early in life, due to a combination of family and peer group influences and the political environment during an individual's first experiences of voting (Miller and Shanks, 1996: 128–32). Once established, party attachments are expected to be highly stable, and become more ingrained over time. One of the main reasons for this stability, according to this view, is that partisanship is causally prior to and has a significant impact on many other political attitudes. In the words of Campbell et al. (1964: 76), 'Identification with a party raises a perceptual screen through which the individual tends to see what is favourable to his partisan orientation.' Partisanship is therefore seen as an exogenous factor exerting enormous influence on long-term electoral trends.

There are a number of important critiques of this argument. A revisionist view assigns much less significance to party identification as a driver of other political attitudes. For Fiorina (1981: 84), partisanship is nothing more than a 'running tally' of an individual's evaluations of party performance. This account treats partisanship as a rational assessment rather than as a psychological attachment. As such, it is much more susceptible to change in response to short-term political events, and not the important explanatory variable that the authors of 'The American Voter' assumed. Thomson (2017) provides evidence in support of this revisionist view of partisanship in the Irish case.

A second line of criticism is that party identification has little meaning outside the United States. The usefulness of party identification as a concept is tied up with its stability: individuals may change their vote in response to short-term factors, but partisanship is far stickier, and hence a better predictor of future behaviour. However, in some European contexts, party identification was found to covary strongly with the vote (Thomassen, 1976; LeDuc, 1981). If party identification is synonymous with the vote, it loses its usefulness as an independent variable to explain long-term electoral patterns. The lack of applicability of the concept to many European countries is generally believed to derive from the very importance of political parties in structuring choice. Particularly in list-based electoral systems, where voters are essentially choosing between parties rather than candidates, voters are very unlikely to vote against their party identification. Furthermore, voters in many European countries have traditionally held strong class and religious identities, and these have been dominant over party identities.

However, these arguments do not necessarily apply to the Irish case, which resembles the United States in a number of ways that makes party identification a more useful concept than it is in many other European countries. Voting in Ireland has traditionally not been driven by strong social group or class identities, so party identities could potentially fill this gap. The Irish electoral system is far more candidate-centred than most other European countries, so how you vote and which party you support are not necessarily the same things. As Marsh notes, 'If party identification proved to be a useful concept anywhere in Europe, Ireland would seem to be a prime candidate' (Marsh, 2006: 491).

Yet there are significant measurement issues that arise when applying the concept of party identification outside the United States, including in Ireland. The original formulation, still used in American National Election Studies, explicitly focuses on the respondent's self-identity ('Generally speaking, do you usually think of yourself as a Republican, a Democrat, an Independent or what?'). This approach has not been widely exported, for a number of reasons. On a practical level, it is difficult to formulate the question in this way in a multi-party context, particularly when there are no widely used nouns to refer to different partisan groups (Green, Palmquist and Schickler, 2004: 169).[1] It is also more likely that individuals will identify with more than one party in a context where several parties are spread out across the ideological spectrum.

It is more common in European surveys to measure party identification in terms of closeness to a party, and this is the approach used in the Irish National Election Study. The sequence of questions is as follows:[2]

1. 'Do you usually think of yourself as close to any political party?'
   - [If yes] 'Which party is that?'
2. [If no] 'Do you feel yourself a little closer to one of the political parties than the others?'
   - [If yes] 'Which party is that'?

While this measure is arguably further removed from the concept of psychological attachment than the original formulation, it does focus the respondent's attention on long-term attachment. Barnes et al. (1988) find that the two approaches produce scales that are highly correlated and similar in terms of reliability.

Most previous research has measured partisanship in terms of the first of these two questions, treating those who reported feeling 'a little closer' to one of the parties as non-partisans (Marsh and Tilley, 2010; Thomson, 2017). However, movement over time from having no party attachment to feeling a little closer to one party (or vice versa) may be an important indicator of realignment or dealignment. This chapter therefore distinguishes between three types of voters: 'partisans' (those answering in affirmative to question 1 above); 'leaners' (those answering yes to the second question above); and 'non-partisans' (those answering no to both questions).

Before proceeding to the main analysis in the next section, I first compare these three different categories of voters using the 2002–2007 INES panel data. The reason for this exercise is to determine whether 'leaners' are more like partisans or non-partisans in terms of their voting behaviour and attitudes. This is an important consideration when it comes to interpreting changing levels of partisanship in the aftermath of the financial crisis.

Partisan stability implies that party identifiers will be more stable in their vote over time compared to non-partisans. Table 5.1 compares the stability of voting preferences of our three categories of respondents in the period 2002 to 2007. Respondents are categorized according to whether they voted for the same party in 2002 and 2007 or changed their vote.[3] The second column shows the percentage of respondents who voted for the same party in both elections. As expected, there are significant differences between those who identified with the party they voted for in 2002 and those who did not. For respondents who felt close to the party they voted for in 2002, 77 per cent went on to vote for the party again in 2007. For those categorized as 'leaners' in 2002, 64 per cent went on to vote for the party in 2007. In contrast, only 43 per cent of those who did not feel close to the party they voted for in 2002 went on to vote for the party again in 2007.

A similar picture emerges when we look at respondents' assessments in 2007 of the probability (on a scale of 1–10) that they will ever vote again for the party that they voted for in 2002. As reported in the right-hand column in Table 5.1, the average probability score is 8.63 for partisans, 7.88 for 'leaners' and 6.94 for non-partisans. In both of these sets of analyses, the difference between non-partisans, 'leaners' and partisans are statistically significant. Both reported vote and probability to vote therefore tell the same story: partisans have more stable vote preferences over time than 'leaners', who in turn have more stable voting preferences than non-partisans.

Table 5.1 Stability of vote preference by party attachment, 2002–2007

	Voted for same party in 2007 as 2002 (% respondents)	*2007 probability to vote for party voted for in 2002 (mean score)*
2002 Partisans	77%**	8.63**
2002 Leaners	64%**	7.88**
2002 Non-partisans	43%	6.94
All	55%	7.54

Source: INES 2002, 2007.

Note: **p < 0.01. Significance calculated in comparison to non-partisans. Partisans/leaners are respondents who said they felt close to/a little closer to the party that they voted for in 2002; non-partisans are respondents who did not feel close to the party they voted for in 2002.

According to the psychological account, party identification is stable in part because it shapes how people interpret new political information. As Zaller put it, 'People tend to accept what is congenial to their partisan values and to reject what is not' (1992: 242). For instance, partisans are expected to exhibit bias in how they perceive objective conditions (Bartels, 2002). INES respondents in 2007 were asked whether they thought various aspects of the country (the economy, the housing situation, crime and the health service) had improved or disimproved over the previous five years. Respondents who identified with the main government party (Fianna Fáil) should, according to the theory, be more likely than other respondents to say that things had improved. To ensure that the direction of causation is not the other way around (i.e. respondents develop an identification with Fianna Fáil because they believed that things had improved), respondents are categorized based on their partisanship in 2002.

Each of the four items (economy, housing, crime, health) is measured on a 5-point scale. Where appropriate the items are reversed so that in all cases lower scores indicate that a respondent believed things had improved, while high scores indicate that a respondent thought things had got worse. As Table 5.2 shows, for all of these items except 'crime', respondents who identified with Fianna Fáil in 2002 were significantly more likely to believe that things had improved in 2007. There is no noticeable difference between partisans and 'leaners' in this regard. In contrast, those who voted for Fianna Fáil in 2002 but did not claim an attachment to the party were no different than other respondents in how they perceived these conditions.

The evidence presented in Tables 5.1 and 5.2 shows that partisanship has a significant effect on both the behaviour and attitudes of Irish voters. Partisans are more likely to be stable in their vote choice from one election to the next, and they are more likely to perceive economic and social conditions in a positive light when their party is in office. What is more, these effects are found

Table 5.2 Perceived changes in conditions between 2002 and 2007 (respondents grouped according to 2002 partisanship)

	Economy (n = 1,149)	Housing (n = 982)	Crime (n = 1,141)	Health (n = 1,137)
Fianna Fáil partisans	1.87**	2.48**	3.98	3.06**
Fianna Fáil leaners	1.90**	2.48**	4.12	3.37**
Fianna Fáil non-partisans	2.24	3.04	4.03	3.83
Other respondents	2.32	3.00	4.10	3.90

Source: INES 2002, 2007.

Note: **p < 0.01. Significance calculated in comparison with 'Other' respondents. Lower scores indicate a more positive view of how conditions have changed.

even among those classified here as 'leaners'. This is in line with research in the United States that finds that voters who describe themselves as 'Independent', but in a follow-on question admit to feeling closer to one or other of the parties, actually behave very similarly to outright party identifiers (Keith et al., 1992). It is therefore important not to ignore 'leaners' when examining trends in party identification over time, which is the focus of the next section.

Changing patterns of party identification in Ireland

As mentioned in the introduction, it is often claimed that the level of mass partisanship is in decline in advanced industrial democracies (e.g. Dalton, 2002; Mair, 2013). One prominent explanation for this is that dealignment occurs as a result of 'cognitive mobilization'. Due to the complexity of politics, making an informed voting decision can be difficult. Rather than making up their minds afresh at each election, voters form long-term attachments to a party, and this serves as a short-cut to help them interpret political information. In this view, party attachments are formed by voters who lack the time and resources to make a fully informed decision. When voters become more politically sophisticated due to higher levels of education and greater access to information, they become less dependent on partisan cues (Dalton, 2002: 29).

However, such broad-brush theories fail to account for the fact that the patterns of dealignment have not been uniform across countries. Indeed, there is evidence to suggest that in some countries the level of partisanship has actually increased in recent years (Andeweg and Farrell, 2017). A more explicitly political explanation is needed to account for such country-specific patterns. One such argument is that the level of party identification is linked to the degree of party polarization in a country (Schmitt and Holmberg, 1995; Hetherington, 2001; Lupu, 2015; Smidt, 2015). Party attachments, in this account, are most likely to form during times when clear ideological and policy differences exist between parties. When parties converge, they arouse more muted emotional responses among voters, and voters who come of age at times of party convergence are less likely to form strong attachments. Growing dealignment is therefore a symptom of the narrowing of the policy space between mainstream parties. In contrast to cognitive mobilization, however, political convergence is not all one-way traffic. Party systems can undergo periods of polarization as well as convergence, and according to this view, we should expect to see increases in party attachment among young voters at such times.

In support of this argument, Hetherington (2001) finds that a resurgence of mass partisanship in the United States has occurred as a result of growing polarization at the elite level. Smidt (2015) finds that Independent voters in the United States have begun to behave more like loyal party supporters as a consequence of party polarization. In a cross-national study, Lupu (2015) finds a strong correlation between the degree of party polarization in a country and the level of mass partisanship.

This political explanation for patterns of partisanship fits neatly with the well-developed literature on realignments. There is convincing evidence from the United States that periods of gradual dealignment have been reversed by 'critical elections' which have revitalized politics and led to an increase in party identification in subsequent years, often along different socio-demographic lines than before. As described by V. O. Key, these are elections 'in which the depth and intensity of electoral involvement are high, in which more or less profound readjustments occur in the relations of power within the community, and in which new and durable electoral groupings are formed' (1955: 4). Critical elections are often associated with an increase in party polarization, which is one of the reasons that they can reinvigorate partisanship (Burnham, 1970).

As argued in the introduction to this chapter, the 2011 election in Ireland bears all the hallmarks of a critical election. As with other critical elections, it was associated with a noticeable increase in party polarization. This is clear from the INES surveys, where voters are asked where they think each party is located on a left–right scale. Party polarization can be measured using the method recommended by Dalton (2008), which takes account of both the policy positions of parties and their size.[4] According to this measure, which has a theoretical range from zero (when all parties occupy the same position) to ten (when parties are equally divided at opposite ends of the left–right spectrum), party polarization in Ireland was 2.3 in 2002, 2.0 in 2007, 2.7 in 2011 and 3.0 in 2016. This is a very substantial increase in polarization, much higher than the vast majority of cases analysed by Dalton, who compared changes in polarization across a wide range of established democracies (2008: 907).

To test the critical election argument, I examine the evolution of partisanship over the full period of the INES series (2002, 2007, 2011 and 2016), paying particular attention to generational differences.[5] If realignment is taking place, we should observe an increase in the *level* of partisanship and changes in the *direction* of partisanship (i.e. which parties people feel close to) in the 2016 election compared to the pre-bailout elections (2002 and 2007), particularly among younger voters. In contrast, if dealignment is continuing, we will observe a pattern of decline in party identification over the period, particularly among younger cohorts.

Turning first to the extent and intensity of partisanship over time, Figure 5.1 divides the electorate in each election year into the three categories introduced previously: partisans, 'leaners' and non-partisans. Figure 5.1 appears to provide some support for the realignment argument. In 2002 and 2007, almost half the electorate expressed no attachment to a party, while the other half were evenly split between partisans and 'leaners'. In 2011, non-partisans made up almost two thirds of the electorate; this was due to a decline in the proportion of partisans (from 27 per cent in 2007 to 21 per cent) and a very sharp decline in the proportion of 'leaners' (from 26 per cent to 15 per cent). This trend was dramatically reversed in 2016. Here we find by far the lowest proportion of non-partisans in the series (at 34 per cent), while the proportion of partisans increased to 31 per cent and the proportion of 'leaners' increased to almost 36 per cent.[6] Given that 'leaners' exhibit many of the traits of more committed partisans in terms of voting behaviour and attitudinal bias, the sharp increase in the number of 'leaners' in 2016 is a potentially important development.

Related to this, parties also evoked stronger feelings among voters in 2016 compared to previous years. Some researchers use the percentage of citizens with positive feelings towards one or more party and negative feelings towards one or more parties as an indicator of partisanship (e.g. Hetherington, 2001). In all INES surveys, respondents were asked what they thought about each party in terms of a scale from 0 (strongly dislike) to 10 (strongly like). In 2002, 56 per cent of respondents indicated that they liked one or more party (gave them a score of 7 or more) and also disliked at least one party (gave them a score of 3 or less). By 2016, this increased to 78 per cent, by far the highest of any year in the series.

The realignment argument implies that increases in partisanship should be strongest among younger cohorts. This would be in stark contrast to previously observed patterns in Ireland. Mair and Marsh (2004) found decreasing levels of partisanship in Ireland both over time and across generations in the period 1978–1994: each generation exhibited lower levels of partisanship than its predecessor, and for each generation they observed a decline in party identification over time. This analysis is replicated in Figure 5.2 using the INES data. Respondents are divided into three cohorts: those born prior to 1960, those born in the 1960s and 1970s and those born after 1979. The top panel shows the percentage of

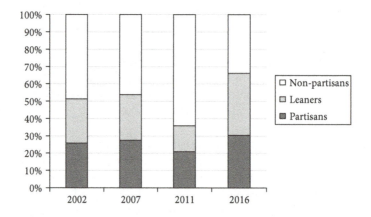

Figure 5.1 Levels of partisanship (INES data), 2002–2016.

Source: INES 2002, 2007, 2011, 2016 (INES2). Data weighted for demographic factors and party vote shares.

respondents who are 'close to' or 'a little bit closer to' a party (i.e. partisans plus 'leaners'), while the bottom panel excludes 'leaners'.

The results using the more encompassing measure of partisanship (the top panel) are quite different from those for the earlier period reported in Mair and Marsh (2004). First of all, as we have already seen, there is no consistent pattern over time in the level of partisanship: a decrease in the number of partisans across all generations in 2011 is followed by a sharp increase across all generations in 2016. Secondly, the generational pattern also changes over time. While in the period 2002–2011, the youngest generation is the least aligned, the reverse is true in 2016. Remarkably, the percentage of aligned voters among

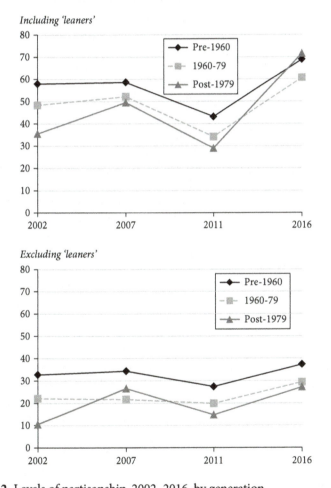

Figure 5.2 Levels of partisanship, 2002–2016, by generation.

Source: INES 2002, 2007, 2011, 2016 (INES2). Data weighted for demographic factors and party vote shares.

the generation born after 1979 (often referred to as the 'millennial' generation) increases from 29 per cent in 2011 to 72 per cent in 2016. This is significantly higher than the figure of 61 per cent for the generation born in the 1960s and 1970s, and marginally above that of the oldest cohort (at 69 per cent aligned). This would appear to be a telling piece of evidence in support of the realignment thesis. However, if we exclude 'leaners' from our measure of partisanship (see the bottom panel in Figure 5.2), this dramatic change among the youngest cohort disappears. Rather, the youngest cohort remains the least aligned of the generations using this narrower measure. This suggests that while many young voters acquired party attachments in the wake of the economic crisis, these attachments are rather weak. It remains to be seen whether or not these attachments become more deeply ingrained over time.

To further test the realignment argument, it is necessary to also examine the direction of partisanship. Figure 5.3 plots the proportion of the electorate indicating attachment to each of the main political parties. As before, the panel on the top shows the percentage of partisans including 'leaners', while the panel on the bottom excludes 'leaners'. It is evident from both graphs that the decline in partisanship in 2011 is accounted for almost entirely by the collapse in the number of voters identifying with Fianna Fáil, from close to 30 per cent (including 'leaners') in 2002 and 2007 to 11 per cent in 2011. Fianna Fáil partisanship rebounded somewhat in 2016, but remained far below the pre-crisis level. In contrast, both Fine Gael and Sinn Féin experienced a steady increase in partisan supporters over the period, with Fine Gael marginally ahead of Fianna Fáil as the party with the highest number of partisan identifiers in 2016. Identification with the smaller parties (the category 'Other' includes at various points the Greens, Progressive Democrats (PDs), AAA-PBP, Social Democrats and Renua) is low for most of the period, but there is a sharp increase in 2016, particularly for the looser measure of partisanship shown in the top panel. Overall, Figure 5.3 shows that the patterns of identification in 2016 are much more fragmented than was the case prior to the economic crash.

The consistent rise in identification with Fine Gael is somewhat surprising, given that the party experienced a sharp decline in its vote share in 2016 compared to 2011. It may be that some people who voted for Fine Gael for the first time in 2011 had by 2016 developed an identification with the party, while others proved to be only one-time voters. This interpretation is borne out by the data. Looking at the 2011 INES, only 18 per cent of new Fine Gael voters (i.e. those who did not vote for the party in 2007) identified with the party in any way. By 2016, a majority (58 per cent) of those who switched to Fine Gael in 2011 and were now voting for the party for the second successive time considered themselves to be close to or a little close to the party. So while Fine Gael's vote share peaked in 2011, the number of Fine Gael partisans grew considerably in 2016. In total, almost half (46 per cent) of Fine Gael partisans

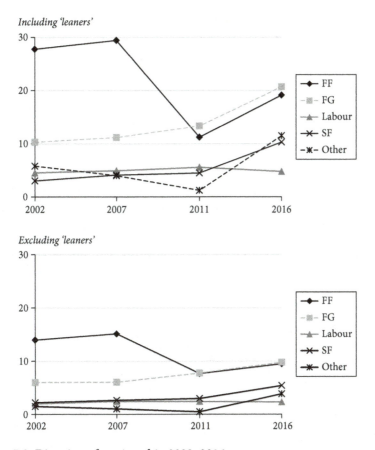

Including 'leaners'

Excluding 'leaners'

Figure 5.3 Direction of partisanship 2002–2016.

Source: INES 2002, 2007, 2011, 2016 (INES2). Data weighted for demographic factors and party vote shares.

and leaners in 2016 were relatively new converts to the party, not having voted for them in 2007; this is far higher than the corresponding figure for Fianna Fáil (at 30 per cent).

As with the level of partisanship, the direction of partisanship can be broken down by generation. According to the realignment hypothesis, we should expect to find that the changes in the direction of partisanship illustrated in Figure 5.3 are most noticeable among the youngest generation. Table 5.3 provides a breakdown of partisanship in 2016 for each of the three generations defined previously. For completeness, smaller parties are now included separately rather than combining them. Each cell in Table 5.3 shows the percentage of respondents from a particular generation that felt some identification with the party in question (i.e. partisans plus 'leaners'; the corresponding figures when 'leaners' are excluded are shown in parentheses). Among the oldest generation, Fianna Fáil and Fine Gael were still the two biggest partisan blocks in 2016 by a considerable margin. Just over half of respondents from this generation identified with or leaned towards one of these two parties, while relatively few identified with any other party. The level of identification with Fianna Fáil and Fine Gael was somewhat lower among the middle generation, and this was not replaced with a noticeable increase in identification with any other party. As expected, it is among the youngest cohort that we find the most striking patterns. Here, identification with Fine Gael was relatively high (20 per cent if 'leaners' are included), but identification with Fianna Fáil (12 per cent) was far lower than it was among the older cohorts. A number of other parties have substantial numbers of partisans and 'leaners' among this cohort, including Sinn Féin (13 per cent), Social Democrats (8 per cent) and AAA-PBP (7 per cent). The increased fragmentation in party identification shown in Figure 5.3 is therefore driven primarily by patterns of identification among the youngest generation.[7]

Table 5.3 Direction of partisanship 2016, by generation

	Pre-1960	*1960–1979*	*1980-*	*All*
Fianna Fáil	26	20	12	19
	(15)	*(9)*	*(5)*	*(9)*
Fine Gael	25	19	20	21
	(13)	*(9)*	*(8)*	*(10)*
Labour	4	5	6	5
	(2)	*(2)*	*(3)*	*(2)*
Sinn Féin	8	10	13	10
	(4)	*(6)*	*(6)*	*(5)*
Green	2	2	2	2
	(1)	*(1)*	*(1)*	*(1)*
AAA-PBP	1	1	7	3
	(1)	*(0)*	*(2)*	*(1)*
Social Democrats	3	3	8	5
	(1)	*(1)*	*(2)*	*(1)*
Other	1	1	2	1
	(1)	*(1)*	*(1)*	*(1)*
Total	69	61	72	66
	(37)	*(29)*	*(27)*	*(31)*

Source: INES2 2016. Data weighted for demographic factors and party vote shares.

Note: Figures without parentheses include 'leaners'; figures in parentheses exclude 'leaners'. AAA-PBP = Anti-Austerity Alliance – People Before Profit.

Conclusion

The literature on realignments distinguishes between critical elections, characterized by dramatic political change, increased polarization and a rupture in the old patterns of party identification, and 'cementing' elections where new patterns become embedded for the next generation of voters (Wattenberg 1996: 138). The findings presented here are not unequivocal, but they do provide some evidence that elections of 2011 and 2016 should be seen in this light. If 2011 was the year where old party attachments (at least as far as Fianna Fáil is concerned) were abandoned, by 2016 young voters in particular had begun to form new political allegiances.

Two pieces of evidence support this conclusion. First, two thirds of respondents in the 2016 INES survey expressed some level of attachment to a party, which was almost double the figure from the previous election. The increase in partisanship in 2016 was most evident among younger voters who came of age during this turbulent period; remarkably, voters born after 1979 were more likely to admit to some party attachment than any other cohort. This is highly unusual in comparison to previous elections, when younger voters were the least aligned.

Second, the distribution of partisan attachments among parties was noticeably different in 2016 compared to the pre-crisis elections. For example, in 2002 and 2007, almost 30 per cent of the electorate identified to some extent with Fianna Fáil and less than a quarter identified with another party; whereas in 2016 only 19 per cent identified in any way with Fianna Fáil and almost half the electorate identified with a different party. Again, these differences are particularly evident among the younger generation. This suggests that the fragmentation of the party system that occurred in 2011 and 2016 is likely to persist. Assuming that party identifiers remain loyal to their party, the extreme volatility of the 2011 and 2016 elections may have been a temporary phenomenon.

Yet while there is evidence of a nascent realignment among Irish voters, it is ultimately too soon after the critical election of 2011 to say with confidence what the long-term implications will be. The increase in party identification in 2016 was primarily of the weaker sort – that is, voters who said they felt only a little closer to one party than others. The analysis presented earlier in this chapter shows that these weak partisans do exhibit many of the same behavioural and attitudinal traits associated with more committed partisans. Nevertheless, it is quite possible that these weak attachments will not survive into the future. This is particularly so given that some of the parties that voters (particularly young voters) expressed an attachment to, such as the Social Democrats, were only a few months in existence at the time of the 2016 election. We should be sceptical of the extent to which voters can form lasting allegiances to parties in such a short space of time.

To conclude, the question of whether the turbulence of the 2011 and 2016 elections should be seen as a symptom of dealignment or realignment can only be answered definitively in retrospect. All we can say from this vantage point is that the evidence to date does not rule out the possibility that we are in the midst of a realignment that will shape Irish elections over the longer term. Given that most observers have expected that partisanship would continue its long-term decline in Ireland, even this tentative conclusion may come as something of a surprise.

Notes

1 Unlike the United States, where voters habitually refer to themselves as Democrats or Republicans, nouns are not used to describe partisanship in Ireland (apart from in a derogatory sense, such as 'Blueshirt' (Fine Gael supporter) or 'Shinner' (Sinn Féin supporter)). One could speculate that the fact that nouns to describe Irish partisan groups are not in common usage is an indication that these groupings are not an important part of people's identity. On the other hand, lacking a word to describe it does not necessarily imply that people do not consider themselves as part of a partisan grouping.
2 An additional question measuring the intensity of partisanship was also asked, but this chapter focuses on these two basic questions.
3 Respondents who did not vote in one or more of the elections are excluded.
4 This measure is based on the weighted average distance between each party and the policy centre on the left–right dimension (where the policy centre is simply the weighted average of party positions).
5 For 2016, the INES2 data are used.
6 There were some differences in the sampling procedures used for each wave of the INES, which might have affected the results. To test this, a sample matching procedure was used (Blackwell et al., 2009) to select a set of respondents from the 2002 and 2016 surveys that were similar in terms of age, education, political interest, turnout and left–right self-placement. Using the matched samples, significant differences still remain in terms of the level of party identification. In the unmatched data reported in Figure 5.1, the level of partisanship (including 'leaners') is 14.8 per cent higher in 2016 compared with 2002. Using the matched data, the corresponding figure is 12.3 per cent. This suggests that the growth in party identification recorded in the 2016 INES2 survey is not primarily due to differences in the nature of the sample. It should be noted, however, that the level of partisanship found in the 2016 INES2 data is slightly higher than that found in the 2016 exit poll (INES1). Specifically, 27 per cent of voters in the exit poll reported to be close to a party, compared to 32 per cent of self-reported voters in the INES2 post-election survey. It is not possible to examine 'leaners' using the exit poll, as the relevant question was not asked.
7 As a robustness check, Table 5.3 was replicated using data from the 2016 exit poll (INES1). The exit poll only asked whether or not a respondent felt close to a party; it did not ask the follow-up question that identified 'leaners' in the analyses in this chapter. Furthermore, the exit poll differs in that it does not include non-voters in the sample. Overall, the generational patterns in party identification in the exit poll are similar to those found in Table 5.3. In particular, party identification among younger respondents in the exit poll is far more fragmented that among older generations. One noticeable difference, however, is that in contrast to the figures shown in Table 5.3, Fine Gael and Fianna Fáil attract roughly equal numbers of partisan supporters among the youngest generation in the exit poll.

References

Andeweg, Rudy B., and David M. Farrell. 2017. 'Legitimacy decline and party decline', in Caroilen van Ham, Jacques Thomassen, Kees Arts, and Rudy Andeweg (eds), *Myth and Reality of the Legitimacy Crisis*. Oxford: Oxford University Press, pp. 76–94.

Barnes, Samuel H., M. Kent Jennings, Ronald Inglehart and Barbara Farah. 1988. 'Party identification and party closeness in comparative perspective', *Political Behavior*. 10: 215–31.

Bartels, Larry M. 2002. 'Beyond the running tally: Partisan bias in political perceptions', *Political Behavior*. 24: 117–50.

Blackwell, Matthew, Stefano Iacus, Gary King and Giuseppe Porro. 2009. 'cem: Coarsened exact matching in Stata', *Stata Journal*. 9: 524–46.

Burnham, Walter Dean. 1970. *Critical Elections and the Mainsprings of American Politics*. New York: Norton.

Campbell, Angus, Philip E. Converse, Warren E. Miller and Donald E. Stokes. 1964. *The American Voter: An Abridgement*. New York: Wiley.

Dalton, Russell J. 2002. 'The decline of party identifications', in Russell Dalton and Martin P. Wattenberg (eds), *Parties Without Partisans: Political Change in Advanced Industrial Democracies*. Oxford: Oxford University Press, pp. 19–36.

Dalton, Russell J. 2008. 'The quantity and the quality of party systems party system polarization: Its measurement, and its consequences', *Comparative Political Studies*. 41: 899–920.

Farrell, David M., and Jane Suiter. 2016. 'The election in context', in Michael Gallagher and Michael Marsh (eds), *How Ireland Voted 2016: The Election that Nobody Won*. Basingstoke: Palgrave Macmillan, pp. 277–92.

Fiorina, Morris P. 1981. *Retrospective Voting in American National Elections*. New Haven: Yale University Press.

Green, Donald P., Bradley Palmquist and Eric Schickler. 2004. *Partisan Hearts and Minds: Political Parties and the Social Identities of Voters*. New Haven: Yale University Press.

Hetherington, Marc J. 2001. 'Resurgent mass partisanship: The role of elite polarization', *American Political Science Review*. 95: 619–31.

Keith, Bruce E., David B. Magleby, Candice J. Nelson, Elizabeth A. Orr and Mark C. Westlye. 1992. *The Myth of the Independent Voter*. Los Angeles: University of California Press.

Key, Valdimer Orlando. 1955. 'A theory of critical elections', *Journal of Politics*. 17: 3–18.

LeDuc, Lawrence. 1981. 'The dynamic properties of party identification: A four-nation comparison', *European Journal of Political Research*. 9: 257–68.

Lupu, Noam. 2015. 'Party polarization and mass partisanship: A comparative perspective', *Political Behavior*. 37: 331–56.

Mair, Peter. 2013. *Ruling the Void: The Hollowing of Western Democracy*. London: Verso Books.

Mair, Peter, and Michael Marsh. 2004. 'Political parties in electoral markets in postwar Ireland', in Peter Mair, Wolfgang Muller and Fritz Plasser (eds), *Political Parties and Electoral Change: Party Responses to Electoral Markets*. London: Sage, pp. 234–63.

Marsh, Michael. 2006. 'Party identification in Ireland: An insecure anchor for a floating party system', *Electoral Studies*. 25: 489–508.

Marsh, Michael, and Gail McElroy. 2016. 'Voting behaviour: Continuing de-alignment', in Michael Gallagher and Michael Marsh. (eds), *How Ireland Voted 2016: The Election that Nobody Won*. Basingstoke: Palgrave Mcmillan, pp. 159–84.

Marsh, Michael, and James Tilley. 2010. 'The attribution of credit and blame to governments and its impact on vote choice', *British Journal of Political Science*. 40: 115–34.

Miller, Warren Edward, and J. Merrill Shanks. 1996. *The New American Voter*. Cambridge, MA: Harvard University Press.

Rosenblum, Nancy L. 2010. *On the Side of the Angels: An Appreciation of Parties and Partisanship*. New Jersey: Princeton University Press.

Schmitt, Hermann, and Sören Holmberg. 1995. 'Political parties in decline?' in Hans-Dieter Klingemann and Dieter Fuchs (eds), *Citizens and the State*. Oxford: Oxford University Press, pp. 95–133.

Smidt, Corwin D. 2015. 'Polarization and the decline of the American floating voter', *American Journal of Political Science*. 61: 365–81.

Thomassen, Jacques. 1976. 'Party identification as a cross-national concept: Its meaning in the Netherlands', in Ian Budge, Ivor Crewe and Dennis Farlie (eds), *Party Identification and Beyond*. New York: John Wiley and Sons, pp. 63–80.

Thomson, Robert. 2017. 'The malleable nature of party identification', in Michael Marsh, David Farrell and Gail McElroy (eds), *A Conservative Revolution? Electoral Change in Twenty-First Century Ireland*. Oxford: Oxford University Press, pp. 123–42.

Wattenberg, Martin P. 1996. *The Decline of American Political Parties, 1952–1996*. Cambridge, MA: Harvard University Press.

Zaller, John. 1992. *The Nature and Origins of Mass Opinion*. Cambridge: Cambridge University Press.

6

Why did the 'recovery' fail to return the government?

Michael Marsh

Introduction

The results of the general election in 2016 came as a shock to most observers, whether in academia, in the media or in politics. While nobody expected that the government would be returned with the sort of majority won in 2011, the view was widespread that the fact that the Irish state had successfully exited the bailout programme into which the previous government had effectively led it, and was well in line to balance its books, would enable the government to come close to getting a second term, even if some additional support was required from Independents. This was the thinking behind the campaign run by Fine Gael in particular (Leahy, 2016): 'Let's keep the recovery going.' The government had led Ireland from the depths of the economic crisis that precipitated the 2011 election, and the opposition parties could not be trusted to keep the country on course. However, the government parties between them won just 32 per cent of the vote, compared with 55 per cent in 2011. The voters did not buy the message. This chapter explores some reasons why.

The fact that the economy is central to deciding elections is a truth if not universally acknowledged at least one accepted widely. It has some obvious illustrations – most commonly Clinton's win over George Bush in 1992 – and fits well into the more general themes of responsible democratic government. In a critique of a growing literature questioning the ability of voters to make rational decisions, V. O. Key (1966) explained how voters did not need a lot of information to know whether things were getting better or worse, and would use that judgement to punish or reward incumbents. Political science has seen a huge literature of studies exploring this link between economic performance and electoral success, and the bulk of the work does confirm a positive relationship (Lewis-Beck and Stegmaier, 2007). Yet results do vary in their findings as to the size of the impact that the economy has on electoral outcomes, and a significant body of work also points to variations in that impact across time and place. Anderson (2007) reviewing the literature, argues that there are individual and institutional factors complicating the relationship and suggests significant conditionalities in the link between economic and political trends. These stem from the link between the real economy and voters' assessments of whether conditions are improving or not and attribution of responsibility for the changes perceived. Institutional factors are those attributes of the political system that might affect the clarity of responsibility for economic trends (Powell and Whitten, 1993). An argument has been made recently that economic voting effects have been different in post-crisis Western Europe (Kriesi, 2012; Hernandez and Kriesi, 2015). There are two reasons for this. The first is the scale of the downturn, which means that people are worse off than they were before the crisis despite the upturn. The second is that party systems are no longer underpinned by extensive party attachments (on this, see also chapter 5). Together this has led to governing parties being more heavily punished and party systems seeing more change, as votes move away from the more established parties, something that was very apparent in Ireland in 2016 and is a wider theme of this volume.

Those looking for economic voting in Ireland have generally found it (Marsh et al., 2008; Marsh and Mihaylov, 2012; Leyden and Lewis Beck, 2017) and 2011 was a classic case of electoral punishment for bad times, but 2016 does not seem to have fitted with expectations. This chapter explores the apparent absence of economic voting in the case of the 2016 Irish election. Some of the academic arguments about conditionality do tie in with elements of the campaign by opposition forces, who questioned both the reality and the extent of the recovery, but also the extent to which the government should be credited with responsibility for any improvements. I will also explore the importance in 2016 of assessments of personal circumstances, typically downplayed in the academic literature, but highlighted in commentary on the election as the absence of a 'feel-good' factor. Things may have been improving, but perhaps they were still short of pre-crisis levels. There were of course other elements in the campaigns by opposition parties, with most arguing that the government had adopted an unfair and unjust approach to resolving the crisis, and that its 'austerity' policies ensured that the worse off carried most of the burden. This, though, is a separate argument to the relatively simple one explored here. Arguably, the election was not just about the economy but was also about many other aspects of government performance, such as public services, taxes and a failure to deal with crime and housing, not to mention the issue of water charges. These, though, are outside of what is thought of as 'economic voting'. I will return to this point in the concluding section.

The organization of the chapter is as follows. First, I will deal with the most basic assumption behind the expectation that the government would do reasonably well, and that is that there really was a recovery, and one which was not simply confined to the capital. Second, I will look at the variations in perceptions of the economy, and here I will look not just at the widely employed 'sociotropic' evaluations of the national economy but also at evaluations of the voter's own household, so-called pocketbook evaluations. In addition, I will make use of a factual question on unemployment which has been used previously to explore the basis of people's judgements about the national economy (Ansolabehere, Meredith and Snowberg 2014). The point here is to see how far judgements might have varied according to personal and local rather than national conditions. Next, I will explore accountability: Did voters attribute responsibility for changing national circumstances to the government? Finally, I will bring these together to see how far variations in economic perceptions and judgements about responsibility account for the failure of the government parties to gain their expected reward.

What recovery?

It is conventional to look for indicators of national economic well-being in terms of unemployment, economic growth and inflation. There are problems with all of these in an Irish context. Growth statistics can be misleading because so many international companies are located in Ireland, and the comings and goings of their paper profits can distort figures. Typically, the emphasis has been placed on Gross National Product (GNP) rather than Gross Domestic Product (GDP) but even the former has been unreliable recently, as growth exceeded 20 per cent in 2016, leading to comments about 'leprechaun economics' and moves by the Central Bank to explore new indicators. However, the fact of significant growth since the crisis is widely accepted internationally. Unemployment rates are also criticized as a measure of well-being on the basis that they are artificially low because of high levels of emigration. Hence, we will look at employment figures as well. Inflation has been very flat for some time and is ignored here.

Figure 6.1 shows the change in these indicators from 2011 up to the start of 2016, when the election took place. The pattern is clear: growth trended upwards from 2013, and at the same time unemployment fell and the numbers in employment rose. GDP by early 2016 was 20 per cent higher than it was at the start of 2013, unemployment was down from almost 15 per cent to just 9 per cent and employment was also up, by almost 150,000. These look like the sort of statistics that should have seen the governing parties rewarded rather than penalized heavily for their efforts.

The improvements shown in Figure 6.1 were questioned during the election. Two of the specific points raised are explored here. The first is the extent to which the recovery was a national phenomenon, or something that was restricted to Dublin. Data are available at regional level, notably for what are called the NUTS 3 units. These regions are unequal in terms of size with the

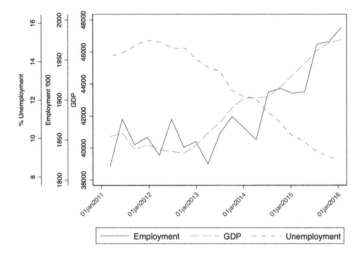

Figure 6.1 Economic indicators 2011–2016.

Source: INES 2002, 2007, 2011, 2016. Data weighted for demographic factors and party vote shares.

largest, Dublin, with over a quarter of the national population, and the smallest, Midlands, with just 6 per cent, but the rest are more similar in size, ranging from the Mid-West (9 per cent) to the South-West (15 per cent). The second is the window through which improvement is judged. Much of the economic voting literature simply considers the very recent past, such as the year before the election, but we can also consider the period since the last election. However, bearing in mind Hernandez and Kriesi's (2015) comments on the crisis, we can also look back much further, to the previous election on the eve of the crisis when, although there were concerns about the future, the present looked very rosy indeed (Marsh and Mikhaylov, 2012).

As of 2016, unemployment was just under 9 per cent for the country as a whole, but ranged from well under that in Dublin and the Mid-East (Meath, Kildare and Wicklow, really the Dublin commuter belt) to 12 per cent in the Midland region (Laois Offaly, Westmeath and Longford) and in the South-East (Carlow Kilkenny, Wexford and Waterford) with the West (Mayo, Roscommon and Galway) also over 10 per cent. Improvements in the previous year were very similar in scale although the Midlands and South East regions saw the smallest ones, and changes since 2011 were broadly similar, from a drop of 7.9 per cent in Mid-West (Clare, North Tipperary and Limerick) to just 4.5 per cent in the Border (Cavan, Donegal, Louth, Leitrim and Sligo). The most striking difference, however, is in relation to changes since 2007. Unemployment nationally was *up* by 3.6 per cent on where it was in spring 2007, but it was up by more than 5 per cent in the West, Midlands and South East regions, and over

Table 6.1 Regional variations in unemployment and employment (figures are percentages)

	Unemployment				Employment		
	2016Q1	Change since 2011Q1	Change in previous year	Change since 2007Q2	Change since 2011Q1	Change in previous year	Change since 2007Q2
Mid-East	5.9	−7.1	−1.9	1.8	+4	−1	−8
Dublin	6.9	−5.8	−1.9	2.0	+12	+5	−3
South-West	7.7	−6.2	−2	3.8	+8	+3	−7
Mid-West	7.9	−7.9	−2.3	2.4	0	+4	−12
Ireland	**8.4**	**−6**	**−1.6**	**3.6**	**+7**	**+2**	**−7**
Border	8.6	−4.5	−1.6	2.7	+5	+3	−12
West	10.2	−6.5	−1.5	5.4	0	0	−13
Midland	11.6	−5.6	−0.9	7.3	+12	+3	−5
South-East	12.5	−5	−−0.3	7.4	+10	+1	−9

Source: Calculations based on CSO statistics for NUTS 3 regions. Unemployment figures are given as percentages of the labour force (ILO: ages 15–74), and employment as changes in absolute numbers. Data are from the Quarterly National Household Survey.

7 per cent in the last two of these, as against less than 2 per cent in the wider Dublin region (Dublin and Mid-East).

Looking at employment levels gives a similar picture in terms of Dublin versus the rest, although the areas showing the biggest decline since 2007 and biggest increase since 2011 are not always the same ones. The Border, West and Mid-West regions all have employment levels down more than 10 per cent on 2007, with the West and Mid-West showing no growth since 2011. In contrast, Dublin employment levels are almost back to 2007 levels.

There was economic inequality before the crisis in terms of employment/ unemployment levels, but this was exaggerated by the crisis, and the recovery, so that the disparity now is significantly greater than it was.[1] The rising tide may have lifted most boats, but many of them in 2016 were still well below where they once had been. Figure 6.2 shows how the regional variation increased with the crisis, and had not decreased much by 2016. For instance, unemployment

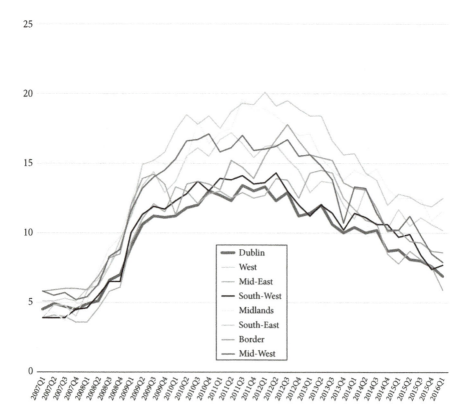

Figure 6.2 Regional levels of unemployment 2007–2016.
Source: Central Statistics Office (CSO), Table QNQ22.

ranged from 4 to 6 per cent in 2007Q2 (it was 5 per cent in Dublin – the heavy black line), but the range extended to 13–18 per cent (Dublin 13 per cent) in 2011Q1 and was 7–12 per cent (Dublin 7 per cent) in 2016Q1. In sum, while a recovery from 2011 is clear, and is clear everywhere, most areas are still well short of pre-crash levels of unemployment. Their recovery is no more than partial.

Perception of recovery

While there has clearly been some degree of recovery in all parts of the country, for this to have a political impact the recovery must be perceived by the voters. There are a variety of questions asked to get at this perception. These vary most importantly in terms of the time window that is used and whether evaluations are retrospective or prospective. One measure of perception is the ESRI/KBC Consumer Sentiment Index, a measure based on a monthly survey of sentiment carried out by the Economic and Social Research Institute in collaboration with KBC Bank. It uses a methodology pioneered by the University of Michigan and includes questions about the national economy and household circumstances, and gathers both backward- and forward-looking evaluations (Duffy and Williams, 2002). The index is standardized to a 1995 baseline, when positive and negative sentiment was evenly distributed, with a slight positive bias, so any figure of over 100 indicates a balance of positive sentiment. As Figure 6.3 shows,

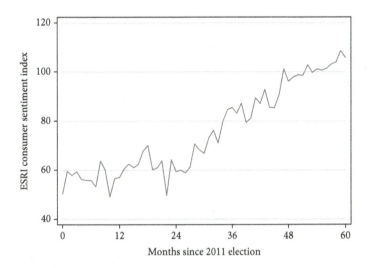

Figure 6.3 Consumer sentiment 2011–2016.

Source: ESR/KBC index.

sentiment improved from late 2012 onwards, topped 100 by late 2014, and was clearly above 100 in February 2016, when it stood at 105.

The February figure of 105 is not only up on Feb 2011 (50) but also well up on the figure on the eve of the 2007 and 2002 elections (92 and 83 respectively) when the incumbent governments were re-elected, but below that in 1997 (118) when the last Fine Gael and Labour coalition was not! Not since January 2006 and January 2005 had that figure been achieved, and prior to 2005 you need to go back to June 2001 – when the index was generally well over 100 since 1995 – to find such a high figure. Clearly there is no simple link between sentiment and election outcomes (see also Marsh and Mikhaylov, 2012). However, the 2002 and 2007 INES surveys showed a balance of evaluations indicating that there had been an improvement in the lifetime of the government, while in 1997 a change of government in 1995 without an election may have muddied the waters (Marsh and Sinnott, 1998).

Two elements in the ESRI/KBC index are evaluations of the state of the economy nationally and of the household. All three INES surveys for 2016 contain questions about the national economy. These ask for retrospective evaluations, with two surveys asking about change in the previous year and one about the last five years. The five-year question also links the window to the lifetime of the Fine Gael and Labour coalition, a wording used in previous INES surveys. Table 6.2 shows the responses. The main point is that all three surveys suggest that people's evaluations are on balance positive. The big difference between the three polls is not down to the window, since the responses in the

Table 6.2 Retrospective perceptions of the country as a whole

	Country in the last year (1)	Country in the last year (2)	Country in last 5 years (3)
[Much] better	46	13	30
[A little] better		55	52
Same	35	25	7
[A little] worse	19	5	5
[Much] worse		3	6
Total	100	100	100
N	1436	999	999

Note: Question wordings (1) INES1: Thinking about the economy as a whole, do you think that the country is better off, worse off or about the same as last year? (2) INES2: Would you say that over the past twelve months, the state of the economy in Ireland has gotten much better, gotten somewhat better, stayed about the same, gotten somewhat worse, or gotten much worse? (3) INES3: Thinking back over the last five years – the lifetime of the 2011 to 2016 Fine Gael/Labour government – would you say that the ECONOMY in Ireland over that period of time got a lot better, got a little better, stayed the same, got a little worse or got a lot worse?

first two columns are fairly similar. The response patterns in the exit poll where only better off/same/worse off responses were provided show the least positive picture. This is understandable to the extent that small improvements might be classed as 'same' as opposed to 'better', but this survey also showed a slightly higher proportion who saw a deterioration.

When it comes to evaluations of personal finances, questions and response wordings show less difference. This is apparent in Table 6.3. Positive and negative evaluations do not differ a great deal across the three surveys, positive ranging from 26 per cent to 30 per cent and negative from 20 per cent to 25 per cent, although the percentage seeing no change is much larger when the time frame is one year. There is a striking contrast with the national evaluations in Table 6.2 in that in all three surveys, the weight of evaluation is broadly neutral with the largest proportion seeing no change and positive and negative evaluations balanced, if tilted slightly towards positive. In essence, the average voter saw the national economy as getting better but was much less positive about their own circumstances. The 'feel-good' factor was absent. Positive evaluations on the national economy were given by 82, 68 and 46 per cent in the three surveys, while positive evaluations of personal finances were given by only 30, 26 and 27 per cent respectively. People seemed to be saying that there was a recovery, but there was not one for me.

Most of the political science literature since the 1980s has downplayed the importance of personal evaluations, following the argument made by Kramer (1971) that changes in personal circumstances were a consequence of a host of factors unrelated to national economic trends. It has also been shown that such

Table 6.3 Retrospective perceptions of the household finances

	In the last year (13)	In the last year (2)	In last 5 years (3)
[Much] better	27	3	4
[A little] better		23	26
Same	48	54	35
[A little] worse	25	15	23
[Much] worse		5	12
Total	100	100	100
N	1436	999	999

Note: Question wordings (1) INES1: Do you yourself feel better off financially, worse off financially or about the same compared to last year? (2) INES2: Would you say that over the past twelve months, the state of financial situation of your household over the past 12 months has gotten much better, gotten somewhat better, stayed about the same, gotten somewhat worse or gotten much worse? (3) INES3: And how about the financial situation of your household over the last five years? Has that gotten got a lot better, gotten a little better, stayed the same, got a little worse or got a lot worse?

evaluations are much more weakly related to voting choice than the national, sociotropic evaluations, as might be expected if there is less reason to hold the government to account for them (see, for example, Anderson, 2000). Indeed, it is notable that the core module of the Comparative Study of Electoral Systems (CSES) includes only sociotropic evaluations. However, the size of the gap we see here between the two types of evaluations is quite unusual from a European perspective (Marsh, 2017). It can perhaps be accounted for by the particular circumstances: a very severe crash in the housing market, which left a high level of indebtedness, and a very large hole in the public finances, which in turn prompted big tax increases and significant cuts in the wages of those in public sector employment as well as general cuts in public services. For many, perhaps, a lack of improvement in their personal circumstances can be attributed to government policy, even if the government might argue that it had little choice but to adopt the path of 'austerity'.

Some recent research has called for a revaluation of Kramer's argument against the randomness of personal evaluations, arguing instead that people's assessments of their own and of the national economy do vary systematically with local conditions and the circumstances of people like them (Ansolabehere, Meredith and Snowberg 2014). The first of the two post-election INES surveys used a question which asked people to report their perception of the unemployment rate. Respondents were told that unemployment had varied between 4 and 17 per cent over the previous 40 years and then were asked to say what it was currently. Figure 6.4 shows the responses. (Responses outside the historical range were recoded to the limits of that range. Eleven per cent indicated a figure of above 17, and 2 per cent a figure of below 6.4.) The most common responses are grouped around the figure of 9 per cent – in line with the official figure at the time – with more than half in the range 8–10 per cent. However, one in six voters thought unemployment was below 8 per cent, while almost one in three thought it was more than 10 per cent. The substantial number suggesting unemployment was over 17 per cent include those giving figures of 20 as well as figures of 40, 50 and even 60 or more in a few cases, suggesting that some respondents were not engaging with the question.

How far do these judgements reflect actual local conditions? This can be explored using the data on regions already discussed above. Two caveats here are first, that these regions are larger than would be ideal to necessarily describe an individual's local experience, and second, that there are minor difficulties in matching respondents to regions. The constituency locations recorded in the survey do not always unambiguously match to regions, but for almost all respondents they do match.[2] A simple regression analysis (predicting the unemployment estimate from the level in the region at the time) does show a significant relationship, with a 1 per cent change in the local unemployment rate at the time of the election linked with a 0.18 change in the unemployment estimate.

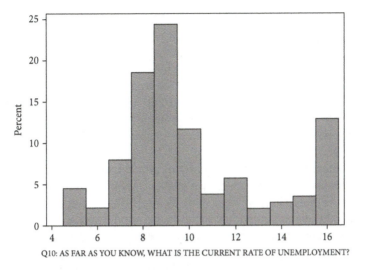

Q10: AS FAR AS YOU KNOW, WHAT IS THE CURRENT RATE OF UNEMPLOYMENT?

Figure 6.4 Respondents' estimates of unemployment in 2016.

Question: The unemployment rate in the Ireland has varied between 4% and 17% between the early 1980s and today. The average unemployment rate during that time was 11%. As far as you know, what is the current rate of unemployment? That is, of the adults in the Republic who wanted to work during the last week of February, what percentage of them would you guess were unemployed and looking for a job? (INES2).

Given that the regional range in unemployment levels runs from 5.9 to 12.5 this means a difference from lowest to highest locally is linked with a difference of 1.2 per cent in the estimate of national unemployment (6.6*0.18). Even so, this factor explains less than 2 per cent of the variation in individual estimates.

There is a stronger link between perceived unemployment and evaluations of the national economy. Again, a simple regression analysis suggests a significant difference of just one point on the evaluation scale across the range of estimated unemployment rates. Those thinking that unemployment is higher have a tendency to see the economy in more negative terms. Even so, those perceiving overly high levels of unemployment are to some degree offset by those using rose-tinted spectacles. If everyone thought unemployment was 9 per cent, it would move the average position in a positive direction on the five-point sociotropic scale (1–5) from 2.1 down to 1.8 – a relatively small shift.[3] Using simple regression assumes that the five points on the scale are evenly spaced. Arguably at least, the differences between 1 and 2 are not the same as between 2 and 3. Re-running the analysis with an ordinal regression that simply assumes this scale is ordered produces similar results. Had everyone thought unemployment was 9 per cent, 33 per cent would have seen the economy as getting much better rather than just 30 per cent, although if nobody had thought that unemployment was *more* than 9 per cent, that figure would have several points higher again.

Introducing other elements into the analysis to track local conditions, such as unemployment change in the last year, last five years or last nine years produces mixed results if we combine all the polls, but the different scales used in each survey arguably make this problematic. Results using ordinal regression suggest respondents in Dublin had more favourable evaluations than those in all other regions apart from those in the Mid-East and South West.[4] Moreover, this is in part explicable in terms of the local record since 2007. But the differences should not be exaggerated. The mean evaluations range from 2.1 to 2.7 in the Border region.

Evaluations of the national economy are arguably also due to variations in the experiences of different groups (Ansolabehere, Meredith and Snowberg, 2014). This can be explored in more detail here by modelling the impact on evaluations of local conditions and individual social background. There are variations across the three polls in what is available, but all have the same measures of social class, age and gender. Several models were estimated using ologit (Ordered Logistic Regression), each including the same social background variables, but changing the measures of the local economy, from current unemployment levels to measures of change in unemployment and employment over the last year, since 2011 and since 2007. The results are shown in Table 6.4. The first main point to emerge from this analysis is that the longer the time window in which change at local level is calculated, the more the explanatory power. This is evident in the fact that the coefficients for both employment and unemployment are significant only when the nine-year window is used, but also in the fact that the model fit, judged by the chi-square figure, is much better for the five- and nine-year window than the single year window, and also marginally better than when current unemployment figures are used.[5] Second, there are significant class and gender differences in evaluations, although age differences are minimal apart from more favourable evaluations by those aged 65 and over: men are more positive, as are the middle class and larger farmers. Figure 6.5 (based on the last model) shows predicted proportions saying the economy has improved a lot: respondents classified as AB – the better off middle class essentially – were twice as likely to be very positive as those in class D, the semi- and unskilled working class. The line for men here is consistently above the line for women, but they are significantly different only for the middle-class AB and lower middle-class C1 groups.

All this suggests that, to some extent, people's evaluations are affected by what they see around them, and that they vary in predictable ways according to local circumstances. While the local effects are slight, they are as expected and surely would be stronger if the local areas were smaller.

Hence the argument that the recovery did not have the same impact in all areas and on all classes has some merit, as does the suggestion that the way the 'real' national economy is experienced in the lives of communities varies across

Table 6.4 Sociotropic evaluations by unemployment and employment levels in region of respondent (ologit estimations)

		Sociotropic evaluations		
	Model 1 Current unemployment	Model 2 Economic change since 2015	Model 3 Economic change since 2011	Model 4 Economic change since 2007
Unemployment (%)	0.0697***	−0.00214	−0.0255	−0.0533***
	−0.0158	−0.00603	−0.0392	−0.00938
Employment (%)		−0.0062	−0.0786***	−0.0301**
		−0.00613	−0.0169	−0.0145
Class (ref AB)				
C1	0.415***	0.427***	0.416***	0.409***
	−0.0875	−0.0875	−0.0875	−0.0877
C2	1.086***	1.107***	1.090***	1.074***
	−0.107	−0.107	−0.107	−0.107
D	1.252***	1.293***	1.273***	1.247***
	−0.116	−0.116	−0.115	−0.116
E	1.048***	1.069***	1.046***	1.036***
	−0.113	−0.113	−0.113	−0.113
Larger farmers	0.295*	0.412**	0.406**	0.354**
	−0.178	−0.175	−0.176	−0.177
Smaller farmers	0.965***	1.066***	1.007***	0.961***
	−0.282	−0.281	−0.281	−0.281
Women	0.234***	0.240***	0.249***	0.236***
	−0.064	−0.0639	−0.064	−0.064
Age (ref 18–24)				
25–34	0.0033	−0.00378	0.0116	0.00111
	−0.132	−0.132	−0.132	−0.132
35–44	0.0803	0.0784	0.0874	0.0815
	−0.127	−0.127	−0.127	−0.127
45–54	0.069	0.0523	0.0759	0.0599
	−0.131	−0.131	−0.131	−0.131
55–64	−0.0863	−0.0775	−0.054	−0.0752
	−0.136	−0.136	−0.136	−0.136
65+	−0.292**	−0.289**	−0.285**	−0.300**
	−0.14	−0.14	−0.14	−0.14

(Continued)

Table 6.4 *Continued*

	Model 1 Current unemployment	*Sociotropic evaluations*		
		Model 2 Economic change since 2015	Model 3 Economic change since 2011	Model 4 Economic change since 2007
Survey (ref INES 3)				
INES1	−0.255***	−0.238***	−0.233***	−0.254***
	−0.082	−0.0819	−0.082	−0.082
INES2	0.238***	0.244***	0.252***	0.237***
	−0.0798	−0.0797	−0.0798	−0.0797
Constant cut1	0.394**	−0.204	−0.672***	0.0911
	−0.186	−0.149	−0.255	−0.152
Constant cut2	1.756***	1.151***	0.692***	1.456***
	−0.188	−0.15	−0.255	−0.154
Constant cut3	3.190***	2.580***	2.130***	2.894***
	−0.193	−0.155	−0.257	−0.159
Constant cut4	3.453***	2.844***	2.394***	3.159***
	−0.195	−0.157	−0.258	−0.161
Observations	3,319	3,319	3,319	3,319
Chi-square test	293.3	275.1	303.5	306.1

Standard errors in parentheses ***$p < 0.01$, **$p < 0.05$, *$p < 0.1$.
Source: INES1 2016, INES2 2016 and INES3 2016.

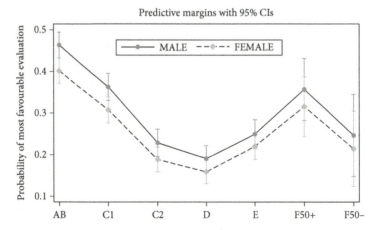

Figure 6.5 Differences in most positive sociotropic evaluations by class and gender based on all INES polls 2016.

those communities, essentially because some are richer than others. Before we go on and look at the impact of these perceptions of party support, we will look at one more factor: accountability.

Who was responsible for the recovery?

There is certainly room for debate about responsibility for the recovery. The government made the case that it was its determination to exercise control over the public finances and make favourable deals with the EU when possible that brought, or was bringing, the country out of the mess it was in. Against that, there are several arguments. One, made by Fianna Fáil in particular, is that the government was just following the path out of the crisis initially laid out by Fianna Fáil between 2008 and 2011. A second is that both Fianna Fáil and the Fine Gael/Labour coalition were just following the policies forced on Ireland under the terms of the bailout, and while they might deserve some credit for enduring the necessary unpopularity that came with austerity, it was not very much. The third counterargument is not so different to the second one, but rather than crediting the government for doing what it had to do, blames it for the subservience to Brussels and for not demanding much heavier sacrifices from those to blame. And in this scenario, it was the financiers, bankers and speculators who should have paid the price, not the ordinary Irish voter.

Following the question evaluating the change in the national economy discussed above, respondents were asked whether the change (for better or worse) was mainly due to the policies of the government, or not.[6] This is a question asked in previous INES surveys and some British election studies. It makes sense to say that if the government was not responsible then national, sociotropic evaluations should have no impact on party choice, and indeed previous evidence suggests that is true: it is the interaction of evaluations and attribution that is important (see Marsh and Tilley, 2010). There may be some room for opposition party supporters who see an improvement to attribute responsibility elsewhere; likewise, government partisans who see little improvement may feel the government was not to blame. Most respondents, 61 per cent, did attribute responsibility – for better or worse – to the government. This was most pronounced among those who thought things had got much better (80 per cent) or had become a little worse (84 per cent) or much worse (91 per cent). Those who did *not* credit the government were in a majority (55 per cent) only among those who thought things had got 'a little better'.

Hence for almost half of the voters, sociotropic evaluations were positive and the government was given credit. For just over a quarter, sociotropic evaluations were positive but the government was not given credit, and for a small group, one tenth of voters, things had got worse and that was down to the government. For the remainder, things were much the same, and half of those gave the government credit/blame for these circumstances. It remains to be seen how each of these groups voted but what is clear here is that there were enough voters who credited the government with bringing about improvement to re-elect it, had they all voted Fine Gael or Labour.

Evaluations and the vote

The primary focus here is on the relationship between sociotropic evaluations and the vote, and how far this is affected by a range of other factors, particularly pocketbook evaluations and the attribution of responsibility. One further factor that needs to be taken into account is the partisanship of each voter. There is ample evidence that partisans do tend to voice evaluations that are favourable to 'their' party. This could simply be because their partisanship influences the way they evaluate information (as allowed by traditional theories of partisanship, see Thomson 2017 for Ireland, and see also chapter 5 in this volume), but it could also be that the voting preference itself is rationalized by the evaluation (for example, Evans and Anderson, 2006). One way to control for this is to use a measure of closeness to a party. However, most Irish voters do not feel close to any party and, in addition, there is sometimes too exact a link between such attachment and how people actually voted when both are measured in the same survey. Instead, here the analysis uses the recalled vote from 2011. This is certainly flawed as recall data always are. In this case too, few recall supporting government parties, particularly Labour. Arguably, the extent that Fine Gael and Labour appear to convert and keep voters is thus exaggerated.

The first analysis examines the link between sociotropic evaluations and the vote controlling for attributions as well as past vote. The object of explanation here is a vote for the government, either Fine Gael or Labour. The main independent variables are sociotropic evaluations and the attribution of economic change to the government or not. An interaction term allows for the impact of evaluation to vary according to whether the government is seen to be responsible. There is also a control for government support in 2011. The findings of this analysis and those that follow are illustrated by figures, but the underlying details are available in the appendix to this chapter. A conventional way to look at the impact of one variable on another is to hold all other variables at a particular value, typically their mean. In this case, the main control variable is vote in 2011, which is either for the government ($gov11 = 1$) or not ($gov11 = 0$). Hence, we show the impact in Figure 6.6 both for those who reported supporting the Fine Gael and Labour government and those who did not. Figure 6.4 shows the impact of sociotropic evaluations on government support for two groups of voters, those who credit/blame the government for the current economic situation and those who do not according to the 2011 vote. The pattern is clear. For those who attribute economic responsibility to the government and voted for it in 2011,

WHY DID THE 'RECOVERY' FAIL TO RETURN THE GOVERNMENT?

the impact of evaluations on likelihood of support for a government party in 2016 goes from just a 3 per cent probability to an 81 per cent probability, as evaluations go from most negative to most positive. When the government is not seen as responsible and the respondent did not vote Fine Gael or Labour in 2011, the range is tiny, from 2 per cent to 12 per cent. The impact of the other two combinations lies between these two extremes, moving support from less than 5 per cent up to around 40 per cent. These changes for the intermediate combinations are not significant except for those in the most positive group, as the confidence intervals around each point show. This certainly supports the theory of economic voting: positive sociotropic evaluations benefitted the government parties to a very significant degree. Moreover, this holds even for those who did not vote for the government in 2011. However, clearly there were people who did not support the government despite positive evaluations and appropriate attribution, even if they supported the government last time. If a voter thought the economy had improved a lot, the chances of them supporting its re-election were much higher than the average (in this sample) of just 32 per cent, but this was not the case of those who thought the improvement was simply 'somewhat better'. Only among those who voted for it last time and attributed responsibility to it for the improvement was there support over that figure.

A second analysis explores intra-government differences. A pattern often seen in the economic voting literature is that support for the main governing party shows the biggest effects. The explanation is that these are the parties most identified with government policy. The Irish experience of minor parties

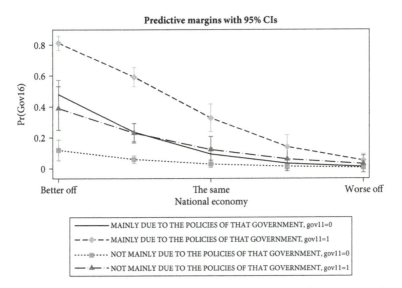

Figure 6.6 Sociotropic effects by attribution and vote in 2011 based on INES3.

in recent coalitions has been negative, with minor parties in government doing particularly badly, although this has happened in good times and in bad. Is there evidence that the economic vote this time went to Fine Gael rather than Labour? There are no data on the differential attribution of responsibility between Fine Gael and Labour, but it is possible to look at the differential impact on Fine Gael and Labour support of positive evaluations. This analysis broadly repeats the previous one, but confines the estimation to government supporters only, with the object of interest being the Labour share of the government vote. There is no control for a specifically Labour vote in 2011. Figure 6.7 shows the effects of sociotropic evaluations on the Labour share of the coalition vote. These are effectively zero: the Labour share does *not* vary by the level of sociotropic evaluation. There is no indication here that the 'recovery' only helped Fine Gael: those who perceived it were no more likely to support the Fine Gael side of the partnership than those who did not. Further explorations, allowing for different relationships according to whether people voted Labour or Fine Gael in 2011, did not change this conclusion. Labour's problem was the government's problem.

Finally, here I will deal with the 'feel-good' factor. Did people's far less positive personal or pocketbook evaluations have a negative effect on government voting, one which was independent of the sociotropic effects already seen and which might account for the electoral weakness of the government parties? As was explained earlier, personal evaluations have been downgraded in the literature. They are seen as having very weak effects at best. (An exception is Nannestad and Paldam, 1995; 1997; but see Borre, 1997; see

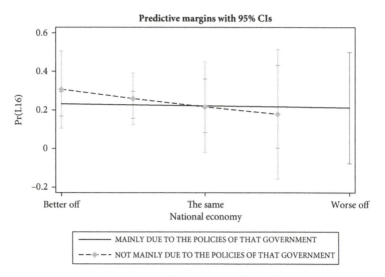

Figure 6.7 Impact of sociotropic evaluations on Labour share of government vote based on all INES polls 2016.

also Killian, Schoen and Dusso, 2008 who argue both are relevant to turnout). This is said to be because personal circumstances may get better or worse for any number of reasons quite disconnected from government decisions, and so such evaluations are a very noisy signal of macroeconomic health (Kinder and Kiewiet, 1981). Yet in the current case, there were government decisions that did mean real income would rise slowly despite growth: the initial cuts in public sector pay at the start of the crisis; restrictions on public sector income increases, with increments frozen for some years; and tax increases, particularly in the form of the universal social charge.

Following on the same lines of the analyses above, the three INES polls are again used here, and the separate effects of sociotropic and pocketbook evaluations are estimated with controls for previous vote and social background factors. Figure 6.8 shows the impact of positive evaluations on voting for a government party, with sociotropic evaluations on the left and pocketbook evaluations on the right. Separate predictions are shown for those who recalled voting for the government in 2011 and those who did not. What is clear is that both types of evaluations have strong effects. More positive sociotropic evaluations move the probability of staying with a government party from just 20 per cent to over 70 per cent, more positive pocketbook evaluations increase the chance of government voting from just below 40 per cent to almost 80 per cent. Pocketbook effects are weaker but they are still very significant. Among voters who did not vote Fine Gael or Labour in 2011, positive evaluations do also make a difference to their vote in 2016, more than doubling the chance

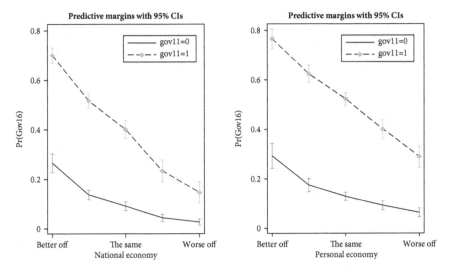

Figure 6.8 Comparison of sociotropic and pocketbook voting effects based on all INES polls 2016.

of a government vote. These findings are in line with patterns found in Irish voting in the local and European elections in 2014, and in opinion poll data in 2015 (Marsh, 2017). The lack of a feel-good factor mattered, but how far can this explain the government's losses? Using the same model, it is possible to simulate what would have happened if only people had been more positive about their own circumstances; for instance, if pocketbook evaluations had been on a par with sociotropic ones. In such a case, how much bigger might the government's vote have been? The polled surveys report a government vote of 32.4 per cent (the actual figure is 32.1). Had pocketbook evaluations been on a par with sociotropic ones, the predicted government share would have been 36.8 per cent, more than 4 per cent higher.[7] This might have proved significant when it came to post-election coalition building, but it would still have left the government parties almost 20 per cent short of the 55.5 per cent won in 2011. Evaluations would have to have been very much more positive for the government to have got much closer to this figure.

Conclusion

This chapter has explored the puzzle of the missing economic vote in the 2016 election which saw a government that was seen internationally to have presided over a recovery that enabled Ireland to exit its bailout successfully punished at the polls. It explores several ways within the general theory of economic voting to resolve the puzzle. These can be summarized here and then I will consider the wider implications of what has been found.

The first possibility is that there was no recovery, but the evidence seems clear enough that, measured in the standard ways, there was growth, unemployment was falling and the numbers in employment were going up, and had been for a couple of years prior to the election. However, the recovery did not happen to the same extent everywhere, and the crisis did bring about a much greater degree of regional inequality that the recovery had done little to correct.

The second possibility is that people did not know about the recovery. But the evidence is that there was a reasonably good public knowledge of the current employment rate, with relatively few people thinking it was still high in comparison with the last 40 years. There were variations here, understandable in the context of local unemployment levels and also variations by class and gender. People acknowledged the recovery in surveys, when asked questions about things such as the progress of the national economy, but also in a wider set of questions that make up consumer sentiment indexes. Sentiment was positive, and most people seemed to acknowledge that the economy was improving. Again, local conditions had some impact here and there was some evidence that people's frames for comparison stretched back to 2011 and even 2007, when things were probably better than in 2016 for many people. This, it is argued, goes some way to explain why people's evaluations of their personal circumstances tended to be much more negative than their evaluations with respect to the national economy. People recognized the recovery, but many did not feel its effects.

A key conditionality with respect to economic voting has been said to be the clarity of responsibility for any upturns and downturns. Key elements are things like the extent to which the economy is under the control of the government, and the extent to which local political authority is recognized. It might be argued that a small open economy and member of the EU, using the Euro, has little control over its economic fortunes, but that is hard to square with the severe punishment meted out to the previous government. Moreover, the Westminster-type of government with weak local authorities does mean power is concentrated at the centre, and shared across just two parties. If the objective indicators suggest responsibility can be identified, the subjective ones concur, with two thirds of voters holding the government responsible for the country's economic fortunes.

Even given all this, it remains possible that the economy did not feature in people's calculations, but several attempts to model the impact of economic assessment on voting behaviour in 2016 did indicate that there was economic voting. The problem for the government was that the impact was simply not great enough, and that too few people had a sufficiently favourable view. A clear majority saw improvement, and the link between assessment and vote is pronounced. Even so, the government failed to keep about one-fifth of its voters who acknowledged a lot of improvement. There is no indication that it was the minor party, Labour, that failed to win votes on the basis of the recovery. Both parties gained and lost equally in this respect.

The economic voting literature has downplayed the 'pocketbook vote' but the analysis here found that it had a very significant and independent effect. It was evident from 2014 onwards that the feel-good factor was absent, despite some recognition that the economy was picking up, and this was very evident during the election. This weakened the impact of the more favourable sociotropic evaluations, and a simple simulation indicated that this could have cost the government parties 4–5 per cent in terms of support. However, even with such a large vote share, the government would still have lost about one in three of the votes won in 2011.

What does this mean?

The central message to take from this analysis is that there is no obvious answer to the puzzle within the context of economic voting theory – if that is not too grand a term for it. The recovery was real, it was acknowledged, and it was relatively easy to credit the government, but that did not happen to the degree that might be expected. The recent literature of post-crash politics does offer another perspective. Hernandez and Kriesi (2015) suggest that the failure of recovery to restore pre-crisis prosperity is one reason why the governments leading their countries out of crisis might not be well rewarded. There is certainly some truth in this in the Irish case, and this gets some support in the analysis above. It also helps explain the way in which household evaluations lagged behind those for the country as a whole. A second factor highlighted by Hernandez and Kriesi is the fact that the party system is more open in an era of dealignment. Party attachment is relatively low in Ireland (even if it may have been up a little in 2016 (see chapter 5)), and in normal times we might expect that to increase economic voting as evaluations are less distorted by attachment (Kayser and Wlezien, 2011). Yet the lack of strong attachments also makes a government more vulnerable when it makes unpopular decisions, and the Fine Gael/Labour government, as must any government in a country dealing with an international bailout, certainly made its share of these. This takes us away from the simplicity of economic voting, although most of the issues apparently troubling voters in 2016 were economic at heart. The economy and the health services were the major ones. There was a range of other ones – from homelessness to the water charges issue that mobilized the biggest protests seen in the lifetime of the government – that would hurt the government parties. The two parties together came close to doubling their 'normal' vote in 2011 because of the unprecedented reaction to the crisis. This was a much larger economic effect than might have been expected (Marsh and Mikhaylov, 2012). That perhaps helps us to understand how they fell back so much in 2016.

A second message is about the assessment of personal economic situations. This analysis echoes previous ones on recent Irish voting, to show a significant and independent effect of personal economic circumstances on behaviour (see Marsh, 2017). This is not to say that the bulk of the literature dismissing these effects is wrong, but perhaps the theory underpinning that rejection needs to be reconsidered. The Irish case shows that it is possible for sociotropic and pocketbook evaluations to diverge systematically, and for perfectly understandable reasons that have implications for political behaviour, not least because opposition parties can exploit the absence of the 'feel-good' factor. It may well be significant, too, that prominence of the 'recovery' in the campaign (Leahy, 2016) and the government's own narrative for some time made the gap between sociotropic and pocketbook evaluations a more significant factor in political choices.

Chapter appendix

Table A6.1 Regression analysis of sociotropic evaluations on vote ... underlying Figure 6.6

Variables	Voting for government party in 2016
Voted government parties in 2011	1.606***
	(0.202)
Sociotropic evaluations (positive to negative)	−1.432***
	(0.413)
Responsibility attribution to government	2.244***
	(0.646)
Sociotropic evaluations * responsibility	−0.311
	(0.337)
Reference class (AB)	
SOCIALCLASS C1	−0.276
	(0.263)
SOCIALCLASS C2	−0.205
	(0.306)
SOCIALCLASS D	−0.768*
	(0.460)
SOCIALCLASS E	0.0228
	(0.328)
SOCIALCLASS Larger farmers	1.382***
	(0.518)
SOCIALCLASS Smaller farmers	−0.760
	(0.734)
Woman	0.248
	(0.192)
Age reference category 18–24	
25–34	−0.425
	(0.465)
35–44	0.268
	(0.449)
45–54	0.676
	(0.456)
55–64	0.0864
	(0.474)
65+	0.195
	(0.475)
Constant	3.061***
	(0.863)
Observations	840
Pseudo R-squared	0.337
LL	−361.5

Standard errors in parentheses.

***p < 0.01, **p < 0.05, *p < 0.1.

LL = log likelihood.

Table A6.2 Regression analysis of sociotropic evaluations on Labour share of coalition vote … underlying Figure 6.7

Variables	Voted Labour rather than FG
Sociotropic evaluations (positive to negative)	−0.257
	(0.576)
Responsibility attribution to government	−0.375
	(1.118)
Sociotropic evaluations * responsibility	0.0840
	(0.627)
Reference class (AB)	
SOCIALCLASS C1	−0.0660
	(0.400)
SOCIALCLASS C2	0.609
	(0.479)
SOCIALCLASS D	-
	-
SOCIALCLASS E	−0.327
	(0.489)
SOCIALCLASS Larger farmers	−1.731
	(1.058)
SOCIALCLASS Smaller farmers	-
	-
Woman	0.285
	(0.298)
Age reference category 18–24	
25–34	0.0435
	(0.566)
35–44	0.622
	(0.486)
45–54	0.326
	(0.483)
55–64	0.622
	(0.485)
65+	-
	-
Constant	−0.848
	(1.132)
Observations	269
Pseudo R-squared	0.0396
LL	−150.1

Standard errors in parentheses.

*** p < 0.01, ** p < 0.05, * p < 0.1.

LL = log likelihood.

Table A6.3 Regression analysis of sociotropic and pocketbook evaluations on coalition vote ... underlying Figure 6.8

Variables	Voted for a government party in 2016
Voted government parties in 2011	2.183***
	(0.267)
Sociotropic evaluations (positive to negative)	−0.506***
	(0.0807)
2011 vote * sociotropic	−0.0294
	(0.0998)
Pocketbook evaluations (positive to negative)	−0.271***
	(0.0679)
2011 vote * pocketbook	−0.0534
	(0.0870)
INES (reference category INES3	
INES1	−0.216*
	(0.116)
INES2	−0.263**
	(0.113)
Reference class (AB)	
SOCIALCLASS C1	0.00974
	(0.122)
SOCIALCLASS C2	0.0946
	(0.152)
SOCIALCLASS D	−0.312*
	(0.179)
SOCIALCLASS E	0.122
	(0.163)
SOCIALCLASS Larger farmers	0.607***
	(0.229)
SOCIALCLASS Smaller farmers	0.582
	(0.390)
Woman	0.253***
	(0.0902)
Age reference category 18–24	
25–34	−0.538***
	(0.203)
35–44	−0.369*
	(0.193)
45–54	−0.0947
	(0.197)
55–64	−0.310
	(0.205)
65+	−0.0541
	(0.208)
Constant	0.244
	(0.258)
Observations	3,192
Pseudo R-squared	0.237
LL	−1543

Standard errors in parentheses.

***p < 0.01, **p < 0.05, *p < 0.1.

LL = log likelihood.

Notes

1 A similar case can be made with respect to disposable income, although figures are not yet available up to 2016. The CSO reported that the gap between average disposable incomes in Dublin and in other regions decreased during the period of peak austerity, but has since widened again. *The Irish Times* 22/3/17.
2 The Tipperary constituency crosses two regions, as does Cavan-Monaghan.
3 Arguably government voters might be inclined to think unemployment is lower, but the relationship is unchanged even if a control for vote in 2011 is introduced.
4 This is most striking when we use the INES Exit poll data (INES1), which employed a 3-point scale, but does hold generally.
5 The first post-election INES poll (INES2) asked about improvements in the last year whereas INES1 and INES3 used the last 5 years, but these results hold regardless of which poll is used.
6 Do you think this was MAINLY due to the policies of that government or NOT MAINLY DUE to the policies of that government?
7 In making this prediction all other variables were held at their mean levels.

References

Anderson, Christopher J. 2000. 'Economic voting and political context: A comparative perspective', *Electoral Studies*. 19: 151–70.

Anderson, Christopher J. 2007. 'The end of economic voting? Contingency dilemmas and the limits of democratic accountability', *Annual Review of Political Science*. 10: 271–96.

Ansolabehere, Stephen, Marc Meredith and Erik Snowberg. 2014. 'Macroeconomic voting: Local information and micro-perceptions of the macroeconomy', *Economic and Politics*. 26: 380–410.

Borre, Ole. 1997. 'Economic voting in Danish electoral surveys 1987–1994', *Scandinavian Political Studies*. 20: 347–65.

Duffy, David, and James Williams. 2002. *Constructing a Consumer Sentiment Index for Ireland*. Dublin: Economic and Social Research Institute (ESRI).

Evans, Geoffrey, and Robert Andersen. 2006. 'The political conditioning of economic perceptions: Evidence from the 1992–97 British electoral cycle', *Journal of Politics*. 68: 194–207.

Hernández, Enrique, and Hanspeter Kriesi. 2015. 'The electoral consequences of the financial and economic crisis in Europe', *European Journal of Political Research*. 55: 203–24.

Kayser, Mark Andreas, and Christopher Wlezien. 2011. 'Performance pressure: Patterns of partisanship and the economic vote', *European Journal of Political Research*. 50: 365–94.

Killian, Mitchell, R. Schoen and Aaron Dusso. 2008. 'Keeping up with the Joneses: The interplay of personal and collective evaluations in voter turnout', *Political Behavior*. 30: 323–40.

Kinder, Donald R., and D. Roderick Kiewiet. 1981. 'Sociotropic politics', *British Journal of Political Science*. 11: 129–61.

Kramer, Gerald H. 1971. Short-term fluctuations in US voting behavior, 1896–1964. *American Political Science Review*. 65(1): 131–43.

Kriesi, Hanspeter 2012. 'The political consequences of the financial and economic crisis in Europe: Electoral punishment and popular protest', *Swiss Political Science Review*. 18: 518–22.

Leahy, Pat. 2016. 'Campaign strategies: How the campaign was won and lost', in Michael Gallagher and Michael Marsh (eds), *How Ireland Voted 2016: The Election that Nobody Won*. Basingstoke: Palgrave Macmillan, pp. 75–97.

Lewis-Beck, Michael S., and Mary Stegmaier. 2007. 'Economic models of voting', in Russell Dalton and Hans-Dieter Klingemann (eds), *The Oxford Handbook of Political Behaviour*. Oxford: Oxford University Press, pp. 518–37.

Leyden, Kevin, and Michael Lewis-Beck. 2017. 'The economy and the vote in Irish National Elections', in Michael Marsh, David Farrell and Gail McElroy (eds), *A Conservative Revolution? Electoral Change in Twenty-First Century Ireland*. Oxford: Oxford University Press, pp. 28–41.

Marsh, Michael. 2017. 'After 2011: Continuing the revolution', in Michael Marsh, David M. Farrell and Gail McElroy (eds), *A Conservative Revolution? Electoral Change in Twenty-First Century Ireland*. Oxford, Oxford University Press, pp. 192–207.

Marsh, Michael, and Slava Mikhaylov. 2012. 'Economic voting in a crisis: The Irish election of 2011', *Electoral Studies*. 3: 478–84.

Marsh, Michael, and Richard Sinnott. 1998. 'The behaviour of the Irish voter', in Michael Marsh and Paul Mitchell (eds), *How Ireland Voted 1997*. Oxford: Westview Press, pp. 151–80.

Marsh, Michael, and James Tilley. 2010. 'The attribution of credit and blame to governments and its impact on vote choice', *British Journal of Political Science*. 40(1): 115–34.

Marsh, Michael, Richard Sinnott, John Garry and Fiachra Kennedy. 2008. *The Irish Voter: The Nature of Electoral Competition in the Republic of Ireland*. Manchester: Manchester University Press.

Nannestad, Peter, and Martin Paldam. 1995. 'It's the government's fault! A cross-section study of economic voting in Denmark, 1990/93', *European Journal of Political Research*. 28: 33–62.

Nannestad, Peter, and Martin Paldam. 1997. 'From the pocketbook of the welfare man: A pooled cross-section study of economic voting in Denmark, 1986–1992', *British Journal of Political Science*. 27: 119–37.

Powell, G. Bingham, and Guy D. Whitten. 1993. 'A cross-national analysis of economic voting: Taking account of the political context', *American Journal of Political Science*. 37: 391–414.

Singer, Matthew. 2011. 'Who says "It's the Economy"? Cross-national and cross-individual variation in the salience of economic performance', *Comparative Political Studies*. 44: 284–312.

Thomson, Robert. 2017. 'The Malleable Nature of Party identification', in Michael Marsh, David M. Farrell and Gail McElroy (eds), *A Conservative Revolution? Electoral Change in Twenty-First Century Ireland*. Oxford: Oxford University Press, pp. 123–42.

7

Party or candidate?

Michael Courtney and Liam Weeks

Introduction

The stock of parties has been declining in value. In part, this is a product both of declining levels of partisanship and of the decreasing salience of social cleavages. Voters are now less attached to parties and social groups, and, in some jurisdictions, are increasingly looking to candidates over parties as cues when voting. In this respect, the comparative experience seems to be following a pattern that has long been evident in Ireland, where since opinion polls first began to ask about voters' motivations, choosing a candidate to represent the interests of the constituency has consistently been of high priority.

The aim of this chapter is to examine the importance of both party and candidate for the Irish voter. The act of voting is often discussed and analysed as if it is a party-centred act, but the reality in Ireland is that it takes place through the prism of candidates. Parties know that they rely on a certain level of, albeit dwindling, party loyalism, but in most cases they need to pick the right candidate to maximize support. The importance of party vis-à-vis candidate has been examined in past studies (Marsh, 2007; Marsh et al., 2008), but the aim here is to bring the discussion up to date for 2016. The financial crisis had a number of important political impacts, and one was to increase the importance of party vis-à-vis candidate in 2011 (Marsh, Farrell and McElroy, 2017). This was because national issues, which parties are more capable of dealing with than individual candidates, became of greater importance. With the gradual recovery of the Irish economy in the latter half of the tenure of the Fine Gael-Labour coalition, we assess if this altered the dynamics of party and candidate. We examine both attitudinal and behavioural assessments of these two incentives, and conclude that voters have returned to the more familiar habit of candidate-centred ballot choices, though significant party-centred behaviour persists. In the final section, we consider voters who reject party entirely and cast their first preferences for Independent candidates. In 2016, a record number of voters chose Independents over party candidates, and we examine whether this constitutes an exceptional form of candidate-centred behaviour.

Party versus candidate

The literature on the importance of candidate intermingles terms such as the personal vote, personalism and candidate-centred voting, but they are all generally discussing the same phenomenon – the ability of candidates to attract a following based on their personal qualities. One factor often cited as influencing the personal vote is the electoral system, with candidate-centred rules more likely to encourage the cultivation of a personal following. There has been some work on the strength of the personal vote in countries that use an electoral system with multi-member constituencies and intra-party choice, such as Finland, Japan and Switzerland (Karvonen, 2004; Swindle, 2002), and also in those with single-member constituencies, such as Canada, the United Kingdom and the United States (Cain, Ferejohn and Fiorina, 1987; Carey and Shugart, 1995). Of course, Ireland having one of the most candidate-centred of electoral systems has led many to assume that a consequence of its single transferable vote is a strong personal vote. The latter has been evident in opinion polls back to the 1960s, which have consistently shown that choosing a candidate to look after the local constituency is of particular importance to voters, with approximately 40 per cent stating it to be their main priority (Chubb, 1992: 144; Sinnott, 1995: 168–71; Marsh, 2010: 183–86). Most Irish political scientists would dispute, however, the extent to which the emphasis on candidates' qualities may be a product of the electoral system. The adoption of STV in Scotland for local elections in 2007 facilitated Marsh and Curtice (2008: 294–95) examining this relationship further, where they found party to be more important than in Ireland. While 27 per cent of Scottish voters said they would still vote for their most preferred candidate if they switched parties, the equivalent Irish figure was 46 per cent, suggesting that the electoral system is not necessarily a decisive factor in a predilection for candidate.

The significant competitor with candidate for the heartstrings of the voter is party, with there being somewhat conflicting evidence concerning the primacy of each. Marsh's (2010: 184) analysis of the INES between 2002 and 2007 found that approximately one third of the electorate was candidate-centred, one third party-centred, with another third influenced by a mix of both. Other studies based on mock-ballots have likewise demonstrated the importance of candidate (Bowler and Farrell, 1991a; b). More recently, Marsh et al. (2008: 24) found that it is now only a minority of voters who vote for all of the candidates of their first preferred party in a sequence. As Marsh and Plescia (2016) have discussed, however, one problem concerns the extent to which opinion poll data suggest the primacy of candidate over party, while aggregate data suggest otherwise. This was evidenced by the general stability of party support, at least up until the 2011 general election, and also by the historically high levels of intra-party transfer rates, which until the 1980s were in excess of 80 per cent (Sinnott, 1995: 209–11), indicating a high degree of partisanship. Since then, this figure has declined to approximately 60 per cent for the major parties, implying that party is less important, and in line with the noted fall in party identification (Marsh, 2006; see also chapter 5 in this volume). The decline in the importance of party, however, does not necessarily imply an equivalent rise in the importance of candidate, as there is a range of competing forces on voters, notably locality as an example (Tavits, 2010), although this is often intermingled with candidate.

It may not necessarily be that it is now party versus candidate. It may be that the two motives are intertwined. That is because, as Marsh (2007) says, personal voting is nested within party voting. This is also the case in Malta, which also uses the candidate-centred STV electoral system. With very few voters casting preferences across party lines (Hirczy de Mino and Lane, 2000: 192–93), it might seem as if Malta is a very party-centred system, but within their choice of party, candidate is very important. For this reason, among others, parties tend to run more candidates than seats, to ensure they have a wide enough variety of candidates to maximize the party vote. So, perceptions of candidates are mingled with perceptions of parties. This raises the issue of endogeneity as parties may pick candidates to cater for this effect. But candidates also have an influence on the relationship, as some of them may cultivate this personalistic demand. By contrast, other candidates may do little personal campaigning, instead relying on party label for support, particularly where the party is strong and if the candidate has a weak profile.

The electoral context of 2016

Although all had not changed utterly in the Easter rising centenary year, there had been a considerable level of movement in the Irish political system, primarily as a consequence of a serious economic recession. At its nadir, in 2011, party had increased in importance as a voting incentive with the electorate more focused on national issues, primarily centred on the economy. There was an economic recovery in the years since, so what is of interest is the effect this had on the importance of party and candidate as voting stimuli. It might be that 2011 marked a critical juncture in electoral behaviour, with party becoming ever more important, as candidate declined in significance. This would be against the aforementioned comparative experience, however, and might not be wholly expected given the decline in support for the traditional parties, and the rise in support for Independents. Three new parliamentary parties had formed in the interim period since the 2011 election, all pretty much focused on national issues, and yet the group with the greatest surge in support was the Independents. Lacking a party brand (although some of the Independent candidates were organized in groups, such as the Independent Alliance and Independents 4 Change), this might suggest that candidate appeal, or the personal vote, remained important.

Voters' motivations: Party or candidate?

To assess the importance of party and candidate we consider two measures: voters' attitudes towards these stimuli, and, in the next section, their behaviour on the ballot, in terms of how they cast their preferences. We base our assessments of voter attitudes and behaviour with reference to patterns over four elections since the first Irish election study in 2002. Voter attitudes concern voters' perceptions of what they believe to be more important when casting their votes, while the second measure deals with their actual behaviour. It is necessary to consider both measures because past studies have shown that while voters may rank candidate over party, when it comes to the ballot, they exhibit significant party-oriented behaviour.

Beginning with voters' attitudes, a number of measures were employed in the election studies that allow us to evaluate the importance of party and candidate. The first was a simple and direct question that asked voters to evaluate which was more important when casting their first preference, responses to which can be compared by party-voter across the four elections in this period (see Table 7.1). As is evident, 2011 constitutes an anomaly, as it is the one election in the timeframe where party was deemed more important than candidate. Rather than indicating a trend, it was more a deviation, as candidate returned to prevalence in 2016, with a 53–44 split. This was not as high as the split in 2002 and 2007, when there was a 3:2 ratio in favour of candidate, but the fact that it reversed the pattern of 2011 indicates the extent to which that election was just a tremor, rather than a full-scale earthquake.

To test the robustness of this direct measure regarding subjective beliefs about party-candidate orientation, a follow-up question asked if voters would still support their first preferred candidate if he or she ran for another party (see Table 7.2). Voters answering in the affirmative is further evidence of an orientation towards candidate, while responses in the negative must be seen to qualify a voter's claim to candidate-centredness. There is a tradition of multi-candidate strategies in Ireland. Voters, particularly supporters of the two main parties, usually have the option of voting for one or more candidates under their preferred party label. Responses indicating candidate-centredness to the party/candidate question may operate within a latent party-centredness, that is, voters

Table 7.1 Reasons for voting: Party or candidate

	2002			2007			2011			2016		
	Candidate	Party	N	Candidate	Party	N	Candidate	Party	N	Candidate	Party	N
FF	57	43	796	55	45	480	48	52	218	55	41	287
FG	66	34	387	65	35	308	41	59	649	46	51	339
GP	41	59	75	43	57	49	37	63	19	63	33	44
Lab	69	31	162	60	40	129	40	60	289	54	45	115
PD/Renua	74	26	57	55	45	40	-	-	-	78	19	36
SF	44	56	88	52	48	54	36	64	162	45	51	237
AAA/PBP	-	-	-	-	-	-	-	-	-	64	35	73
SD	-	-	-	-	-	-	-	-	-	78	20	50
Total	59	41	2155	60	40	1237	42	58	1387	53	44	1221

Note: Don't know/no reply and not applicable not included. Data are drawn from INES 2002, 2007, 2011 and INES1 2016.

FF = Fianna Fáil; FG = Fine Gael; GP = Green Party; Lab = Labour; SF = Sinn Féin; PD = Progressive Democrats; SD = Social Democrats; AAA-PBP = Anti-Austerity Alliance – People Before Profit.

Table 7.2 Would vote for the same candidate if he or she stood for a different party

	2002				2007				2011				2016			
	Yes	*Depends*	*No*	*N*	*Yes*	*Depends*	*No*	*N*	*Yes*	*Depends*	*No*	*N*	*Yes*	*Depends*	*No*	*N*
FF	43	15	43	796	38	10	52	480	35	26	39	218	47	12	42	298
FG	59	11	31	387	45	11	44	308	28	34	39	649	42	17	41	350
GP	16	26	58	75	14	10	76	49	21	47	32	19	32	17	50	46
Lab	45	23	33	162	42	15	43	129	38	33	29	289	42	20	38	116
PD/Renua	49	24	27	57	44	13	44	40					48	11	41	37
SF	37	19	44	88	38	23	40	54	33	31	36	162	33	19	48	247
AAA/PBP/SP						13	21	53		46	21	28	28	28	50	74
SD													45	34	21	51
Total	46	16	38	2155	41	13	46	1115	32	32	36	1438	40	18	42	1221

Source: INES 2002, 2007 and 2011 and INES1 2016.

Note: Responses to the question: 'Would you vote for your first preferred candidate if they ran for another party?'

FF = Fianna Fáil; FG = Fine Gael; GP = Green Party; Lab = Labour; SF = Sinn Féin; PD = Progressive Democrats; SD = Social Democrats; AAA-PBP = Anti-Austerity Alliance – People Before Profit.

make their choice of candidate within party. This follow-up question puts that latency to the test.

Voters could choose one of three responses: 'Yes, I would vote for the same candidate', 'No' and 'Depends on the party they stood for'. Voters may be so opposed to particular parties that, while they demonstrate an affinity with the candidate, their affinity has some limitations. A Fine Gael voter, for instance, may support the candidate if they ran for Labour or Fianna Fáil, but not Sinn Féin. In 2016 (see Table 7.2), 40 per cent of party voters would support the candidate if they stood for a different party, 42 per cent would not do so and 18 per cent responded that it depends on the party. This is roughly in line with trends in the pre-crisis elections of 2002 and 2007. The 2011 election is an outlier, with responses broken down almost evenly into the three response categories. In this regard, 2016 represents a continuity of traditional voting behaviour, rather than change.

Following the methodology of previous studies in this area (Marsh et al., 2008: 148), these two questions on the importance of party and candidate can be combined to construct an index of attitudinal candidate-centredness. The index itself has three categories: candidate-centred, party-centred and mixed. A voter is coded as candidate-centred if they choose candidate over party, and would unequivocally follow the candidate to another party. A voter is coded as party-centred if they responded that they are party-centred to the first item, and would not vote for another party in order to continue their support for the candidate. If a voter gave alternative response combinations, 'depends' in the second item, they are categorized as 'mixed' overall. As evident in Table 7.3, the proportion of candidate-centred voters is surprisingly in decline. We say surprisingly because this is not something that was evident in either Tables 7.1 or 7.2. In 2002, almost 39 per cent of voters were candidate-centred, falling to around 32–33 per cent for the 2007–2011 elections, and falling again to 29 per cent in 2016. Apart from 2007, the proportion of party-centred voters has remained fairly consistent, at around 28 per cent.

Voters for the small parties have been the least candidate-centred, especially those voting for the Greens, although this rose in 2016. While Sinn Féin's vote is less candidate-centred, this is not reciprocated by a rise in its party-centred vote, but rather by the proportion of voters with mixed incentives. Table 7.3 also confirms the considerable decline in the candidate-centred nature of Fine Gael voters, which was 50 per cent in 2002, fell as low as 20 per cent in 2011, but increased slightly to 28 per cent in 2016. The same pattern is replicated for Labour, for whom 47 per cent of its voters in 2002 were candidate-centred, a proportion that declined to 33 per cent in 2016 (again, as for Fine Gael, an increase on 2011). Fianna Fáil voters, on the other hand, seemed to have leaned away from candidate in 2007 and 2011, before reverting back to their 2002 levels in 2016.

Table 7.3 Candidate/party index from close-ended questions

Party	2002				2007				2011				2016			
	CC	PC	M	N	CC	PC	M	N	CC	PC	M	N	CC	PC	M	N
FF	36	30	34	796	29	37	34	480	26	30	43	218	36	28	36	298
FG	50	23	27	387	35	29	36	308	20	32	48	649	28	30	41	350
GP	16	45	39	75	10	55	35	49	11	26	63	19	26	26	48	46
Lab	47	24	30	162	32	29	40	129	25	22	53	289	33	29	39	116
PD/Renua	49	18	33	57	35	38	28	40					41	11	49	37
SF	27	41	32	88	32	35	33	54	20	32	48	162	21	32	48	247
AAA/PBP									32	11	57	28	18	27	55	74
SD													41	14	45	51
Total	39	28	33	2155	32	32	36		33	28	39	4775	29	28	43	1221

Note: PC = party-centred, CC = candidate-centred, M = mixed incentives. All figures bar the N columns are percentages. Party-centred are those for whom party is more important and who would not have voted for their first preferred candidate if they had run for a different party. Candidate-centred voters are those for whom candidate is more important and who would still for have voted for their first preferred candidate if they had run for another party. Those with a mix of party and candidate incentives are in the mixed category. Data are drawn from INES 2002, 2007 and 2011 and RTE exit poll 2016.

FF = Fianna Fáil; FG = Fine Gael; GP = Green Party; Lab = Labour; SF = Sinn Féin; PD = Progressive Democrats; SD = Social Democrats; AAA-PBP = Anti-Austerity Alliance – People Before Profit.

The relationship between attitudes and behaviour

How voters report their motivations and intentions in a survey may not be a strong predictor of their behaviour. Attitudes and behaviour are distinct concepts so, empirically, they can correlate highly or diverge to a considerable extent. Voters may report certain attitudes but behave in a way that is even contradictory to those attitudes as other intervening factors break the link between attitudes and behaviour (Fishbein and Azjen, 1975). With this in mind, we move away from the discussion of attitudes to focus on voters' behaviour in terms of how they complete the ballot. We examine the patterns by which preferences are cast to determine if voters are candidate or party-centred, in particular, by focusing on the level of intra-party solidarity, that is the extent to which supporters of one party candidate continue to cast preferences for the running mate(s) of that candidate (Gallagher, 1978).

In the context of this analysis, people may report being candidate-centred but, at the same time, exhibit party-centred behaviour by prioritizing high preferences for candidates of the same party, or vote for all available party candidates somewhere on the ballot. We look at the relationship between attitude orientations, towards candidate or party and solidarity voting from two angles. The first operationalization of solidarity voting is whether all available candidates from a voter's first preferred party are marked immediately following the first preference until no more candidates are available from that party. We call these complete sequential preferences. This is a demanding test for voters, particularly where parties run more than two candidates. The second measure of solidarity voting is not as strong and considers whether voters gave a preference anywhere on the ballot to all available candidates from the party of their first preference. We call these complete non-sequential preferences. We then link these dynamics to how people responded to the attitudinal questions about their motivations to assess the strength of the relationship between attitudes and behaviour. Given the demanding requirements of the first measure of solidarity voting, there should be a weaker relationship between survey responses and sequential voting solidarity than between survey responses and non-sequential solidarity. If attitudes and behaviour are consistent, candidate-motivated voters should be less likely to cast sequential preferences than party-motivated voters. One note of caution is that it is wholly possible that candidate-centred voters express non-sequential solidarity voting, particularly if they are inclined to cast preferences for most candidates on the ballot. Nevertheless, we expect such voters to cast preferences for all party candidates at a lesser rate than those claiming to be party-centred. We replicate and extend the analysis presented by Marsh et al. (2008: 149) to determine whether there have been any major shifts in the relationship between subjective beliefs about candidate-centredness and reported voting behaviour in the elections since 2002.

Table 7.4 Patterns of sequential party voting by candidate-centredness of the first preference vote (per cent), 2002–2016

Sequential vote in	Motives for first-preference vote		
	Candidate-centred	Mixed	Party-centred
2002	27	38	66
2007	27	46	65
2011	25	45	53
2016	33	46	60

Using the data presented in Table 7.3, for the four Dáil elections between 2002 and 2016, we examine the level of sequential and non-sequential voting according to the three types of attitudinal measures. These include whether voters are candidate- or party-motivated, or have mixed motivations. Beginning with sequential voting, we indicate in Table 7.4 that, as expected, those who say they are candidate-centred are less likely than other respondents to cast sequential preferences. In 2002 and 2007, 27 per cent of voters who claimed to be candidate-centred voted sequentially where their first preference party ran multiple candidates. This figure decreased to 25 per cent in 2011, but increased to 33 per cent in 2016. This suggests a divergence of attitudes and behaviour as respondents provide candidate-centred responses but, more recently, exhibit more party-centred behaviour. Voters with mixed motives also exhibit more party-centric behaviour at recent elections, with the proportions casting sequential lists increasing since 2002, but holding steady at around 46 per cent over the past three elections. The proportion of voters claiming to be party-centred and also voting for a complete party list fell in 2011 by twelve percentage points, but increased again in 2016, suggesting a restoration of more party-centric behaviour. This could also be seen as a slight convergence of behaviour between candidate- and party-centred voters, with candidate-centred voters paying more attention to party labels, and party voters giving greater weight to candidate profiles.

In Table 7.5, we perform a similar analysis, except the focus is on non-sequential party voting, where someone casts a preference for all the candidates of their first preference party, but not in a sequential order. Similar patterns to those identified in Table 7.4 are evident, with non-sequential voting declining across all three categories in 2011 before rising again in 2016. The primary difference is that the proportions are almost twenty percentage points higher than those engaging in sequential voting. In 2016, 50 per cent of candidate-centred voters cast preferences for all the candidates of their first preference party, with as many as 80 per cent of party-centred voters doing so.

Table 7.5 Patterns of sequential party voting by candidate-centredness of the first preference vote (per cent), 2002–2016

	Motives for first-preference vote		
Non-sequential vote in	Candidate-centred	Mixed	Party-centred
2002	44	54	75
2007	44	62	82
2011	36	54	63
2016	50	64	79

Notes: All figures are proportions. They indicate the level of non-sequential voting (i.e. those who cast non-sequential preferences for all candidates of their first preference party) by attitudinal response category. Candidate-centred voters are those who report that candidate is the primary factor in their first preference vote and say that if their candidate had run for some other party they would still have voted for him; and party-centred voters are those who say party is the primary factor in their first preference vote and that they would not have voted for the candidate if he or she had not run for that party; all others are classified as having mixed motivations. Includes only instances where a party fielded more than one candidate. Data are drawn from INES 2002, 2007, 2011 and 2016 (INES1).

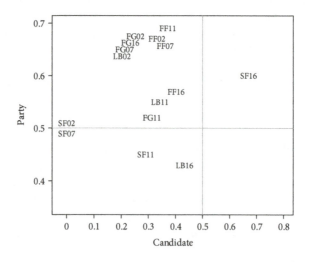

Figure 7.1 Proportions of party- and candidate-centred voters casting sequential party ballots by year and party.
Source: INES 2002, 2007, 2011 and 2016 (INES1).

The likelihood of voters casting sequential and non-sequential preferences can be explored further at the party level. For each party/election combination, Figure 7.1 plots the proportion of party-centred voters casting a sequential ballot against the proportion of candidate-centred voters who did so. For example, in 2016, 65 per cent of party-centred Fianna Fáil voters cast sequential ballots, compared with 40 per cent of Fianna Fáil candidate-centred voters. All things being equal, we should expect to see the scores on the party index (y-axis) around twenty points greater than those on the candidate index (x-axis), based on the findings from Tables 7.4 and 7.5. It is therefore no surprise that most of the results cluster around 60–65 per cent for party-centred voters and 30–40 per cent for candidate-centred voters.

There are some interesting deviations, however, within individual parties. Among Fianna Fáil voters, for example, a disconnect between attitudes and behaviour has emerged. The proportion of candidate-motivated voters casting sequential ballots for the party has risen over time, from 33 per cent in 2002 to 40 per cent in 2016, while the proportion of party-motivated voters doing so fell from 67 to 57 per cent. Fine Gael voters in 2016, save for some anomalous behaviour in 2011, report attitudes and cast ballots as consistently as they did in 2002, with 23 per cent of candidate-motivated voters casting sequential ballots and 67 per cent of party-motivated voters doing so. While the dynamics of the relationship between attitudes and behaviour for Labour voters mirrored those of Fine Gael in 2002, by 2016 the likelihood of its party-centred voters casting sequential ballots had decreased dramatically, from 65 per cent in 2002 to 43 per cent in 2016. Over time, Sinn Féin voters' behaviour has disengaged from their attitudes. In 2002 and 2007, no candidate-motivated voter for the party cast a sequential ballot, while 50 per cent of party-motivated supporters did so. In 2011 the proportion of candidate-motivated voters casting sequential ballots increased to 29 per cent and, in 2016, to 67 per cent, even higher than the proportion of party-motivated voters casting sequential ballots.

Across all combinations of party affiliation and attitude orientation, the general trend is that voters exhibit more party-centred behaviour compared to the 2002 figures. Of these twelve combinations, only four exhibit less party-oriented 'straight ticket' voting: Fianna Fáil party-centred voters, Fine Gael candidate-centred voters and Labour voters with mixed and party-centred attitudes. This suggests a deepening of partisanship in Irish politics, or at least, an increase in Mair's 'clientelistic partisans' – voters committed to a candidate, but willing to support the full ticket (Mair, 1987; Marsh et al., 2008).

Independent voters

One of the most prominent changes in voting behaviour at recent elections has been the rise in support for Independent candidates. Independents have always been a feature of the Irish political landscape (Weeks, 2015; 2017), but support for them began to grow in the 1990s. Apart from a blip in 2007, support for Independents increased at every Dáil election since the 1990s, from 6 per cent in 1992 to almost 10 per cent in 2002, up to 2016 when one in six voters cast a first preference for Independent candidates of varying hues, with twenty-three of them winning seats. While the virtually unique presence of Independents in the Dáil might suggest they are a form of Irish exceptionalism, they may instead be a variant of the more common comparative phenomenon of populism. In other European countries this has taken the form of parties, such as the Five Star Movement in Italy, the Party of Freedom in the Netherlands and UKIP in Britain, but no such party has yet emerged in Ireland (on the 2011 election, see Bowler and Farrell, 2017). Although Independents are in no way a far-right movement, as is the case with a number of populist groups, candidates running under this banner exhibit some typically populist characteristics. For example, Taggart (2000: 2) defined a number of themes associated with populists, including that they are 'reluctantly political', identify with an 'idealized heartland', adapt to the colours of their environment and provoke a strong reaction to a sense of crisis, all of which have been exhibited by Independents in the Irish context. They are, by definition, anti-party, usually focus on localized issues specific to their constituency, and, in the absence of a party whip, can easily adapt their position to the prevailing public mood on an issue. In addition, there is no one strand or distinct specific type of populism, with the only common theme being 'appeals to the people' and 'distrust of elites' (Taggart, 2000: 21), messages which often form the central theme of Independents' campaigns.

One caveat concerning these populist comparisons is that they apply to the political actors, that is, the Independent candidates themselves. When it comes to the type of support they attract, there is little evidence that Independent voters are similar in their socio-economic make-up to populist voters in other countries. Typically, the latter tend to be disproportionately represented among the white, older and less educated groups, and tend to be conservative in their outlook, resenting the onset of liberal, progressive values. More detailed studies of Independent voters have shown them to lack ideological and social bases (Bowler and Farrell, 2017; Weeks, 2011). While this may well be due to the heterogeneity of Independent candidates, when they are treated as an aggregate Weeks (2011; 2017) found that when differentiating categories of Independents, including those from a party background, those more locally focused, and those with an ideological streak, there is little evidence of a social base to their support.

Returning to the core question of this chapter on whether voters are motivated by party or candidate, it could easily be assumed that the rise in support for these Independents is an indicator of the growing strength of candidate-centred voting. So, while the previous section indicated that candidate-centred voting has not increased in prominence over the past few elections, and has actually decreased among some party voters, it may be that this has been masked by the rise in support for Independents, and that they are attracting the bulk of those who prefer candidate over party. A counter-argument is that voters for Independents are instead drawn to the 'Independent' brand. By definition, this is something different to a party orientation, which is why Independent voters need to be treated separately. After all, one of the assumed attractions of this brand is that the candidate, and ultimately TD, is not constrained by a party whip. The candidate, if elected, will also have more scope to speak publicly about issues affecting the constituency, without retaliation from a party machine. Therefore, Independent voters may consider themselves candidate-centred, but are attracted to the 'Independent' brand, meaning that they would not follow that candidate if they ran for a party.

The same set of questions as used above was also addressed to Independent voters in 2002 and in 2007 who were asked if they voted for party or candidate, and if they would still vote for their preferred Independent should they run for a party. Obviously, the value of the first measure can be questioned, since, by implication, those voting for Independents cannot be basing their decision on party, given their preferred candidate's non-party status. Nevertheless, it is still useful to include the responses to compare with party voters. Not surprisingly, almost all Independent voters in 2002 and 2007 based their vote on candidate and not party. Given Independents' lack of a party label, the only surprise is that a small proportion (6 and 7 per cent) of those voting for them prioritized party over candidate. In 2011 and 2016, Independent voters were asked a separate question, namely whether their vote for an Independent was because of the candidate or because he or she was an Independent. In both election years, 27 per cent of those voting for Independents did so because of their attraction to the brand, implying that it is not necessarily all about the candidate for Independent voters. The proportion willing to continue to vote for their Independent candidate if they joined a party increased in 2007 to 66 per cent, but in 2016 it fell back to 2002 levels of 56 per cent. Combining these two questions into an Independent versus candidate-centred index, it appears that Independent voters have become more brand-centred, although this may be due to the changed question wording in 2011.

One might quite reasonably query the validity of treating Independents as a brand, because although some of them ran as part of loose alliances in 2016, particularly the Independent Alliance and Independents4Change, they comprise, for the most part, separate candidacies. Historically, Independents came from a variety of backgrounds, with Weeks (2009) identifying six broad Independent 'families', including some who left a party, some who ran as localized community candidates, and others who sought to highlight a single issue. Little united these candidates other than that they ran on a non-party platform. For these reasons, there was little to link the support bases of these individual candidates, and as has been mentioned previous studies of Independents both as a whole and as separate categories found few socio-economic or attitudinal bases to their vote. This is not the appropriate arena to repeat a similar analysis for 2016, and in any case, the suggestion that the 'Independent' brand is growing

Table 7.6 Independent voters

Party or candidate											
2002			**2007**			**2011**			**2016**		
Candidate	*Party*	*N*	*Candidate*	*Party*	*N*	*Candidate*	*Party*	*N*	*Candidate*	*Party*	*N*
94	6	140	93	7	54	75	25	144	73	27	205

Vote for Independent if they ran for a party															
2002				**2007**				**2011**				**2016**			
Yes	*Depends*	*No*	*N*	*Yes*	*Depends*	*No*	*N*	*Yes*	*Depends*	*No*	*N*	*Yes*	*Depends*	*No*	*N*
57	24	19	176	66	13	21	53	52	23	25	155	56	19	25	215

Independent-centred or candidate-centred															
2002				**2007**				**2011**				**2016**			
CC	*IC*	*M*	*N*	*CC*	*IC*	*M*	*N*	*CC*	*IC*	*M*	*N*	*CC*	*IC*	*M*	*N*
51	1	47	140	65	6	30	54	47	11	42	155	44	17	39	205

Note: IC = Independent-centred, CC = candidate-centred, M = mixed incentives. All figures bar the N columns are percentages. Independent-centred are those for whom non-party status is more important and who would not have voted for the Independent if they run for a party. Candidate-centred voters are those for whom candidate is more important and who would still for have voted for an Independent if they had run for a party. Those with a mix of Independent and candidate incentives are in the mixed category. Data are drawn from INES 2002, 2007 and 2011 and RTE exit poll 2016.

lessens the necessity for such an unpacking, particularly when the sample sizes for each category of Independent would be pretty small.

Conclusion

This chapter has explored how the 2016 election relates to trends in party- and candidate-centred voting in Ireland. The analysis examined both attitudinal and behavioural measures, with a focus on how voters perceive these factors to guide them at the ballot box, followed by a comparison with how they actually behave. We found that candidate has somewhat surprisingly continued to decline in importance. Where in 2002 a plurality of voters (40 per cent) were candidate-centred, the equivalent figure in 2016 was just under 30 per cent. This has not been matched by a concomitant rise in the number of party-centred voters. Instead the proportion of voters with mixed incentives has increased, suggesting that there is a greater conflict between party and candidate for the heartstrings of voters. The results also suggest that partisanship, although not on the rise, is not in decline as had been thought. In spite of all the electoral volatility, the proportion of party-centred voters has remained rather stable.

We found that attitudes are not pure predictors of behaviour, as those who declared themselves to be guided by candidate over party demonstrated party-centric behaviour on the ballot. In particular, our finding that 30 per cent of voters with candidate-centred attitudes cast sequential party preferences suggests that candidate-centred voting may be nested within party choice. In other words, those who profess to be guided by candidate are doing so within the context of their preferred party. This does not necessarily imply that voters are confused when making choices or that they tell lies to pollsters. Rather, those for whom choice of party is a fixed act (that is, they tend to vote for the same party) view their vote as an intra-party choice, and are thus likely to see candidate as the main influence on their ballot choice.

A particularly exceptional form of candidate-centred behaviour in the Irish context is the support for Independents. Pariahs in most other comparative jurisdictions, Independents have been an ever-present feature of the Irish political scene, but in recent elections their vote has accelerated considerably. While in the past supporters of these candidates saw little attraction in the 'Independent' brand and were mainly lured by the qualities of the respective candidate, this has begun to change. In 2011, and especially in 2016, the Independent label has become more of a valuable commodity, with as many as one in four Independent voters stating this to be a stronger incentive than factors specific to the candidate. Although lacking a party brand, it should not be assumed that Independents are either a symptom of a declining partisanship or a rising level of populism. While Independent politicians are certainly accused of exhibiting populist tendencies, there is little evidence of their attracting a right-wing populist vote akin to that witnessed elsewhere in Europe in recent years.

In general, both party and candidate remain locked in conflict for the hearts and minds of Irish voters. A party cannot afford to ignore candidate and must select individuals of merit and ability for its ticket in order to attract votes. Likewise, a candidate cannot ignore the appeal party has to some voters. The general findings from our analysis suggest that it is not a binary choice for most voters, that is, they do not decide solely on party or candidate, but rather these factors have a joint influence. This is borne out by the rise in the proportion of voters with mixed motivations and also by the number of candidate-centred voters exhibiting party-oriented behaviour. From this perspective, the 2016 election was more a case of continuity than change.

Chapter appendix

Table A7.1 Data for Figure 7.1

Party	Year	Candidate-centred	Mixed	Party-centred
Fianna Fáil	2002	48	62	75
Fianna Fáil	2007	52	65	81
Fianna Fáil	2011	44	49	76
Fianna Fáil	2016	57	72	71
Fine Gael	2002	47	61	77
Fine Gael	2007	43	64	82
Fine Gael	2011	45	63	61
Fine Gael	2016	42	73	85
Labour	2002	39	52	75
Labour	2011	49	63	75
Labour	2016	43	43	43
Sinn Féin	2002	0	67	50
Sinn Féin	2007	11	0	50
Sinn Féin	2011	43	75	55
Sinn Féin	2016	92	89	80

Notes: All figures are proportions. They indicate the level of sequential voting (i.e. those who cast sequential preferences for all candidates of their first preference party) by attitudinal response category. Candidate-centred voters are those who report that candidate is the primary factor in their first preference vote and say that if their candidate had run for some other party, they would still have voted for him or her; and party-centred voters are those who say party is the primary factor in their first preference vote and that they would not have voted for him or her if their candidate had not run for that party; all others are classified as having mixed motivations. Includes only instances where a party fielded more than one candidate. Data are drawn from INES 2002, 2007, 2011and 2016 (INES1). Labour did not run multi-candidate tickets in any constituency in 2007.

References

Bowler, Shaun, and David Farrell. 1991a. 'Voter behavior under STV-PR: Solving the puzzle of the Irish party system', *Political Behavior*. 13: 303–20.

Bowler, Shaun, and David Farrell. 1991b. 'Party loyalties in complex settings: STV and party identification', *Political Studies*. 39: 350–62.

Bowler, Shaun, and David Farrell. 2017. 'The lack of party system change in Ireland in 2011', in Michael Marsh, David Farrell and Gail McElroy (eds), *A Conservative Revolution? Electoral Change in Twenty-First Century Ireland*. Oxford: Oxford University Press, pp. 83–101.

Cain, Bruce, John Ferejohn and Morris Fiorina. 1987. *The Personal Vote. Constituency Service and Electoral Independence*. Cambridge, MA: Harvard University Press.

Carey, John M., and Martin S. Shugart. 1995. 'Incentives to cultivate a personal vote: A rank ordering of electoral formulas', *Electoral Studies*. 14: 417–40.

Chubb, Basil. 1992. *The Government and Politics of Ireland*. 3rd edition, London: Longman.

Fishbein, Martin, and Icek Azjen. 1975. *Belief, Attitude, Intention and Behaviour: An Introduction to Theory and Research*. Reading, MA. Addison-Wesley.

Gallagher, Michael. 1978. 'Party solidarity, exclusivity and inter-party relationships in Ireland, 1922–1977: The evidence of transfers', *Economic and Social Review*. 10: 1–22.

Hirczy de Mino, Wolfgang, and John C. Lane. 2000. 'Malta: STV in a two-party system', in Shaun Bowler and Bernard Grofman (eds), *Elections in Australia, Ireland and Malta under the Single Transferable Vote. Reflections on an Embedded Institution*. Ann Arbor: University of Michigan Press, pp. 178–204.

Karvonen, Lauri. 2004. 'Preferential voting: Incidence and effects', *International Political Science Review*. 25: 203–26.

Mair, Peter. 1987. *The Changing Irish Party System: Organisation, Ideology and Electoral Competition*. London: Frances Pinter.

Marsh, Michael. 2006. 'Party identification in Ireland: An insecure anchor for a floating party system'. *Electoral Studies*. 25: 489–508.

Marsh, Michael. 2007. 'Candidates or parties? Objects of electoral choice in Ireland'. *Party Politics*. 13: 500–27.

Marsh, Michael. 2010. 'Voting behaviour', in John Coakley and Michael Gallagher (eds), *Politics in the Republic of Ireland*. London: Routledge and PSAI Press, pp. 168–97.

Marsh, Michael, and John Curtice. (2008). 'How did they vote? Voters' use of the STV ballot paper in the 2007 Scottish local elections', *Representation*. 44: 285–300.

Marsh, Michael, and Carolina Plescia. 2016. 'Split-ticket voting in an STV system: choice in a non-strategic context', *Irish Political Studies*. 31: 163–81.

Marsh, Michael, David Farrell and Gail McElroy (eds). 2017. *A Conservative Revolution? Electoral Change in Twenty-First Century Ireland*. Oxford: Oxford University Press.

Marsh, Michael, Richard Sinnott, John Garry and Fiachra Kennedy. 2008. *The Irish Voter: The Nature of Electoral Competition in the Republic of Ireland*. Manchester: Manchester University Press.

Sinnott, Richard. 1995. *Irish Voters Decide: Voting Behaviour in Elections and Referendums since 1918*. Manchester: Manchester University Press.

Swindle, Stephen. 2002. 'The supply and demand of the personal vote theoretical considerations and empirical implications of collective electoral incentives', *Party Politics*. 8: 279–300.

Taggart, Paul. 2000. *Populism*. Buckingham: Open University Press.

Tavits, Margit. 2010. 'Effect of local ties on electoral success and parliamentary behaviour. The case of Estonia', *Party Politics*. 16: 215–35.

Weeks, Liam. 2009. 'We don't like (to) party. A typology of independents in Irish political life, 1922–2007', *Irish Political Studies*. 24: 1–27.

Weeks, Liam. 2011. 'Rage against the Machine. Who is the Independent voter?', *Irish Political Studies*. 26: 19–43.

Weeks, Liam. 2015. 'Why are there Independents in Ireland?', *Government and Opposition*. 51: 580–604.

Weeks, Liam. 2017. *Independents in Irish Party Democracy*. Manchester: Manchester University Press.

8

Political fragmentation on the march: Campaign effects in 2016

Theresa Reidy and Jane Suiter

Introduction

Knowing when voters decide who they are going to vote for is a vital part of understanding how elections work. Early behavioural studies of elections often considered campaigns to be of limited consequence in shaping voter decision-making. Declining partisanship and increased choice at elections have driven a reconsideration of this assessment. Campaigns have become more decisive in shaping voter decisions by raising awareness of new parties and candidates and providing vital information on the policy positions of competing actors. Manifesto launches, party leader debates and intense scrutiny of opinion polls have become the cornerstones of modern election campaigns. However, the ways in which campaigns can shape voter decisions vary and need to be investigated at each election.

Ireland was one of the countries most affected by the great recession. The troika bailout agreed in 2010 required significant economic retrenchment and elections in 2011 and 2016 were marked by high degrees of voter volatility. The essential case that we make in this chapter is that the economic crisis had a polarizing effect on a large number of voters. Most particularly, in 2016, voters moved away from the government parties of Fine Gael and Labour which had become associated with the politics of austerity. Fianna Fáil made a small recovery but it was the smaller parties and non-party candidates that experienced a surge in support. We argue that some of these dynamics can be identified in the timing of voter decision-making.

Successive waves of the RTÉ exit poll carried out on polling day at each election confirm that a growing proportion of voters report making their final vote choice during the election campaigns. Using the exit poll, we classify voters into four distinct groups in accordance with the time at which they made their final vote choice: election day deciders, campaign deciders, early deciders and partisans. Election day deciders are those who report that they made their final decision within 36 hours of the election while campaign deciders are those who made up their mind during the three-week campaign. Early deciders report that they made their decision some time before the election was called and partisans are voters who said that they are committed to a political party and always vote for them. The analysis in this chapter is driven by three questions: Who are the voters in each of these groups (i.e. what are their demographic profiles), what parties did each cohort support and what issues influenced their choices?

We present four hypotheses in the next section which provides an overview of how campaigns can affect election outcomes. The subsequent section documents the main events during the course of the 2016 campaign and provides an overview of the issues which dominated public debates. We then detail the empirical analysis confirming that a large proportion of voters report making their final voting choice during the campaign period. Indeed, more than half of the voters in INES1 (the RTÉ/INES exit poll) arrived at their final decision at some point during the campaign. Finally, some implications of the findings for our understanding of voting behaviour and the party system in Ireland are advanced.

Literature review

The earliest studies of voting behaviour tended to consign campaigns to the end of the list of factors which shaped voter decision-making (Lazarsfeld, Berelson and Gaude, 1968) but recent decades have brought a re-evaluation of the hierarchy of voter influences and campaigns have moved closer to the foreground. Declining partisanship is central to understanding the increased relevance of political campaigns. As voter loyalties to the old parties in political systems have weakened, new factors have become more important in shaping voter decisions. The research literature speaks to two main effects: priming and persuasion (Blais et al., 1999). Campaigns may prime voters to think more or less about specific issues, candidates or leaders. The personality of constituency candidates and party leaders, new political issues and constituency service can all be part of campaign communications and ultimately contribute to evolving voter decision-making. Essentially, campaigns operate as a vehicle of communication for all of the aforementioned aspects, as well as providing opportunities for random events to play out (Farrell and Schmitt-Beck, 2002).

Irish election campaigns have become highly professionalized since the 1970s with parties investing extensive resources in managing local and national activities, both on the ground (personal canvass, leaflet drops, postering) and on the air (broadcasting and most recently social media). Importantly, the advent of campaign panel studies has been critical in facilitating our growing understanding of when and how voters make up their minds during campaigns (Faas, 2015).

We know that campaigns do not have a uniform impact (Blais et al., 1999). There is widespread agreement that they matter more to voters who have no party attachment (Kenski, Hardy and Jamieson, 2010; Jacobson, 2015). Decades of research have demonstrated that this group of voters is increasing in size and diversity (Dalton and Wattenberg, 2002; Schmitt-Beck and Partheymuller, 2012). Furthermore, we know that a growing share of voters are waiting until close to election day to make their voting choice and these voters, often termed late deciders, may be particularly susceptible to election campaigns (McAllister, 2002; Blais, 2004; Dassonville, 2012). Partisan dealignment has been identified by McAllister (2002) as the major factor driving later decision-making by voters. Party attachment in Ireland is low by international standards (Marsh, 2000; 2006; chapter 5 in this volume) and the data from four waves of RTÉ exit polls demonstrate that the proportion of campaign deciders has been growing over recent elections, although not in a linear trajectory. The exit poll is a rich data source and allows us to look at late deciders in considerable detail. Late deciders are broken into two categories: election day deciders who made up their minds in the 36 hours before the election; and campaign deciders who arrived at their vote choice at any point from the start of the campaign up to 36 hours before the election.

Following McAllister (2002) we hypothesize that voters who make up their minds during the campaign are more likely to vary their voting preferences across elections. Election day and campaign deciders are less likely to have a firm party affiliation, and arrive at their decisions based on their experiences and information they acquire over the course of the electoral cycle and – by definition – particularly during the campaign. We argue that they should be most likely to switch their voting choice over the five-year election cycle. This leads us to our first hypothesis:

H1: Election day deciders and campaign deciders are more likely to have changed their voting preference to another party since the last election.

Not all campaign deciders will be created equal. In common with countries across Europe and around the world, Ireland has experienced a significant disenchantment with politics, and growing populism, mostly of a left-wing and anti-elite or anti-establishment variety (Aalberg et al., 2017; Reidy and Suiter, 2017). Thus, the voters driving volatility will be both those who made their decision during the campaign and those who have been motivated by deeper-seated preferences based on more long-standing changes in the nature of politics.

In hypothesis two, we argue that opposition to austerity policies took hold from 2008, but peaked in 2013–2015 as a result of a concentrated campaign opposing water charges (Murphy, 2016). This campaign was led by populist parties and alliances from the far left, most prominent among them the Socialist Party, People Before Profit and the campaign group Anti-Austerity Alliance.[1] Sinn Féin quickly followed their lead and also adopted an anti-water charges position. We hypothesize that voters who voted for the early movers in the water campaign, the Socialist Party, People Before Profit and the Anti-Austerity Alliance were more likely to have arrived at this decision during the water protests and would be described as early deciders using the classification structure of the analysis presented in this chapter.

> *H2: Voters for the early movers in the anti-water charge campaign (SP, AAA, PBP and SF) are more likely to be early deciders.*

Political campaigns vary in intensity and effectiveness and are influenced by the type of electoral contest, closeness of the race and the regulatory environment. They can be decisive in shaping voter decisions by raising awareness of new candidates and parties and providing vital information on the policy positions of the competing actors (Jacobson, 2013; Andersen, Tilley and Heath, 2015). The 2016 election was particularly unpredictable; several new parties and alliances had formed since 2011 and the polls projected a fragmented political landscape many months ahead of the election. The new parties were spread across the political spectrum and included the Social Democrats on the centre-left and Renua on the centre-right. Additionally, Ireland has a very high number of Independent candidates, who contest elections without a party affiliation (see chapter 7 for more discussion). In 2016, a number of these candidates came together to form loose alliances, and these included the ideologically diverse group known as the Independent Alliance and a far-left cluster which registered as a party but contested as a collective of Independents, Independents 4 Change. Some of these groups contained candidates who were incumbent members of parliament but who re-designated for the 2016 campaign so the designation 'new' must be taken loosely. We expect that the campaign should be especially important for the voters of these new political parties and alliances. Campaign debates and media coverage offer an opportunity for new parties to engage with voters and present their ideas in a concentrated way. Consequently, we hypothesize that new parties and alliances should be the big winners among election day and campaign deciders:

> *H3: New parties should receive the largest share of their support from election day and campaign deciders.*

Irish politics has long been characterized by a tendency among voters to focus exclusively on local issues when making their vote choice. A significant minority of voters (upwards of 40 per cent in some surveys), claims that candidates who 'deliver for' or 'look after' the needs of their constituency are preferred to those with a national policy focus. Levels of constituency service by public representatives are quite high in Ireland (Chubb, 1963; Martin, 2010; O'Leary, 2011; see also chapter 10 in this volume). Partisanship is low, and the electoral system facilitates a candidate-centric approach to voting (for more discussion, see chapter 7). Garvin (1991) described an 'uncivic' mentality among Irish voters and, writing in the aftermath of the 2011 election, Peter Mair (2011b) spoke of an amoral localism in Irish politics. He argued that the legacy of colonialism had left many citizens feeling that they did not own their own state and 'getting one over' on the state was something that was celebrated. Localism was criticized extensively in the 2011 campaign and data from the 2011 INES show that there was a sharp drop in the number of voters who cited local considerations as a factor in their decision-making. As the crisis has faded, we argue that localism should re-emerge. We contend that localist voters are more likely to have made their decision in advance of the campaign. Knowing the candidate personally and the candidate's local contribution are most important for localist voters and therefore the campaign is less likely to matter for these voters leading us to our final hypothesis:

H4: *Early deciders and partisans are more likely to cite local considerations as the primary factor which shaped their vote choice.*

Campaign 2016

Ireland has a highly regulated campaign environment. There are strict spending limits for election candidates, broadcast political advertising is not allowed and there are clear guidelines on balance which must be adhered to by the broadcast media (Reidy and Suiter, 2015). Print media are reasonably free of campaign-specific restrictions, but partisanship is not an especially prevalent feature among print titles. Personal contact with voters is an important aspect of campaigning in Ireland and has been shown to be decisive in shaping voter choices (Marsh et al., 2008). It is especially important for voters with a localist orientation.

The 2016 election campaign period itself was quite short, at just over three weeks. However, Ireland has endogenous election timing and speculation about the date of the election had been at fever pitch for many months, and had been particularly heightened in autumn 2015 when there were heavy indications that an early election might be called. This background is important only in so far as many commentators described the 2016 campaign as a muted affair. For example, Fiach Kelly in *The Irish Times* recorded that 'a dull and boring general election has yet to catch the public imagination' (13 February 2016).[2] There was a strong sense in the media that the protracted election speculation may have led to declining voter interest. It is worth mentioning that the long-drawn-out path to the election may have been followed closely by politicians, journalists and commentators but as is well established in the research literature, voter knowledge and interest in politics can be very variable (Bartels, 1996; Achen and Bartels, 2016). Many choose to engage in the decision-making process only as election day approaches. Partisans may have a long affiliation with their political party and may indeed pay close attention to political affairs, but for a growing proportion of voters, who are not committed to a political party, the campaign matters a great deal and it is often only as the campaign progresses that these voters engage with the choice ahead.

In some respects, the 2016 campaign was unremarkable. Campaign launches, candidates debates and an extensive ground campaign were all present, but there were few stand out moments (Murphy, 2016). As the campaign got underway in early February, all of the political parties had media-focused campaign launches, manifesto events and regular press briefings at national level while a great many candidates also had individual launch events in their own constituencies (Leahy, 2016).

The government parties campaigned on their record in office and Fine Gael relied on a much-derided 'keep the recovery going' slogan. The slogan had been developed over a number of months by strategists who had drawn heavily from focus group research and had been influenced by strategists from the successful UK Conservative Party campaign in 2015. In essence, the party sought to sell a message of effective economic governance and a promise of stability into the future. After many years of economic retrenchment, the core argument of 'steady as she goes' put forward by Fine Gael was lost in the election milieu as taxation, water charges, health care, law and order and quality of life issues all predictably crowded into the debates. The extent and scale of the economic recovery became a topic of some disputation with many arguing, particularly those in rural areas, that the recovery was imbalanced and heavily favoured Dublin (for a more extended discussion, see chapter 6).

The main opposition parties sought to highlight the social impact of expenditure cuts, stressing the damage to social services over the years of the economic crisis and promising a more rapid return to social investment along with a fairer distribution of economic benefits. Specifically, Fianna Fáil campaigned on the theme 'a fairer recovery is possible'. Entering the election campaign, many commentators confidently predicted that once the campaign began to focus on economic issues, there would be an improvement in the opinion poll support levels for Fine Gael and it was expected that the party could approach 30 per cent by election day. This was based, of course, on the old adage that 'it's the economy, stupid' but as Michael Marsh argues in chapter 6, the improved economic performance did not deliver the expected support bounce for the governing parties.

By election day, both Fine Gael and Labour recorded votes substantially below their 2011 results and below most of the poll figures recorded during the campaign. While many commentators lamented a boring campaign, opinion polls logged important changes in the overall support levels for many of the parties during the campaign period. And as our analysis will show, quite substantial numbers of voters reported having made up their minds during the campaign. To that extent, we can say that there were winners and losers from the campaign. However, disentangling the precise dynamics is beyond the scope of this chapter and not possible to pursue given the limitations of the data available for Irish election research.

Figure 8.1 outlines the overall party support figures from the beginning of 2016 up to and including the election result. Fine Gael, Labour and Sinn Féin trended down during the campaign, while Fianna Fáil and Independents and others trended up. Substantial numbers of voters declared themselves undecided during campaign polling. Typically, in opinion polls, undecided voters fall into three categories, the first of whom are voters that are about to make up their mind: they may have a pre-existing inclination towards a party or may be disenchanted partisans but they are voters and will arrive at their decision before polling day. The second group are undecided: they have no pre-existing preference, may not be very engaged with politics and current affairs and for this group the campaign is vital. The third group of undecideds have not made a decision on their preference and are unlikely to vote at all. Pollsters will often adjust their final party support numbers to take account of intention to vote and those with a low intention are commonly excluded. The data used in

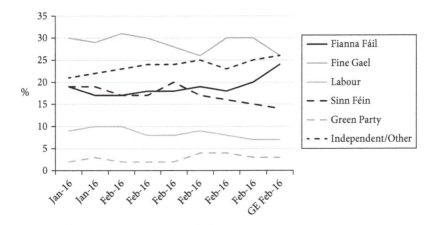

Figure 8.1 Party support levels during January and February 2016, and election result.
Source: RedC Marketing and Research http://www.redcresearch.ie

this chapter allow us to avoid the complications of the last group as the sample is an exit poll, which, by definition, consists solely of voters.

While there was some movement away from the government parties during the campaign, to a great extent the die had been cast for them long before the campaign was initiated. The general consensus of campaign 2016 was that the political messaging and policy platforms, most especially of the government parties, failed to ignite much public interest (Gallagher and Marsh, 2016). However, campaigns matter in a variety of different ways. For new parties, small parties and non-party candidates, they are vital. Strict broadcast rules mean that small parties are included in many current affairs programmes during the campaign period, providing them with a platform to connect with voters not available to them on a consistent basis outside of election periods. The leaders of several small parties were included in a televised leaders' debate. Data from the RTÉ/INES exit poll (INES1) show that at least 66 per cent of voters reported having watched one or more of the leaders' debates.

Broadcast and print media are usually at the core of research on election campaigns, but in Ireland, the ground campaign is also a vital component (Gallagher and Marsh, 2011; Gallagher and Marsh, 2016; Marsh, Farrell and McElroy, 2017). Parties and candidates engage in an extensive canvass of homes in constituencies and this is always accompanied by literature drops and the ubiquitous poster campaign. Posters of candidates and party leaders bedeck the country for the duration of the campaign at every election. Again, we argue that this aspect is most especially important for new entrants to the political arena, both individuals and parties. Often, it provides their main opportunity to announce directly to voters their presence in the election.

The campaign presents very similar opportunities to Independent candidates as it does to small parties. The Independent vote is often understood as being shaped by local factors, but in 2016 the sharp increase in the support levels for Independent candidates was a notable feature of the pre-election period and received considerable discussion both at national and local level. While poll figures do not speak to specific individual Independent candidates, national debates raised the prospect that several of them, including some of the alliances of non-party candidates, could be decisive in forming the incoming government. While some voters may have decided to support a specific Independent some time before the election, the heavy media attention immediately before, and during, the campaign may have encouraged some voters to lean Independent with the campaign offering them the time to choose among the large array of Independent candidates in each constituency. When a voter decides to vote for a small party, there is usually only one candidate from that party on the ballot. The same is not true for Independents: they are drawn from across the ideological spectrum and most constituencies had several Independent candidates. While the national campaign may not have delivered any 'knock-out moments', the campaign at local level, most especially postering and the ground canvass, presented opportunities for new and less well-known Independent candidates to make themselves known to voters.

Campaigns provide an important forum for parties and candidates to discuss policy. Manifesto launches usually provide the cornerstone event for most parties, but parties also manage their campaigns so that particular policy areas are prioritized on specific days over the course of the campaign. Taxation, healthcare and law and order policy documents will often have individual launches and these are usually parsed and analysed in the print and broadcast media. The evidence from campaigns is that local media tend to follow the policy trajectory of national media (Aldridge, 2007). This aspect of the election campaign is important as it underpins our argument in hypothesis 4. National issues tend to dominate in election campaigns. Parties and candidates need to maximize the number of voters they reach, so media discussion tends to focus on questions of national policy. Of course, some items relating to local service delivery or investment developments are communicated in the course of the campaign, but it is likely that voters attuned to local issues will have heard those messages before the campaign was initiated.

Campaigns have come to form a more critical part of the process of political socialization than in previous generations. Social class was never an especially strong predictor of the vote in Ireland and declining levels of partisanship mean that the old cues of family party association are not as meaningful as they once were (though, see chapter 4 for a somewhat divergent pattern in 2016). Secondary agents of socialization, most particularly the media, are moving to the fore (Amna, 2012). The growing prominence of social media in campaigns and arrival of news aggregation sites may also be important when we look at the way in which younger voters arrive at their decision. New entrants to the political marketplace and increased emphasis on national policy-making all serve to underscore the need to examine the dynamics of decision-making during the campaign.

When voters decide and why?

This chapter uses INES1 the RTÉ/INES exit poll, which was conducted on election day at polling stations around the country. The total sample size exceeds 4,000 but the analysis presented here is drawn from a subsample of 1,416 respondents who were asked about the timing of their decision. The dependent variable in the analysis is the timing of vote decision. We divide the responses to this question into four groups: election day deciders who arrived at their decision within 36 hours of voting; campaign deciders who make up their mind during the campaign period but before election day, early deciders who arrived at their decision prior to the start of the election campaign, and partisans who say they always vote the same way. We begin by looking at changes in the overall timing of decision-making by voters at recent elections. We provide a demographic profile of each group before proceeding to look at differences among these cohorts in relation to their voting decision, and, finally, we investigate what factors influenced decision-making among the three groups.

Going back to the start of the series in 1997, RTÉ exit polls have asked voters to identify when they made their final voting decision. From Figure 8.2 we can see that there is an upward trend in the number of voters who report making their final decision during the campaign and on election day. It is not a linear pattern, and unsurprisingly, the trend peaked in 2011 at that most turbulent of elections. But that election aside, there is still a small but noticeable trend upwards, and 54 per cent of voters reported making their final vote decision during the election campaign. Specifically, in 2016, 15 per cent reported that they made their final decision on election day.

Partisans were only separated out as a group in this data series from 2007, but we can see that there was a sharp drop in the number of voters who considered themselves to be long-term supporters of a political party between 2007 and 2011. This is no doubt capturing the huge drop in the Fianna Fáil vote at the 2011 election and the small recovery it experienced in 2016, but it is worth pointing out that partisans now account for a small proportion of voters, and less than 20 per cent of voters reported in 2016 that they always vote for the same party. There are important implications from the drop in the number of partisans and the growth in the number of voters who make their final vote choice during the campaign or indeed on election day, not least of which is the increased unpredictability of election outcomes.

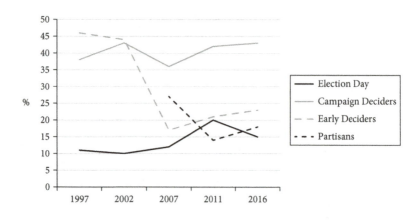

Figure 8.2 Timing of vote decision 1997–2016.

Source: RTE Exit Polls 1997, 2002, 2007, 2011; INES 1 (RTE/INES Exit Poll) 2016.

Although the overall numbers of voters who make their choice during the campaign seem high, the trend is consistent with international research that suggests that a growing share of voters are making their decisions during election campaigns. The measure is commonly used in comparative studies and the trend is more important than the absolute numbers. The general trend accords with the overall picture of volatility which was a feature of at least the last two elections in Ireland and notable from data in previous waves of the INES (Mair, 2011a; Farrell and Suiter, 2016; Marsh, Farrell and McElroy, 2017).[3]

We begin with a demographic breakdown of the four cohorts: election day deciders, campaign deciders, early deciders and partisans. Table 8.1 provides data on the age, gender and urban/rural location of each cohort. To begin, we see that age is important. Among election day deciders, there is a strong age trend with many more younger voters than older voters in this group. A similar pattern is evident for campaign deciders. The greater propensity of young voters to make their decision during the campaign concurs with the research literature. Furthermore, some of these voters would have been first-time voters in 2016 and for those that had previously cast a ballot, the 2011 earthquake election could

Table 8.1 Demographic profile of election day deciders, campaign deciders and early deciders

Age	Election day	Campaign decider	Early decider	Partisan	Total
18–24	32.1	42.0	14.8	11.1	100
25–29	20.9	55.8	13.9	9.3	100
30–34	17.8	49.5	21.5	11.2	100
35–44	14.8	47.9	22.8	14.5	100
45–49	16.3	39.2	25.9	18.7	100
50–64	13.6	40.9	25.7	19.8	100
65+	9.3	41.4	23.2	26.2	100
Total	15.3	44.1	22.9	17.7	100
Gender	Election day	Campaign decider	Early decider	Partisan	Total
Male	15.3	41.5	24.4	18.8	100
Female	15.3	47	21.3	16.4	100
Total	15.3	44.1	22.9	17.7	100
Area	Election day	Campaign decider	Early decider	Partisan	Total
Urban	17.2	44.7	22.4	15.7	100
Rural	11.3	42.9	24.1	21.7	100
Total	15.3	44.1	22.9	17.7	100

Source: INES1 2016.

have been their first election. Their political socialization would have taken place against a backdrop of considerable political flux, the collapse in support for the long-dominant Fianna Fáil and the arrival of several new political parties. That they reserved their final judgement until close to election day was not unexpected. The data on partisanship show an almost exact inverse with the number of voters who report always voting for the same party growing with age.

Turning to gender, we see in Table 8.1 that women are more likely than men to make up their mind during the election campaign although the difference for election day deciders is negligible. Women are less likely to report that they always vote for the same party. Party identification levels are lower among women in Ireland and the data presented here are in line with successive waves of the INES. Galligan and Knight (2011) have argued that lower levels of partisanship among women are a consequence of late politicization of women's issues in the 1970s.

The final demographic factor considered is urban–rural location (Table 8.1). Traditional voting patterns have held more strongly in rural areas and Fianna Fáil, experienced a large part of its recovery in rural Ireland. Looking at the decision of voters along this dimension, it is interesting to see how long-standing loyalties are a little more common in rural areas, with 21.7 per cent of rural voters reporting that they always vote for the same party and 15.7 per cent of urban voters reporting the same.

Proceeding to vote preference, our expectation from hypothesis one is that voters who change their vote from the last election are more likely to make up their mind on election day or during the election campaign. This hypothesis is supported. Table 8.2 shows that voters who voted for a different party in 2016 from the one they supported in 2011 were much more likely to arrive at their decision on election day (18.1 per cent) or during the campaign (51.4 per cent). It is also clear that considerable numbers of voters who made their decision during the campaign voted for the same party in 2016 as in 2011. Partisans were much more likely to vote the same way as they had done before, although again a small proportion report having changed their vote. This may be capturing some of the Fianna Fáil vote dynamic as partisans returned to the party in 2016.

The overall number of campaign deciders is high and that was especially clear in the demographic data which showed that a majority of men and

Table 8.2 Timing of vote choice by vote decision

	Election day	Campaign decider	Early decider	Partisan	Total
Changed vote	18.1	51.4	22.2	8.2	100
Voted same	9.8	34.4	25.4	30.4	100
Total	13.4	41.8	24.0	20.8	100

Source: INES1 2016.

women, those in all age groups, and urban and rural voters made their voting decision during the election campaign.[4] We know that overall levels of vote switching were high at the 2016 election (Farrell and Suiter, 2016) and these figures underline this point.

We move to hypothesis two. The 2016 election delivered a notable increase in the vote share for anti-establishment parties which include the Anti-Austerity Alliance – People Before Profit and Sinn Féin. As we have argued earlier, protests throughout 2013–2015 were very important in mobilizing citizens against the new water charges. These protests were initiated by the Anti-Austerity Alliance which was strongly supported by the Socialist Party – with which it later merged – and People Before Profit. Sinn Féin was to join the protests a little later, after much speculation about its loss in the Dublin South West by-election (Gallagher and Marsh, 2016). We argue that the water protests should have been decisive in shaping vote choice for anti-establishment parties. Voters for the Anti-Austerity Alliance – People Before Profit and Sinn Féin should be more likely to fall into the categories of early decider or partisan, although it must be stated that the Anti-Austerity Alliance – People Before Profit grouping was a 'new-ish' grouping of far-left parties from the 2011 election albeit with mostly the same personnel and some of the same constituent parties, so partisanship figures need to be interpreted cautiously.

The hypothesis is not supported, as the data in Table 8.3 show that the largest proportion of voters for the Anti-Austerity Alliance and People Before Profit arrived at their vote decision during the campaign. The second largest proportion for both parties made their decisions before the campaign started, with relatively few deciding on election day, especially for Sinn Féin.

Hypothesis three argued that new parties were more likely to benefit from the campaign period. For parties formed in the years immediately before the election, the campaign provided a major opportunity to introduce their policies, candidates and leaders. Using the register of political parties, the new parties included were the Social Democrats, Renua and Independents 4 Change. We also include the Independent Alliance. Although the group did not register as a party, it did operate as a formal collective with all candidates agreeing to a charter of principles and it used the group designation in media contributions. The Social Democrats and Renua stressed their new organizational structures and policies during the campaign but candidates from Independents 4 Change operated as a group of Independents. A further note of clarification is required as all of these parties/groups had incumbent TDs, most of whom had re-designated during the Dáil term. None was entirely 'new' in the sense that all had very well-known incumbent candidates. It is arguable whether the Green Party should be added to this list of 'new' parties. It is a much older party, but it had no representation in the Dáil from 2011–2016 and was making a return to national politics.

Table 8.3 Timing of vote choice by party

	Election day	Campaign decider	Early decider	Partisan	Total
Fianna Fáil	14.3	42.5	19.7	23.5	100
Fine Gael	13.9	40.8	23.5	21.8	100
Labour	12.1	54.9	17.6	15.4	100
Greens	29.6	31.5	25.9	12.9	100
Sinn Féin	9.6	37.7	27.6	25.1	100
Independent	15.9	54.6	23.1	6.1	100
AAA-PBP	12.2	45.9	32.4	9.7	100
Renua	24.2	63.6	12.1	0	100
Social Democrats	31.2	39.3	21.3	8.2	100
Independent Alliance	22	54	18	6	100
Independents4Change	22.2	33.3	16.7	27.8	100
Other	6.7	53.3	33.3	6.7	100
Total	15.3	44.1	22.9	17.7	100

Source: INES1 2016.

AAA-PBP = Anti-Austerity Alliance – People Before Profit

The data in Table 8.3 give some support to hypothesis three. Voters for the most substantively new parties were much more likely to arrive at their vote choice during the election campaign. Between 70 and 80 per cent of voters for Renua and the Social Democrats made their choice during the campaign with particularly high figures for election day (Renua, 24.2 per cent; Social Democrats, 31.2 per cent). The figures for election day and campaign deciders are also quite high for the Independent Alliance (22 per cent – election day; 54 per cent – campaign period) but much lower for Independents 4 Change during the campaign at 33.3 per cent, although 22 per cent of their voters arrived at their vote choice on election day. Reflecting the point that these are only partly new parties, many of these groups also had small numbers of partisans. These voters may have supported the candidates under their previous affiliations and this is likely to have been particularly true for Independents 4 Change although its overall number of supporters was low.

The very high proportion of voters who indicated that they decided on their preference during the campaign is also evidenced in the table: the figures for deciding during the campaign are also high for the establishment parties of Fine Gael (40.8 per cent), Fianna Fáil (42.2 per cent) and Labour (54.9 per cent), albeit with much lower figures for election day decision. Fianna Fáil picked up a greater percentage of election day and campaign deciders than Fine Gael, a finding which accords with the general impression that Fine Gael underperformed compared with its closest rival in the campaign (Gallagher and Marsh, 2016). Of the older parties in the system, Sinn Féin had the fewest campaign and election day deciders perhaps reflecting a poor campaign performance.

To investigate the impact of events during the entire electoral cycle in more detail, we present data on the most important issue for voters at the 2016 election according to the timing of their decision. We distil some of the most important issues cited by voters into broad categories to simplify the analysis. The social issues category includes crime, childcare, abortion, health, homelessness and education. The economic issues category includes mortgages, unemployment, taxation and economic management. Issues also included in Table 8.4 are stable government, local constituency issues and water charges.

Despite the large street protests of 2013–2015, the introduction of water charges was an important consideration in shaping vote choice for only a modest proportion of voters. The data reported in Table 8.4 confirm that among early deciders, the water charges issue was more important than the other items listed. Voters who cited local issues were least likely to have made up their mind on election day, by quite some distance, and local issues were also cited most frequently by partisans.

The exit poll included a number of questions which explored the issues that were foremost in the minds of voters when they were making their vote choice. In Table 8.5 we look more specifically at the argument set out in hypothesis four, that local considerations should be more important for early deciders and partisans. In the variable reported, local issues are included as a single response option while national issues included choosing who will be Taoiseach, the policies set out by the party and the set of ministers who will make up the government.

The data presented confirm some of this effect. Among election day deciders, more voters are likely to cite national issues than local issues and the same is true for campaign deciders. However, the differences are quite small and, again, the overall impression is that a large proportion of voters made up their mind during the campaign. To a great extent, the data in Tables 8.4 and 8.5 point to considerable diversity of issue priorities among election day and campaign deciders.

To consider these relationships further, the results of an ordered logit are reported in Table 8.6. The dependent variable is the timing of vote decision. The variables in brackets indicate the direction of coding and the model includes controls for age, urban/rural location and gender. From the data presented we can see that local issues are more important to early deciders. This allows us to confirm hypothesis four. Voters who make their vote choice early are also much less likely to switch their vote choice from the previous election and the data also confirm that older voters are much more likely to be partisans.

Table 8.4 Timing of vote choice and most important issue at the election

	Election day	Campaign decider	Early decider	Partisan	Total
Social issues	15.8	45.4	23.5	15.4	100
Economic issues	16.1	45.1	22.1	16.7	100
Stable government	14.5	42.8	20.6	22.1	100
Water charges	16.1	38.9	25.4	19.5	100
Local issue	5.9	47.1	21.2	25.9	100
Total	15.1	44.6	22.7	17.6	100

Source: INES1 2016.

Table 8.5 Timing of vote choice by national or local policy considerations

	Election day	Campaign decider	Early decider	Partisan	Total
National issues	15.9	46.2	22.9	15.1	100
Local issues	14.6	42.1	23.3	20	100
Total	15.3	44.4	23.1	17.2	100

Source: INES1 2016.

Table 8.6 Regression: Timing of vote choice

	Coefficient	z	P > t
National–local issue preference (local)	0.27*	2.25	0.024
Political issue (local)	0.13**	2.78	0.006
Switch: Change vote between elections (no switch)	1.01***	8.19	0.000
Age (older)	0.15***	1.51	0.000
Area (rural)	0.19	−0.94	0.130
Gender (female)	−0.11	3.98	0.348
Number of observations = 981			
Log likelihood = −1215.9277			

Source: INES1 2016.

Note: ***p < 0.001; **p < 0.01; *p < 0.05.

Conclusion

The Irish 2016 election delivered a fragmented political landscape which yielded an unstable minority government. From the analysis presented in this chapter, we can confirm that many voters delayed their voting decision until the campaign period. The number of voters making their decision during the election campaign has been increasing over recent elections. It peaked in 2011 but fell back just a little in 2016. Ireland is following a trend of late voting decision-making which is evident across democracies.

Specifically, in relation to Irish elections, there are a number of points which emerge from the empirical analysis. More vote switchers arrive at their decision during the course of the election campaign, and overall a greater proportion of those who made up their mind during the campaign changed their preference from the previous election. We conclude that the campaign period does matter, and election results may become more unpredictable as larger proportions of voters arrive at their final decision close to election day, making early campaign opinion polls more problematic as predictors of final outcomes.

Campaigns matter for new parties and groups. Large proportions of Social Democrats and Renua voters made up their minds during the campaign period, although overall, the performance of these parties was mixed. More significantly, Independent candidates also performed well among campaign deciders. The campaign in 2016 differed from previous contests in that there were groups of Independents (Independent Alliance, Rural Independents) which were included in national media debates and, as usual, the ground campaign offered the opportunity for new Independent candidates to bring the candidacy and issue priorities to the attention of voters. More than half of Green Party voters made up their mind during the election campaign, even though some of the media coverage the party received stemmed from its complaints that it was not receiving enough media coverage and was excluded from the leaders' debates.

Anti-establishment sentiment had become deeply embedded in Irish politics by 2016 and this is a recurring theme in many of the chapters in this book. The analysis in this chapter demonstrates that a large proportion of voters who supported anti-establishment parties had arrived at their voting decision long before the campaign was formally initiated, although their supporters were also most likely to decide to support them during the campaign.

The 2011 election witnessed an intense debate about the predominance of local political issues in national politics, and survey data showed that there was a fall in the numbers of voters who cited local issues and 'looking after the needs of the constituency' as a priority when picking their candidate. Interestingly, we have seen that in 2016, local issues regained some of their prominence as a priority for voters; this point is addressed in more detail in chapter 10. The evidence presented here demonstrates that a larger proportion of campaign deciders were concerned with national issues than was the case among voters who had made their choice before the election. Only a very small number of election day deciders cited local issues as a consideration in their voter decision-making.

Overall, the analysis confirms that large numbers of voters made their final decision during the election campaign. The campaign matters for all parties and there were winners and losers in 2016. The campaign brought big benefits for new parties with most of their voters deciding to vote for them during the campaign period, although their overall numbers are small. The data also speak to a small movement to the left in Irish politics. Some centrists were persuaded to vote left by the Greens and Social Democrats during the campaign. Fine Gael underperformed at the campaign, picking up smaller proportions of campaign deciders than its main rival, Fianna Fáil, although Sinn Féin had the poorest performance, securing the lowest proportion of its voters during the campaign. Election campaigns tend to be predominantly national in character, with a big focus on social and economic issues and the analysis confirms that, among campaign deciders, these types of issues carry more weight than local considerations which remain important for early deciders and partisans.

Notes

1 These groups subsequently merged with the creation of the Anti-Austerity Alliance – People Before Profit group.
2 Fiach Kelly, 'General Election 2016: Long term plans put to test in final sprint', *The Irish Times*. 13 February 2016.
3 The figure for vote switching for the 2016 election is 23.6 per cent, indicating significant volatility. However, some care is needed when interpreting these type of data as it is not uncommon for voters to misremember voting at the previous election and to recall their vote inaccurately, and so generally underreport actual change.
4 Caution must be used when interpreting specific levels reported in Table 8.2. INES2 also included a question on timing of vote decision. It is not possible to conduct the full analysis using these data as not all variables required for the analysis are present in that dataset. However, the analysis for hypothesis one was replicated using these data with similar results, but with a much smaller overall proportion of voters reporting that they changed their vote from the previous election, and the numbers indicating that they made their choice during the campaign also lower. The direction of the relationship was the same but the effects smaller.

References

Aalberg, Toril, Frank Esser, Carsten Reinemann, Jesper Stromback and Claes De Vreese (eds). 2016. *Populist Political Communication in Europe*, Vol. 1. New York: Routledge.
Achen, Christopher H., and Larry M. Bartels. 2016. *Democracy for Realists, Why Elections Do Not Produce Responsive Government*. Princeton: Princeton University Press.
Aldridge, Meryl 2007. *Understanding the Local Media*. Berkshire: McGraw-Hill Education.

Amna, E. 2012. 'How is civic engagement developed over time? Emerging answers from a multidisciplinary field', *Journal of Adolescence.* 35: 611–27.

Andersen, R., J. Tilley and A. Heath. 2015. 'Political knowledge and enlightened preferences: Party choice through the electoral cycle', *British Journal of Political Science.* 35: 285–302.

Bartels, L. M. 1996. 'Uninformed votes: Information effects in presidential elections', *American Journal of Political Science.* 40: 194–230.

Blais, A. 2004. 'How many voters change their minds in the month preceding an election?', *PS: Political Science and Politics.* 37: 801–03.

Blais, André, Richard Nadeau, Elisabeth Gidengil and Neil Nevitte. 1999. 'Campaign dynamics in the 1997 Canadian election', *Canadian Public Policy/ Analyse de Politiques.* 25:2: 197–205.

Chubb, B. 1963. '"Going about persecuting civil servants": The role of the Irish parliamentary representative', *Political Studies.* 11: 272–86.

Dalton, R., and M. Wattenberg. 2002. *Parties Without Partisans: Political Change in Advanced Industrial Democracies.* Oxford: Oxford University Press.

Dassonneville, R. 2012. 'Electoral volatility, political sophistication, trust and efficacy: A study on changes in voter preferences during the Belgian regional elections of 2009', *Acta Politica.* 47: 18–41.

Faas, T. 2015. 'Bring the state (information) in: Campaign dynamics in the run-up to a German referendum', *Electoral Studies.* 38: 226–37.

Farrell, D., and R. Schmitt-Beck (eds). 2002. *Do Political Campaigns Matter? Campaign Effects in Elections and Referendums.* London: Routledge/ECPR.

Farrell, D., and J. Suiter. 2016. 'The election in context', in M. Gallagher and M. Marsh (eds), *How Ireland Voted 2016, the Election that Nobody Won.* Basingstoke: Palgrave Macmillan, pp. 277–92.

Gallagher, M., and M. Marsh (eds). 2011. *How Ireland Voted 2011, The Full Story of Ireland's Earthquake Election.* Basingstoke: Palgrave Macmillan.

Gallagher, M., and M. Marsh (eds). 2016. *How Ireland Voted 2016, the Election that Nobody Won.* Basingstoke: Palgrave Macmillan.

Galligan, Y., and K. Knight. 2011. 'Attitudes towards women in politics: Gender, generation and party identification in Ireland', *Parliamentary Affairs.* 64: 585–611.

Jacobson, G. C. 2013. *The Politics of Congressional Elections.* New York: Pearson.

Jacobson, G. C. 2015. 'How do campaigns matter?', *Annual Review of Political Science.* 18: 31–47.

Kenski, K., B. Hardy and K. H. Jamieson. 2010. *The Obama Victory: How Media, Money and Message Shaped the 2008 Campaign.* New York: Oxford University Press.

Lazarsfeld, P. F., B. Berelson and H. Gaudet. 1968. *The People's Choice. How the Voter Makes Up His Mind in a Presidential Campaign.* 3rd edition, New York: Columbia University Press.

Leahy, P. 2016. 'Campaign strategies: How the campaign was won and lost', in M. Gallagher and M. Marsh (eds), *How Ireland Voted 2016, the Election that Nobody Won*. Basingstoke: Palgrave Macmillan, pp. 75–97.

Mair, P. 2011a. 'The election in context', in M. Gallagher and M. Marsh (eds), *How Ireland Voted 2011: The Full Story of Ireland's Earthquake Election*. Basingstoke: Palgrave Macmillan, pp. 283–97.

Mair, P. 2011b. 'We need a sense of ownership of our state', in Joe Mulholland (ed.), *Transforming Ireland 2011–2016: Essays from the 2011 MacGill Summer School*. Dublin: Liffey Press.

Marsh, M. 2000. 'Candidate centered but party wrapped: Campaigning in Ireland under STV', in S. Bowler and B. Grofman (eds), *Elections in Australia, Ireland and Malta Under the Single Transferable Vote*. Michigan: Michigan University Press, pp. 114–30.

Marsh, M. 2006. 'Party identification in Ireland, An insecure anchor for a floating party system', *Electoral Studies*. 25: 489–508.

Marsh, Michael, David M. Farrell and Gail McElroy (eds). 2017. *A Conservative Revolution? Electoral Change in Twenty-First-Century Ireland*. Oxford: Oxford University Press.

Marsh, M., R. Sinnott, J. Gary and F. Kennedy. 2008. *The Irish Voter: The Nature of Electoral Competition in the Republic of Ireland*. Manchester: Manchester University Press.

Martin, S. 2010. 'Electoral rewards for personal vote cultivation under PR-STV', *West European Politics*. 33: 369–80.

McAllister, I. 2002. 'Calculating or capricious? The new politics of late deciding voters', in D. Farrell and R. Schmitt-Beck (eds), *Do Political Campaigns Matter?: Campaign Effects in Elections and Referendums*. UK: Routledge/ECPR, pp. 22–40.

Murphy, Gary 2016. 'The background to the election' in *How Ireland Voted 2016*. Cham: Palgrave Macmillan, pp. 1–26.

O'Leary, E. 2011. 'The constituency orientation of modern TDs', *Irish Political Studies*. 26: 329–43.

Reidy, T., and J. Suiter. 2015. 'Do rules matter? Categorizing the regulation of referendum campaigns', *Electoral Studies*. 38: 159–69.

Reidy, T., and J. Suiter. 2017. 'Who is the populist Irish voter?' *Journal of the Statistical and Social Inquiry Society of Ireland*. XLVI(170): 117–31.

Schmitt-Beck, R., and J. Partheymuller. 2012. 'Why voters decide late: A simultaneous test of old and new hypotheses at the 2005 and 2009 German federal elections', *German Politics*. 21: 299–316.

9

The impact of gender quotas on voting behaviour in 2016

Gail McElroy

Introduction

In 2016, the Republic of Ireland joined over fifty countries worldwide in the adoption of candidate gender quotas. Introduced via the *Electoral Reform Act* of 2012, this quota stipulated that the slate of candidates running for each party be composed of no less than 30 per cent of either gender, which effectively meant Irish parties had to find a lot more women to run in a very short space of time. Parties failing to reach this threshold would be punished by the halving of their state funding for the duration of the upcoming legislative term. Given the heavy reliance of political parties on state monies and the possible negative electoral consequences for failing to nominate sufficient numbers of women, it is not surprising that there was a large increase in the number of female candidates selected to run in 2016. In 2011 a mere eighty-six women ran for election, compared with 163 five years later. This sudden influx of a very large number of female nominees into the candidate pool offers us an excellent opportunity to definitively examine whether Irish voters are truly gender blind.

Previous research (McElroy and Marsh, 2010; 2011) has found little evidence of voter prejudice against female candidates. Nonetheless, as recently as January 2016, the country had the ignominious honour of ranking 111th in the world in terms of the number of women it elected to its lower house (a position it shared with both Koreas). The upward trend, visible in other European democracies in the past two decades, in the percentage of women elected to national assemblies had not been mirrored in Ireland, where the percentage of female TDs had stagnated in low double digits for years. The question of why a country which does rather well on other measures of gender equality (e.g. the World Economic Forum's Gender Index) and where voters are seemingly gender blind does not manage to elect more women to its parliament is puzzling. Ireland is a better country than most in which to be a woman, in terms of education, health and economic indicators, but this is not reflected in levels of political representation.

Much of the blame for this lack of progress has been levelled at political parties failing to nominate women to run (McGing, 2013) and the new gender quota was designed to resolve this very issue. But a lingering question over voter bias remains. International experimental research regularly demonstrates voter bias against female candidates (Fox and Smith, 1998; Smith, Paul and Paul, 2007), but aggregate and public opinion analysis fails to replicate this (Seltzer, Newman and Leighton, 1997; Dolan, 1998; Black and Erikson, 2003). Recent attempts to reconcile these seemingly contradictory findings suggest that there is a quality gap between male and female candidates and that failure to control for this for the puzzling results (Anzia and Berry, 2011; Fulton, 2012). This emerging body of work argues that male and female candidates are not equivalent; women who run for office are, on average, more accomplished and capable than their male contenders and this quality gap masks voter bias. Female candidates confront greater hurdles in the selection process for any number of reasons: a lack of self-belief (Lawless and Fox, 2005), greater competition to be chosen (Lawless and Pearson, 2008) or outright selectorate bias (Sanbonmatsu, 2006). Thus, women who manage to get selected and survive the ardours of the campaigning process are of very high quality and voters, recognizing this, reward them with their vote. However, with the introduction of the quota in 2016, we essentially have an exogenous shock to the system: parties were forced to find a large number of women very quickly, so the recruitment pool is likely to have more 'average' women in it. As such, we can now test for true bias among the Irish electorate.

In what follows, we first examine the aggregate data for evidence of voter bias, both historically and in 2016. We then explore the individual level survey evidence from the exit poll data, and finally, we use some new individual-level data on voter traits to examine if there is a personality type that is predisposed to voting for female candidates.

The historical context

The number of women running in Irish elections has, historically, been very low, so low in fact that until the 1970s the absolute number of women competing at election time rarely reached double digits and, even then, many of these were what might be classified as 'honorary men' – the widows, daughters and sisters of dead male TDs. For instance, of three women elected to the Dáil in 1965, one was a daughter and two were the widows of former TDs (indeed one of them – Brigid Hogan Higgins – was also married to a sitting male TD). Similarly, in 1954 only five women were elected to the Dáil and four of these were the widows of former TDs, first elected after a husband's death left the spot vacant.

However, there was a significant increase in the number of women running for election in the 1970s and 1980s, as illustrated in Figure 9.1, in parallel with

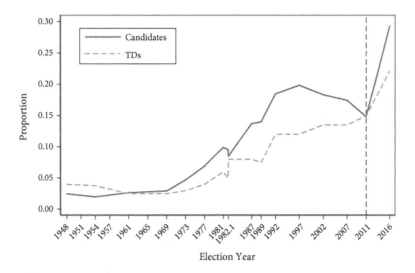

Figure 9.1 Proportion of women running and elected in Irish elections 1948–2016.
Source: Author's own data.

the rise of the international women's movement and Irish membership of the European Economic Community.

In the 1973 general election only 5 per cent of candidates for the Dáil were women but by 1992 this figure had risen to 18 per cent. However, the number of women running for office plateaued in the mid-1990s and there was even a decline in the percentage of women running in the first three elections of the twenty-first century. In 2011, a mere eighty-six of the 566 candidates on the ballot were women, representing slightly more than 15 per cent of the total. The two largest parties, Fianna Fáil and Fine Gael, particularly struggled to nominate women in recent elections. As Figure 9.2 demonstrates, the number of women running for both of these parties never exceeded 18 per cent from 2002 to 2011.

In part, the problem is that incumbency is such a strong predictor of getting re-elected in Ireland (Matland and Studlar, 2004) and most incumbents are men (especially in the two largest parties). Parties naturally re-nominate these candidates as part of their seat maximization strategy. On the other hand, 85 per cent of non-incumbents running in 2011 were also men. In a gender-neutral environment, even with deference to the reselection of incumbent male TDs, one might reasonably expect non-incumbents to divide roughly equally (with some volatility) among male and female candidates. In 2011, only 20 per cent of non-incumbent Fianna Fáil candidates were women (the equivalent figure for Fine Gael was also 20 per cent, while it was 23 per cent for Labour). Until 2016, the main political parties were simply not selecting women to run. An

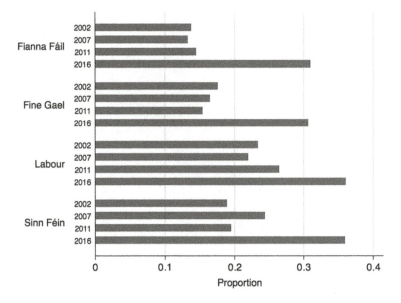

Figure 9.2 Proportion of women running for the four main parties 2002–2016.
Source: Author's own data.

exploration of the reasons for this failure to nominate women is beyond the scope of this chapter, but runs the gamut from outright bias to a lack of women candidates coming forward. Here we will focus on what happens when women actually do run. Have Irish women done as well as men when their names are on the ballot?

The first cut at this question examines the evidence from the aggregate data on all candidates who ran for the Dáil from the early 1970s onwards (given how few women ran prior to this, there is little point in extending the analysis further back in time). In total there were 3,668 candidacies across the twelve elections held between 1973 and 2011, of which just under 16 per cent were female. Using a logit model where the dependent variable simply captures whether or not a candidate won a seat (with win coded as 1; 0 otherwise) and only three independent variables that capture the gender of the candidate (1 if female; 0 otherwise), their incumbency status (1 if an incumbent; 0 otherwise) and their party affiliation (plus an interaction term between incumbency and gender), we find gender is almost never significant in explaining who wins in Irish elections. The sample is divided into two different time periods, 1973 to 1989 and 1992 to 2011, to reflect the significant societal changes that occurred in the almost forty years under exploration. The odds ratios for women winning across the two periods are presented in Figure 9.3.

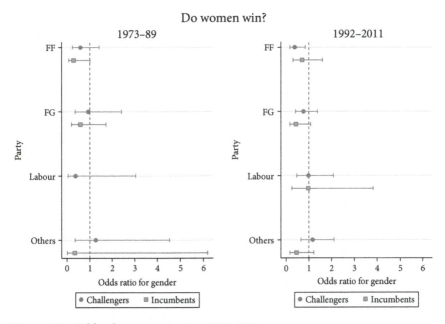

Figure 9.3   Odds of women winning 1973–2011.

Source: Author's own data.

Note: Odds ratios from logit analysis where dependent variable is losing (0) or winning (1).

Even in this simple model, the results indicate that women were not statistically significantly less likely to win than men, across either time period. The only exception is for female challengers running for Fianna Fáil in the post-1992 era, where femaleness does appear to be a slight disadvantage. Furthermore, this Fianna Fáil effect also verges on significance for the party's incumbents in the pre-1992 era. It is, additionally, worth noting that the sign on gender is negative for almost all parties in Figure 9.3, for both challengers and incumbents in the main parties across both time periods, though the effect is not strong enough to have appreciable consequences for winning or losing. The aggregate historical analysis, thus, suggests women do tend to do a little worse in most parties but only significantly so in Fianna Fáil. The fact that there remain so few women in the Dáil appears to largely have been a problem at the nomination, as opposed to the election, stage. So what happens when a lot more women run?

Aggregate analysis 2016

The anticipated impact of the gender quota was the subject of considerable media coverage in the run-up to the election. In particular, speculation was rife as to whether the two biggest parties would be able to meet the 30 per cent threshold or whether they would, at the close of nominations, simply run a bunch of 'no-hoper' female candidates to satisfy the requirement. Fianna Fáil was particularly challenged, in that they had failed to elect a single woman in 2011. To meet the gender quota, party headquarters had to introduce a gender directive to compel local selection conventions to nominate more women (in some cases quite controversially, e.g. Longford-Westmeath). As was clearly demonstrated in Figure 9.2, the rise in the percentage of women running was highest for both of the largest parties, Fianna Fáil and Fine Gael. Fine Gael ran twenty-seven women in 2016 compared with only sixteen in 2011, while Fianna Fáil doubled the number of women it ran from eleven to twenty-two. A total of 551 candidates competed in the general election in 2016, 163 women and 388 men; this represents an increase of over seventy female candidates on the previous election.

As an aside, we find that there was quite a gendered difference in attitudes to the introduction of the quota among candidates. Figure 9.4a indicates that there was a clear disparity in the levels of support for the quota among male and female candidates, with over twice as many female candidates strongly supporting (point 10 on this 0–10 scale) the initiative, compared with male candidates.[1] This gender difference was not evident among voters, as data from the exit poll (INES1) presented in Figure 9.4b indicate (using the same scale). Overall, however, support for the quota was higher among candidates with 44 per cent strongly supporting the initiative (giving a response of 8, 9 or 10) compared with just 31 per cent of voters. That being said, there was very little opposition to the quota either with only 13 per cent of voters and 19 per cent of candidates being strongly opposed (a 0, 1 or 2 response).

To test whether or not gender affected electoral performance in 2016, we again use aggregate data on all the candidates, but this time include a larger set of variables in the model to try and capture how quality, in particular, may interact with gender to affect the inclination to vote for a woman. Additionally, the dependent variable is also a little more nuanced, taking two forms; first, we use the percentage of a quota that each candidate achieved, and second, we calculate the degree to which each candidate's total vote deviated from the mean first preference vote in the constituency.[2] This latter variable captures the extent to which a given candidate exceeds (or falls below) the average number of first preference votes received by other candidates in his or her constituency. Specifically, the dependent variable (V_{dev}) measures candidate i's deviation from the mean candidate first preference vote in his or her constituency, where V_{cmean} gives the mean vote for candidates in a constituency and V_{ci} gives candidate i's vote total:

$$V_{dev} = (V_{ci} - V_{cmean}) / V_{cmean}$$

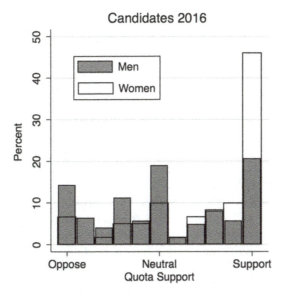

Figure 9.4a Support for gender quota among general election candidates.
Data source: Irish Candidate Study 2016.

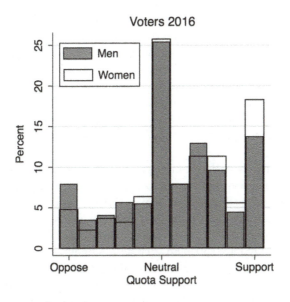

Figure 9.4b Support for gender quota among voters.
Data source: INES1 2016.

This approach is intended to capture how well a candidate did, in terms of his or her total number of first preferences, relative to other candidates in the election, controlling for the different number of votes cast in each constituency. The correlation between the two dependent variables is, as one might expect, very high, but we use both as they capture slightly different aspects of electoral performance.

The key variable of interest in the analysis is, again, the candidate's gender but we also control for a number of other characteristics. In particular, we are interested in measuring the 'quality' of a candidate, though the concept is notoriously difficult to operationalize, especially for challengers. In general, the literature has focused on quality as measured in terms of political experience, especially incumbency status (Squire, 1992; Kulisheck and Mondak, 1996; Van Dunk, 1997) and has found that this has a positive impact on election outcomes. We thus control for the incumbency status of each candidate and additionally ministerial experience (arguably those chosen for ministerial positions should be of even higher quality than backbenchers). Of course, these two variables may not measure quality per se, but rather may capture name recognition or an ability to deliver pork (the latter is especially relevant for the ministerial variable). And, even more importantly, neither of these variables helps us differentiate between high-quality and mediocre non-incumbents. While incumbent performance is directly observable to voters and thus should be easy for them to evaluate (see, however, the discussion in Wlezien, 2016) the question of how to assess challenger quality is more problematic. To attempt to get some further leverage over candidate quality, we also control for whether or not the candidate has served as a county or city councillor. This measure may also be tainted by a degree of name recognition, but it does capture some aspect of quality for challengers or, at least, an ability to win a race. Fifty-one per cent of candidates in 2016 were or had been councillors at some stage, although only 43 per cent of women had been councillors, compared with 56 per cent of male contenders.

Finally, we also control for campaign spending (measured as per cent of the spending limit) as previous research has found a positive relationship between spending and votes (Benoit and Marsh, 2010), especially for challengers. Arguably the ability to raise significant funds is also a measure of candidate credibility and quality or, at a minimum, campaign effort (admittedly, very safe candidates may have to spend very little money, but given the low limits on campaign spending in Ireland, this endogeneity issue is perhaps less of an issue than in the United States). None of the candidates running in 2016 breached the constituency spending limits and over 80 per cent spent less than half the permissible amount.[3] There appear to be no significant gender differences in spending, even if we confine the analyses to the four main parties. But incumbents spend far more than non-incumbents in general, though this divergence disappears if we confine our analyses to the big players (Sinn Féin, Labour, Fine Gael, Fianna Fáil). The model also includes a series of interaction terms: we interacted candidate gender with incumbency, ministerial status and party affiliation.

A linear regression model was run using both dependent variables and, as is clear from Figure 9.5, the gender of the candidate is once more insignificant.[4] Incumbency is a strong predictor of vote-getting, as is being a councillor. Campaign spending was also highly predictive of getting a bigger percentage of the quota or a higher than average number of first preference votes. None of the interaction terms reached standard levels of significance with the interesting exception of gender interacted with running for Fianna Fáil, which was again negatively signed (see models 1 and 2 in Table A9.1). Thus, it does seem to be the case that women running for Fianna Fáil do worse than their male co-partisans. This pattern corroborates what we saw from the analysis on the previous twelve elections. Fianna Fáil voters do seem to prefer male candidates, which does not bode well for the party's prospects of regaining their position as the poll topper, in light of the gender quota increasing to 40% seven years after the 2016 election.

In an ideal world, we would have far better measures of candidate quality, such as details like candidate work histories and educational attainment, though whether voters have this level of knowledge about challengers and act on it is debatable. In the field of economics, candidate quality is typically measured in terms of years in full-time education (e.g. Baltrunaite, 2014), and in future work, collecting and coding this variable for all candidates will be worthwhile. But as one final check of the impact of quality on election outcomes, we also ran a model with a crude control for educational attainment. Given the difficulty

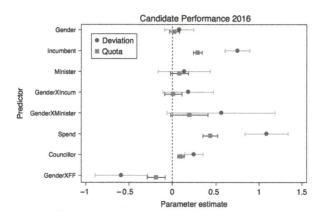

Figure 9.5 Impact of gender on candidate success 2016.
Source: Author's own data.

of collecting these data, the sample is much smaller, with information available for only 273 of the candidates (just under 50 per cent of the total). This includes all those who were elected (for whom biographical information is more readily available) and 129 of the unsuccessful candidates. This trichotomous variable differentiates between those who do and do not have a primary degree and those with advanced qualifications. Exactly 50 per cent of this sample had a primary degree or equivalent and 23 per cent had an advanced degree, with the remaining 26 per cent having a primary school, secondary school or non-degree level qualification. There was a distinct gender division on this variable, with 31 per cent of female candidates having a postgraduate qualification compared with just 20 per cent of men.

With due consideration to the caveat that the analysis is only run on half the universe of candidates and this is almost certainly not a representative sample, the same regression models were run as before with the inclusion of the variable for educational achievement (and a term interacting education and gender).[5] The results are presented in Figure 9.6: yet again, the gender of the candidate is not significant but having served as a councillor, total spend and incumbency remain so. Education is, additionally, a predictor of obtaining a higher percentage of the quota, even when measured crudely in this trichotomous fashion (though the interaction of education with candidate gender is not, as is demonstrated in models 3 and 4 in Table A9.1).[6] Thus candidate quality, however measured, does seem to matter to Irish voters; however, it does not seem to have a gendered dimension to it. There is clearly considerable scope for exploration of this quality dimension in future work and, in particular, data on years in full-time education for all candidates should be collated.

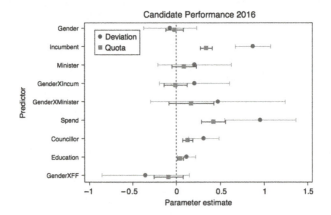

Figure 9.6 Impact of candidate gender and education on success 2016.
Source: Author's own data.
Note: Sample size 272.

All in all, it would seem that the introduction of a large number of women into the mix in 2016 did not reveal any previously hidden biases among Irish voters. Female candidates are not disadvantaged in the bid to get elected (except for Fianna Fáil); what matters is already having a seat in the Dáil, prior political experience at the local level and having money to spend. In the next section, we move beyond the aggregate data and analyse INES data to investigate if the individual level data reveal any discrimination against female candidates, or to establish if there is a particular type of voter who is more inclined or disinclined to vote for a woman.

Individual-level voting data

The aggregate analysis did not reveal anything to suggest that female candidates do systematically worse than their male counterparts in elections in Ireland, but is it the case that there are types of voters that are more or less disposed to voting for female candidates? Are there individuals who are biased in their voting behaviour? Are women more likely to vote for female candidates, for instance, or are those with a right wing leaning more likely to favour men? These questions can only be answered by examining the individual level data from the post-election INES surveys (INES2 and INES3).

We make use of two separate dependent variables in the analysis that follows. The first, PREFERENCE, captures whether or not the respondent expressed any preference for a female candidate; the second, HIGH PREFERENCE, captures whether or not the respondent gave a top preference (a first, second or third) to the candidate in question. The independent variables in the analysis include the demographic and attitudinal characteristics of voters that might influence their propensity to vote for a woman candidate: WOMAN VOTER, AGE, EDUCATION, CLASS, QUOTA SUPPORT, IDEOLOGY, PARTY ID and PARTY CENTRED VOTER, and we also control for whether the candidate voted for was an INCUMBENT or a PARTY CANDIDATE. The key variable of interest is WOMAN VOTER, which is intended to capture the propensity of women to vote for women (measured as a standard dichotomous variable: 0 if the respondent is male and 1 if female). AGE is measured across eight cohorts (ranging from the youngest group of voters aged 18–22 to the oldest, who are 65+). The expectation is that younger people will be more open to voting for women. EDUCATION is a trichotomous variable that distinguishes those who did not complete secondary school education, from those with a secondary level qualification from those with a third level qualification, with the latter theorized to be most likely to vote for female candidates. CLASS is a dichotomized variable that divides the population between the middle class ABC1 group and the rest.[7] Surprisingly, this latter variable is not especially highly correlated with education (0.4), perhaps reflecting the crude measurement of both. QUOTA SUPPORT is an 11-point scale capturing the voters' attitudes towards the introduction of the gender quota (0 strongly oppose, 10 strongly support). Given the brevity of the surveys, there are no specific ideological questions that capture a voter's attitudes to feminist issues but we do control for IDEOLOGY, as measured through general left–right self-placement, reasoning that more left-wing voters will have more progressive attitudes to issues such as the election of women to the Dáil (though see McElroy, 2017 for a discussion of how the super dimension left–right in Ireland is not underpinned by coherent ideological dispositions). We also include a variable, PARTY ID, which measures the strength of the respondent's party identification; we reason that where this is strong, the voter will be driven to vote the party line regardless of the gender of the candidate. PARTY ID is measured using a dichotomous variable, where 1 is feeling close to a particular party and 0 is not. PARTY CENTRED VOTER captures how important the candidate rather than the party is for the respondent. This measure is a three-point scale and ranges from −1 (candidate centred) to 1 (party centred).[8] Given the results of the aggregate analysis, we also control for whether the candidate was an INCUMBENT and running for a party to which the voter was close (PARTY CANDIDATE). We also include interactions between female respondent and all of these variables to see if there are some particular types of female respondents who are more inclined to vote for women.

Figure 9.7a and 9.7b present the results of this analysis for the two separate logit models. It is important to note that the analysis here is confined to female candidates, but results are equivalent to a model in which both male and female candidates are included.[9] As is clearly evident from these figures, the results fail to find any evidence in favour of the hypothesis that women voters favour female candidates; nowhere does WOMAN VOTER reach significance. Similarly, AGE, IDEOLOGY and QUOTA SUPPORT are all insignificant. Attitudes to the introduction of the quota do not seem to impact on a voter's propensity to vote for a female candidate, nor is ideological self-placement significant: there is no difference between right- and left-wing voters in their willingness to vote for a woman. Nor do we find evidence that any particular sub-group of women respondents is more inclined to vote for women candidates (none of the interaction terms are significant in either of the models and as such are not presented in the figures, but full results are presented in Table A9.2 in the appendix for the interested reader). We do, however, find that more educated and middle-class voters are slightly more inclined to express a preference for a woman and education is on the verge of significance for high preference voting also (though the class effect is not). But overall, what seems to matter to voters when they choose to give a vote to a woman, echoing the findings from the aggregate analysis, is that the candidate in question is an incumbent and running for a party they are close to.

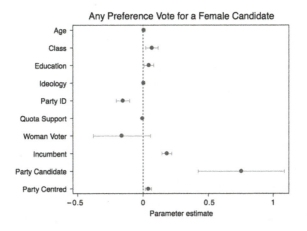

Figure 9.7a Factors affecting voting for female candidates (any preference). Figure 9.7a displays the results of a logit regression model that examines the relationship between individual voter characteristics and casting any preference for a female candidate. The dots represent the point estimates, while the horizontal lines depict 95 per cent confidence intervals. The range of parameter estimates is displayed on the x-axis.

Data source: INES1 2016.

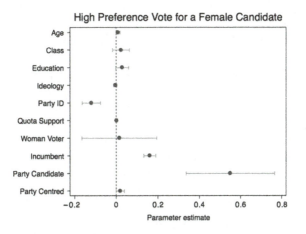

Figure 9.7b Factors affecting voting for female candidates (high preference). Figure 9.7b displays the results of a logit regression model that examines the relationship between individual voter characteristics and casting a high preference vote (1–3) for a female candidate. The dots represent the point estimates, while the horizontal lines depict 95 per cent confidence intervals. The range of parameter estimates is displayed on the x-axis.

Data source: INES1 2016.

On the whole, the analysis in this section suggests that there are few identifiable characteristics of voters that make them more inclined to vote for a female candidate. These results echo much international survey research, which finds that voters do not differentiate between candidates on gender grounds. In the final section, we explore whether there are any distinguishing personality traits of those who vote for women.

The psychology of voting for women

In the previous section, we found that standard demographic characteristics such as class, age and ideology have little to no explanatory power in predicting who will vote for a female candidate. But are there certain types of people who are more likely to vote for women, in terms of their general personality dispositions?

A large body of research in psychology has established that there are five basic elements that account for differences in personality: openness, conscientiousness, extraversion, agreeableness and emotional stability. The general hypothesis that personality affects all types of human behaviour is well established in empirical work and the five-factor model has become the cornerstone of trait psychology since the 1980s. While there are other approaches, these five broad elements are now largely accepted as jointly covering the majority of personality structure. Openness refers to 'the breadth, depth, originality, and complexity of an individual's mental and experiential life' (John, Naumann and Soto, 2008: 120). Conscientiousness is identified as 'socially prescribed impulse control that facilitates task- and goal-directed behaviour, such as thinking before acting, delaying gratification, following norms and rules, and planning, organizing, and prioritizing tasks' (John, Naumann and Soto, 2008: 120). People with high scores for extraversion have 'an energetic approach to the social and material world [and it] includes traits such as sociability, activity and assertiveness, and positive emotionality' (John, Naumann and Soto, 2008: 120). Agreeable individuals are 'pro-social and communal in orientation as opposed to antagonistic to others, they display traits such as modesty, tender mindedness, trust and altruism' (John, Naumann and Soto, 2008: 120). Finally, emotional stability (also referred to as neuroticism) contrasts traits such as nervousness, sadness and anxiety with even-temperedness and general emotional well-being.

Three decades of study have finely tuned both the meaning and measurement of these concepts and this 'Big Five' model is now the 'the most widely used and extensively researched measure of personality' (Gosling, Rentfrow and Swann., 2003: 506). Recent work in political science, drawing on this literature, has established that there is a significant relationship between these personality traits and ideological dispositions and, to a lesser extent, levels of political participation (Mondak, 2010; Gerber et al., 2011). In particular, it has been established that conscientiousness is associated with conservative political values in voters (Gosling, Rentfrow and Swann, 2003; Jost et al., 2003; 2007; Alford and Hibbing, 2007; Mondak, 2010), while those who are open to new experiences tend to be more liberal (Schoen and Schumann, 2007; Carney et al., 2008). The findings with regard to the other three traits – agreeableness, extraversion and neuroticism – are, as of yet, less settled. While agreeableness has been associated with, for instance, more liberal values in Italy and Germany, the result has not been found to hold in studies of US voters. Although emotional stability has been found to predict ideological self-placement in both the United States and Germany, the relationship is in the opposite direction, with high levels of neuroticism being associated with centre-left voting in Germany but voting for the Republicans in the United States (Schoen and Schumann, 2007; Mondak and Halperin, 2008). Finally, while extraversion has been linked to levels of political participation, such as turnout, it has not been systematically associated with voter ideology, though those who score high on extraversion are more likely to be strong party identifiers (Gerber et al., 2011; 2012).

There is very little research on the 'Big Five' and Irish voters; however, a brief battery of questions, which aimed to measure these traits in Irish voters, was included in the 2016 INES3, and here we examine if any of these personality dispositions are predictive of voting for women. The standard battery of ten questions that captures the main underlying predispositions of personality was included in the telephone recall survey, conducted by Red C, and we utilize these data to examine whether or not voting for women is associated with certain personality types (see Appendix Table A9.3 for the full set of questions).

First, we explore whether we see similar patterns in personality difference between men and women in Ireland. Sex differences in personality traits have been found to be larger and more consistent (across time and culture) than sex differences in other domains such as cognitive ability or self-esteem (Hyde, 2005; Else-Quest et al., 2006). These differences in personality have been found to cross national borders. Feingold (1994) found that women in Canada, China, Finland, Germany, Poland and Russia scored higher than men on scales related to the personality traits of neuroticism, agreeableness and conscientiousness. Men scored higher in the extraversion-related trait of assertiveness. One slightly odd finding is that sex differences in personality traits are often larger in developed countries (Europe and North America) with egalitarian cultures, compared with Asian and African states (Costa, Terracciano and McCrae, 2001; McCrae, 2002; Schmitt et al., 2008). Generally, the psychology literature has demonstrated that men tend to be more assertive than women, and women are generally higher than men in anxiety and tender-mindedness/sensitivity (Feingold, 1994; Lynn and Martin, 1997; Kring and Gordon, 1998; Brody and Hall, 2000). And indeed, as illustrated in Figure 9.8, we find that there are gendered differences on two of the five factors in Ireland – neuroticism and agreeableness – with women more like to describe themselves as sensitive than

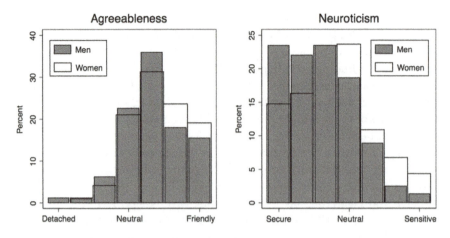

Figure 9.8 Irish voter 'Big Five' trait distribution.
Data source: INES3 2016.

men but also more friendly.[10] However, there are no significant differences in levels of conscientiousness and extraversion, which is at odds with the findings from most other advanced industrial democracies.

Given these questions on personality were asked in a short telephone survey, conducted in the weeks after the election (INES3), we unfortunately do not have access to the full range of voting preferences provided by the mock ballots (INES1), which we used in the previous section. Respondents were, however, asked to name the candidate to whom they gave their first preference, and in the following analysis we take advantage of this information to see if we can isolate personality traits that make a voter more likely to vote for a woman than for a man.[11] Given that the earlier analysis confirmed the importance of party for voters' first preference choice, we confine our analysis to those respondents who could choose between a male and female candidate running for the same party. This approach is necessarily restrictive and reduces the sample considerably, as Fine Gael only ran a male and a female candidate in nineteen out of forty constituencies, while the equivalent figure for Fianna Fáil is seventeen, for Sinn Féin is six and for Labour is just two. There were Independent candidates of both genders running in twenty-three constituencies. Furthermore, we are forced to make the limiting assumption that party trumps gender in this particular model. We also do not have access to questions that would permit us to differentiate party centred from non-party centred voters. With these caveats in mind, we run a logit where the dependent variable codes voting for a female candidate as 1 (0 otherwise). The key variables of interest are the 'Big Five', as detailed above. Given other work in political science that finds openness is correlated with liberal attitudes and conscientiousness with conservative values, our expectation is that these will have the strongest influence on propensity to vote for female candidates (openness should be positively signed and conscientiousness negatively signed). Extraversion has not been found to correlate with voter ideology and the results on neuroticism and agreeableness vary by country, and as such we have no strong expectations related to these three traits. We again control for the age, class, gender, education and ideology of the voter, plus their attitude to the quota. We also control for whether or not the party (or Independents, taken as a group) to which the respondent gave his or her first preference had an incumbent female in the constituency, as incumbency has been found to be such a strong predictor of vote-getting in the earlier sections.

The results of the logit model suggest that few of the 'Big Five' traits are significant predictors of giving a first preference to a woman. The only variable that was significantly related to giving a first preference to a female candidate was openness to experience, which captures a respondent's willingness to try new things and a degree of unconventionality. Extraversion is, surprisingly, negatively related to giving a first preference to a woman but this effect is only significant at the 0.1 level; in future work, with a larger sample and a more refined dependent variable, we will see if this relationship holds. Unsurprisingly, if the party of the candidate the respondent voted for has a female incumbent, the voter is more likely to vote for a female and interestingly, QUOTA SUPPORT does reach significance in this model. As is clear from Figure 9.9 most of the other variables in the model fail to reach standard levels of significance, but once more, education and class are positively signed, a pattern that fits with the analysis in the previous section. Overall, the analysis suggests the more curious

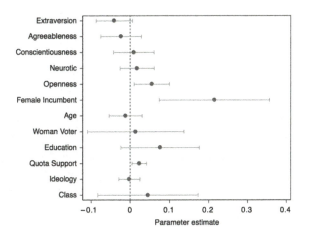

Figure 9.9 Impact of 'Big Five' traits on casting a first preference for a female candidate.
Data source: INES3 2016.

and less conventional are more likely to cast a vote for a female candidate. However, it is worth repeating, that this analysis of Irish voter traits and their impact on voting behaviour is in its infancy and future work, with higher quality data, is required.

Discussion

The introduction of a gender quota bill in the Dáil in December 2011 by then Minister for the Environment Phil Hogan was unexpected in its timing. The Fine Gael–Labour government elected in February 2011 was dealing with an economy in meltdown and tasked with implementing punitive austerity measures, as a condition of the international financial bailout. Gender quotas, for an election that was likely to be more than four years down the line, did not seem like a top priority. While a handful of women's groups and academics had been lobbying for their introduction for some years, there was little public interest in or awareness of the gap in representation. Gender has never been very politicized in Irish electoral campaigns or, indeed, politics more generally. Furthermore, the quota was likely to pose a problem for the main governing party, Fine Gael, though clearly not as much of a problem as for its main rival, Fianna Fáil. Nonetheless, the bill became law in July 2012 and the 2016 general election was the first to operate under its provisions.

The quota had an immediate impact: the number of women running for and elected to the Dáil increased quite dramatically, though at just over 22 per cent of legislators, Ireland still falls well behind most other Western European states in the rankings of women in parliament.[12] And while there was not much public demand for the introduction of the quota, there does not appear to have been any significant opposition to it once the legislation was enacted. There was no change in voting behaviour. Previous work has found the Irish electorate to be gender blind and 2016 was no different; people cast their ballot for candidates on the basis of their party affiliation, their political experience and their quality, more generally. We cannot find a subtype of voter, either in demographic or personality type, who is systematically more inclined to vote for a woman. Ideology, class and age do not consistently predict propensity to vote for women, nor does quota support. What matters most is that the candidate is a known entity; especially that he or she is an incumbent. The responsibility for so few women being elected in Ireland does not rest with the electorate, with, perhaps, the notable exception of those voting for Fianna Fáil. The aggregate and individual level data clearly suggest that this party's voters do actually have a preference for male candidates.

Chapter appendix

Table A9.1 Aggregate analysis 2016

	Model 1 Deviation	Model 2 Per cent of quota	Model 3 Deviation	Model 4 Per cent of quota
Gender	0.0771	0.0246	−0.0245	0.0384
	(0.91)	(0.85)	(−0.09)	(0.42)
Incumbent	0.747***	0.289***	0.874***	0.344***
	(10.16)	(11.52)	(8.51)	(10.11)
Minister	0.133	0.0817	0.205	0.0865
	(0.87)	(1.57)	(0.96)	(1.22)
Gender incumbent	0.179	0.0105	0.201	−0.0136
	(1.22)	(0.21)	(0.98)	(-0.20)
Gender X minister	0.562	0.194	0.482	0.182
	(1.77)	(1.79)	(1.23)	(1.40)
Campaign spend	1.086***	0.434***	0.957***	0.423***
	(8.54)	(9.99)	(4.60)	(6.14)
Councillor	0.247***	0.0970***	0.313***	0.132***
	(4.63)	(5.33)	(3.57)	(4.52)
Fianna Fáil	0.933***	0.307***	0.804***	0.241***
	(10.22)	(9.84)	(6.21)	(5.61)
Fine Gael	0.154	0.0241	−0.0100	−0.0563
	(1.56)	(0.72)	(-0.07)	(−1.17)
Labour	−0.368**	−0.167***	−0.363	−0.184*
	(−2.92)	(−3.87)	(−1.57)	(−2.41)
Sinn Féin	0.737***	0.259***	0.594***	0.201***
	(7.31)	(7.52)	(3.80)	(3.87)
Greens	0.0617	0.0298	−0.0810	−0.00941
	(0.58)	(0.82)	(−0.44)	(−0.15)
Renua	−0.109	−0.0482	−0.279	−0.119
	(−0.88)	(−1.13)	(−1.36)	(−1.74)
Anti-Austerity Alliance	0.206	0.0522	0.00657	−0.0523
	(1.66)	(1.23)	(0.02)	(−0.59)
Gender X Fianna Fáil	−0.589***	−0.185***	−0.346	−0.0798
	(−3.81)	(−3.50)	(−1.35)	(−0.93)
Gender X Fine Gael	−0.125	−0.0299	0.0611	0.0541
	(−0.80)	(−0.56)	(0.25)	(0.67)
Gender X Labour	−0.244	−0.0258	−0.718*	−0.164
	(−1.17)	(−0.36)	(−2.07)	(−1.42)
Gender X Sinn Féin	−0.208	−0.0833	−0.0490	−0.0306
	(−1.22)	(−1.43)	(−0.18)	(−0.34)

(*Continued*)

Table A9.1 *Continued*

	Model 1 Deviation	Model 2 Per cent of quota	Model 3 Deviation	Model 4 Per cent of quota
Gender X Greens	−0.0577	−0.000157	0.00730	0.0137
	(−0.30)	(−0.00)	(0.02)	(0.13)
Gender X Renua	−0.188	−0.0479	−0.0792	−0.00942
	(−0.83)	(−0.61)	(−0.13)	(−0.05)
Gender X AAA	−0.153	−0.0127	−0.0197	0.0870
	(−0.77)	(−0.19)	(−0.05)	(0.70)
Education			0.123	0.0562**
			(1.97)	(2.70)
Education X gender			−0.0234	−0.0290
			(−0.20)	(−0.76)
Constant	−0.829***	0.0457**	−0.880***	−0.00756
	(−17.85)	(2.88)	(−6.24)	(−0.16)
N	551	551	272	272

Source: Author's own data.

Note: *t* statistics in parentheses: $^{*}p < 0.05$, $^{**}p < 0.01$, $^{***}p < 0.001$. OLS Regression with deviation from average number of first preferences in constituency as dependent variable in Models 1 and 3. In models 2 and 4, the dependent variable is per cent of quota obtained by the candidate. AAA – Anti-Austerity Alliance.

Table A9.2 Casting a (high) preference for a female candidate, 2016

	Model 1 Any preference	Model 2 High preference
Woman respondent	−0.837	0.102
	(−1.45)	(0.16)
Party candidate	3.912***	3.892***
	(4.47)	(5.07)
Ideology	0.0181	−0.0288
	(0.71)	(−0.99)
Party ID	−0.790***	−0.846***
	(−5.85)	(−5.19)
Class	0.353**	0.161
	(2.79)	(1.11)
Age	0.0260	0.0606
	(0.89)	(1.78)
Education	0.233*	0.203
	(2.41)	(1.83)
Quota support	−0.0286	0.00972
	(−1.58)	(0.47)

	Model 1 Any preference	Model 2 High preference
Party centred	0.207***	0.135
	(3.34)	(1.92)
Incumbent	0.942***	1.136***
	(9.61)	(10.83)
Woman X party candidate	0.0243	0.154
	(0.04)	(0.30)
Woman X ideology	−0.0450	0.0611
	(−1.08)	(1.29)
Woman X party ID	0.155	−0.312
	(0.72)	(−1.13)
Woman x class	−0.231	0.0322
	(−1.23)	(0.15)
Woman X age	0.0521	−0.0270
	(1.13)	(−0.52)
Woman X education	0.211	−0.0912
	(1.34)	(−0.52)
Woman X quota support	0.0361	−0.00728
	(1.21)	(−0.21)
Woman X party centred	−0.157	−0.0376
	(−1.62)	(−0.34)
Constant	−1.917***	−2.499***
	(−5.98)	(−6.71)
N	3,658	3,658

Source: Author's own data.

Note: *t* statistics in parentheses *p* < 0.05, **p* < 0.01, ***p* < 0.001.

Table A9.3 Big Five questions

I am going to read some statements that describe people. Please indicate whether you completely agree, somewhat agree, partly agree, partly disagree, somewhat disagree or completely disagree with each of the statements. I …

	Trait Measured
am reserved	Extraversion (reversed)
am generally trusting, believe in the good in people	Agreeableness
tend to be lazy	Conscientiousness (reversed)
am relaxed, handle stress well	Neuroticism (reversed)
have few artistic interests	Openness (reversed)
am outgoing, sociable	Extraversion
tend to find fault with others	Agreeableness (reversed)
do a thorough job	Conscientiousness
get nervous easily	Neuroticism
have an active imagination	Openness

Notes

1. Exact question wording was as follows: 'Candidate gender quotas for political parties were introduced for these elections to the Dáil. How much do you support the use of gender quotas for national elections on a scale from 0 to 10 where 0 means strongly oppose and 10 means strongly support?'
2. Under the Single Transferable Vote system, measuring candidate 'success' is not trivial. While winning a seat is what candidates ultimately care about, this dichotomous measure is somewhat crude and loses a lot of the information available on candidate performance. There are several alternative measures available such as share of the vote, share of a quota, absolute number of votes (controlling for votes cast in each constituency), deviation from the average share won by candidates from a district and deviation from the average share won by the candidate's party in a district. These measures are correlated with each other but far from perfectly, and this matters when we are examining levels of significance. Given no strong theoretical reason to use one measure over another, we deploy three alternative measures of success in this chapter.
3. Campaign spending limits were as follows: €30,150 in three seat constituencies, €37,650 in four seaters and €45,200 in five seaters.
4. Not all variables in the model are presented in Figure 9.5. For those, see Table A9.1 in the Appendix.
5. In particular, we almost certainly underrepresent less-educated challengers, Independents especially. If this is the case, we expect the effect of the education measure to be attenuated.
6. Interestingly, the interaction term between gender and Fianna Fáil drops from significance in these models.
7. An alternative categorization of large farmers (50+ acres) with the ABC1 grouping does not affect the results.
8. For more details see Marsh et al. (2008, chapter 8) and Courtney and Weeks, this volume.
9. By including male as well as female candidates, we would have to include third-order interaction terms, which only serve to obscure the central findings.
10. Distributional differences are statistically significant using a Kolmogorov–Smirnov test for openness and neuroticism.
11. Just slightly over three quarters of respondents could (or were willing to) name their first preference candidate, thereby reducing the sample.
12. For instance, of the fifteen pre-2004 member states of the European Union, the only country with a lower figure at the time of writing – August 2017 – was Greece (at 18.3 per cent).

References

Alford, J. R., and J. R. Hibbing. 2007. 'Personal, interpersonal, and political temperaments', *The Annals of the American Academy of Political and Social Science*. 614: 196–212.

Anzia, S. F., and C. R. Berry. 2011. 'The Jackie (and Jill) Robinson effect: Why do congresswomen outperform congressmen?', *American Journal of Political Science*. 55: 478–93.

Baltrunaite, A., P. Bello, A. Casarico and P. Profeta. 2014. 'Gender quotas and the quality of politicians', *Journal of Public Economics*. 118: 62–74.

Benoit, K., and M. Marsh. 2010. 'Incumbent and challenger campaign spending effects in proportional electoral systems: The Irish elections of 2002', *Political Research Quarterly*. 63: 159–73.

Black, J. H., and L. Erickson. 2003. 'Women candidates and voter bias: Do women politicians need to be better?', *Electoral Studies*. 22: 81–100.

Brody, L. R., and J. A. Hall. 2000. 'Gender, emotion, and expression', in M. Lewis and J. M. Haviland-Jones (eds), *Handbook of Emotions: Part IV: Social/ Personality Issues*. 2nd edition, New York: Guilford Press, pp. 325–414.

Carney, D. R., Jost, J. T., Gosling, S. D. and Potter, J. (2008). 'The secret lives of liberals and conservatives: Personality profiles, interaction styles, and the things they leave behind', *Political Psychology*. 29(6): 807–40.

Costa Jr., P., A. Terracciano and R. R. McCrae. 2001. 'Gender differences in personality traits across cultures: Robust and surprising findings', *Journal of Personal Social Psychology*. 81: 322–31.

Dolan, K. 1998. 'Voting for Women in the "Year of the Woman"', *American Journal of Political Science*. 42: 272–93.

Else-Quest, N. M., J. S. Hyde, H. H. Goldsmith and C. A. Van Hulle. 2006. 'Gender differences in temperament: A meta-analysis', *Psychological Bulletin*. 132: 33.

Feingold, A. 1994. 'Gender differences in personality: A meta-analysis', *Psychological Bulletin*. 116: 429.

Fox, R. L., and E. R. Smith. 1998. 'The role of candidate sex in voter decision-making', *Political Psychology*. 19: 405–19.

Fulton, S. A. 2012. 'Running backwards and in high heels: The gendered quality gap and incumbent electoral success', *Political Research Quarterly*. 65: 303–14.

Gerber, A. S., G. A. Huber, D. Doherty, C. M. Dowling, C. Raso and S. E. Ha. 2011. 'Personality traits and participation in political processes', *Journal of Politics*. 73: 692–706.

Gerber, A. S., G. A. Huber, D. Doherty and C. M. Dowling. 2012. 'Personality and the strength and direction of partisan identification', *Political Behavior*. 34: 653–88.

Gosling, S. D., P. J. Rentfrow and W. B. Swann. 2003. 'A very brief measure of the Big-Five personality domains', *Journal of Research in Personality*. 37: 504–28.

Hyde, J. S. 2005. 'The gender similarities hypothesis', *American Psychologist*. 60: 581.

John, O. P., L. P. Naumann and C. J. Soto. 2008. 'Paradigm shift to the integrative big five trait taxonomy', *Handbook of Personality: Theory and Research*. 3: 114–58.

Jost, John T., Jack Glaser, Arie W. Kruglanski and Frank J. Sulloway. 2003. 'Political conservatism as motivated social cognition', *Psychological Bulletin*. 129(3): 339.

Jost, John T., J. L. Napier, H. Thorisdottir, S. D. Gosling, T. P. Palfai and B. Ostafin. 2007. 'Are needs to manage uncertainty and threat associated with political conservatism or ideological extremity?', *Personality and Social Psychology Bulletin*. 33(7): 989–1007.

Kring, A. M., and A. H. Gordon. 1998. 'Sex differences in emotion: Expression, experience, and physiology', *Journal of Personality and Social Psychology*. 74: 686–703.

Kulisheck, M. R., and J. J. Mondak. 1996. 'Candidate quality and the congressional vote: A causal connection?' *Electoral Studies*. 15: 237–53.

Lawless, J. L., and R. L. Fox. 2005. *It Takes a Candidate: Why Women Don't Run for Office*. Cambridge: Cambridge University Press.

Lawless, J. L., and K. Pearson. 2008. 'The primary reason for women's underrepresentation? Reevaluating the conventional wisdom', *Journal of Politics*. 70: 67–82.

Lynn, R., and T. Martin. 1997. 'Gender differences in extraversion, neuroticism, and psychoticism in 37 nations', *The Journal of Social Psychology*. 137: 369–73.

Marsh, M., R. Sinnott, J. Garry, J. and F. Kennedy. 2008. *The Irish Voter*. Manchester: Manchester University Press.

Matland, R. E., and D. T. Studlar. 2004. 'Determinants of legislative turnover: A cross-national analysis', *British Journal of Political Science*. 34: 87–108.

McCrae, R. R. 2002. 'Neo-PI-R Data from 36 Cultures', in R. McRae and J. Allik (eds), *The Five-Factor Model of Personality Across Cultures*. New York: Springer, pp. 105–26.

McElroy, G. 2017. 'Party competition in Ireland', in M. Marsh, D. Farrell and G. McElroy (eds), *A Conservative Revolution? Electoral Change in Twenty-First Century Ireland*. Oxford: Oxford University Press, pp. 61–82.

McElroy, G., and M. Marsh. 2010. 'Candidate gender and voter choice: Analysis from a multimember preferential voting system', *Political Research Quarterly*. 63: 822–33.

McElroy, G., and M. Marsh. 2011. 'Electing women to the Dáil: Gender cues and the Irish voter', *Irish Political Studies*. 26: 521–34.

McGing, C. 2013. 'The single transferable vote and women's representation in Ireland', *Irish Political Studies*. 28: 322–40.

Mondak, J. J. 2010. *Personality and the Foundations of Political Behavior*. Cambridge: Cambridge University Press.

Mondak, J. J., and Karen D. Halperin. 2008. 'A framework for the study of personality and political behaviour', *British Journal of Political Science*. 38: 335–62.

Sanbonmatsu, K. 2006. 'Do Parties Know That "Women Win"? Party Leader Beliefs about Women's Electoral Chances', *Politics & Gender*. 2: 431–50.

Sanbonmatsu, K. 2010. *Where Women Run: Gender and Party in the American States*. Ann Arbor, MI: University of Michigan Press.

Schmitt, D. P., A. Realo, M. Voracek and J. Allik. 2008. 'Why can't a man be more like a woman? Sex differences in Big Five personality traits across 55 cultures', *Journal of Personality and Social Psychology*. 94: 168.

Schoen, H., and S. Schumann. 2007. 'Personality traits, partisan attitudes, and voting behaviour: Evidence from Germany', *Political Psychology*. 28: 471–98.

Seltzer, R., J. Newman and M. V. Leighton. 1997. *Sex as a Political Variable: Women as Candidates and Voters in US Elections*. New York: Lynne Rienner Publishers.

Smith, J. L., D. Paul and R. Paul. 2007. 'No place for a woman: Evidence for gender bias in evaluations of presidential candidates', *Basic and Applied Social Psychology*. 29: 225–33.

Squire, P. 1992. 'Legislative professionalization and membership diversity in state legislatures', *Legislative Studies Quarterly*. 17: 69–79.

Van Dunk, E. 1997. 'Challenger quality in state legislative elections', *Political Research Quarterly*. 50: 793–807.

Wlezien, C. 2016. 'On causality in the study of valence and voting behavior: An introduction to the symposium', *Political Science Research and Methods*. 4: 195–97.

10

What do Irish voters want from and think of their politicians?

David M. Farrell, Michael Gallagher and David Barrett

Introduction

The 2016 election revealed a lot of flux in people's voting behaviour. How did this translate in terms of attitudes to representative politics in Ireland? What do voters think of the system of representative politics today? What do they want from their TDs? The INES 2016 data allow us to explore three main dimensions of interest. First, we examine attitudes to the role of members of parliament, and the extent to which long-established patterns of support for a strong constituency orientation from TDs are evolving over time. It is clear from previous research that Irish voters expect a strong constituency orientation from their elected representatives (for a recent review see Gallagher and Suiter, 2017). Given that the 2016 election saw the worst ever electoral outcome for the old, established parties, and the entry into the Dáil of a large coterie of new TDs – some representing new parties on the left, many independent of any party – it is timely to explore whether traditional attitudes to the role of a TD are changing. We ask to what extent such attitudes are affected by the type of TD voters support (notably the difference between supporters of established parties versus those supporting new parties or Independents). Second, we examine patterns of contact between voters and TDs and assess whether these are being affected by other changes over time, such as the emergence of social media.

In the third section of the chapter, we switch from a focus on what voters want of their elected representatives to one on what they think of them overall. Frequently, negative media coverage of politicians, coupled with the continuing fallout from the economic collapse of 2008, provides good reason to expect that voters will have a pretty dim view of the political class generally. A series of INES 2016 questions (deployed as part of a battery of CSES questions) allows us to explore in detail for the first time what voters think about representative politics in Ireland; whether they believe that politicians are corrupt; and how attitudes to questions like this may have influenced voting behaviour in 2016.

Expectations regarding the background and
role of parliamentary representatives

In discussing voters' expectations of what TDs should be doing, and the nature of their contact with TDs, we will have frequent recourse to where voters stand on what we term the localist–cosmopolitan dimension.[1] We measure this by asking respondents whether they agree or disagree with the statement 'I find the things that happen directly in my local area more interesting than news about national and international developments'. Altogether, 33 per cent agreed with this, 52 per cent disagreed and the other 14 per cent neither agreed nor disagreed.

Broadly speaking, those who see national and international events as the more interesting (we might term this the 'cosmopolitan' end of the spectrum) tend to be more educated and better off. They tend to think that their area has been doing better than the rest of the country over the past five years (67 per cent of them believe this, with only 48 per cent believing that it has been doing worse than the rest of the country). In contrast, those who regard local events as more interesting than national or international ones (the 'localists') tend to have less education, and to be working class or farmers. They are much less inclined to believe that their area has been doing better than the rest of the country: only 21 per cent of them believe this, with 42 per cent feeling it has done worse.[2] Among supporters of the various political groups, Sinn Féin supporters are the most localist (average score of 2.9 on a scale where 1 is the most localist and 5 the least localist), followed by supporters of Independent candidates (3.1). Supporters of Fine Gael and Fianna Fáil are in a median position. The least localist are supporters of the Green Party (4.0), followed by the Social Democrats (3.8) and Labour (3.6). As we shall see, this variable is strongly related to most aspects of perceptions of TDs' roles. We should note, though, that we cannot relate this to the discussion in the third section of the chapter, because this question was not asked of respondents to the questions analysed there.

Under Ireland's STV electoral system, voters are able to rank order all candidates on the basis of whatever factor seems most important, which may be party (although even then they will often have to make a choice among several candidates of their favoured party) or may be anything else. Voters might attach most importance to what the candidates seem likely to *do*, assessing their perceived ability to contribute to national politics and/or to tend to constituency needs, or, alternatively, they might attach most importance to what the candidates *are*, looking for candidates who possess certain socio-demographic characteristics. The latter was tested by asking respondents how important it was to them that 'your TD' possess a number of characteristics; the results are shown in Table 10.1.

Table 10.1 Importance of parliamentary representatives' possession of certain characteristics

Characteristic	Average score
Has the same political viewpoint as you	6.15
Has the same level of education that you have	4.75
Is from the same area as you	4.71
Is from the same social class as you	4.00
Is of approximately the same age as you	2.40
Has the same religious views that you have	2.35
Is of the same sex as you	1.68

Source: INES3 2016.

Note: Minimum score is 0 (not at all important) and maximum is 10 (very important). In this and in all other tables, data are weighted appropriately. N = 1,000.

Given that 5 is the mid-point of the scale, it is clear that most of these characteristics are regarded as having no great importance.[3] The only one generally perceived as important is sharing a political viewpoint, and the surprising aspect of this is that the score is not closer to 10. Altogether, 22 per cent of respondents indicated, by giving a score of less than 5, that they regarded this factor as unimportant, emphasizing that elections are about much more than policy proximity. Education is the most highly rated socio-demographic characteristic, though on balance it is seen as not important and there is little sub-group variation.

The third most important is that a TD is from the same area as the respondent. This matters most to supporters of the largest three parties and is least important to those who voted for a minor party. This may not reflect any different orientation on the part of voters for different parties but simply result from the larger parties, particularly Fine Gael and Fianna Fáil, often running more than one candidate and thus compelling their supporters to make a choice on the basis of candidate factors. As is well known, candidates, especially in rural areas, poll most strongly around their home base (for the example of Donegal see Sacks, 1970; for Mayo, Gallagher, 2014: 773–75). Those with a predominantly local orientation are much more inclined to attach importance to this (average score of 5.9) than are those with a more cosmopolitan outlook (average score 4.0). As we might expect, those who attach most importance to the constituency aspects of TDs' roles, such as getting resources for the constituency and looking after the needs of individual constituents, are especially inclined to see this factor as important. It is also significantly more important to those who believe that 'the area around here' has been doing worse than the rest of the country since the 2011 election (average score 5.3) than to those who think the area has been doing better (average score 3.8). This is very much part of a pattern: respondents who believe that their area has been doing worse than the rest of the country prioritize the local aspects of TDs' roles and are generally more locally oriented in their outlook.

Relatedly, those closer to the local end of the local–cosmopolitan spectrum, and by extension those who especially value the local roles of TDs, are more inclined to attach importance to several descriptive characteristics: it is significantly more important to them that their TD be of the same social class as themselves, holds the same religious views and is approximately their age. Descriptive representation of this sort is consistently least important to middle-class respondents, to those with a university education, to men and to Dublin voters. That, at least, is what they say; of course, for such people, their representatives are already quite like them, and were their TDs to have a significantly different profile, such respondents might suddenly find that they cared a great deal more about the backgrounds of their TDs.

Finally, and topically given the introduction of candidate gender quotas at this election (see Buckley, Galligan and McGing, 2016, and chapter 9 in this volume), very little importance was attached to the candidate's gender; most respondents (52 per cent of them) gave this a score of zero, and only 7 per cent gave it a score of more than 5. In some ways it may seem paradoxical or ironic that the criterion seen as least important by the voters is the one to which most political attention has been paid through the introduction of candidate gender quotas, as has been observed for the UK (Cowley, 2013: 158–59; for discussion see Buckley and Galligan, 2018: 216–17). However, it should be noted that even if the voters do not seem very exercised by the gender of their own TD, they still believe that there should be more women in parliament; the INES survey of 2011 found that 62 per cent of respondents believed that there should be more women TDs, 29 per cent thought the current number was about right, 6 per cent had no opinion and only 3 per cent wanted fewer women in the Dáil, a pattern of responses that could be interpreted as validation of the gender quotas initiative. While in 2016 no group saw the gender of candidates as, on balance, important, there was quite a bit of statistically significant sub-group variation. Middle-class respondents, those with university education and less locally oriented respondents were the least inclined to attach any importance to it. Women (who gave it a score of 2.1), rated this factor more highly than men (who gave it a score of 1.2), and this difference remains constant even when we control for class, education and region. The effect of this is that not only is there no bias against women among voters as a whole, but, in fact, voters collectively have a preference for female candidates, other things being equal, albeit not having strong feelings on the subject (Keenan and McElroy, 2017; for more, see chapter 9 in this volume).

These findings are very similar to the pattern in Britain (Cowley, 2013: 148). There, too having the same political views was seen as the most important criterion, with an almost identical score to that in Ireland, and the order of the other criteria was much the same, with being of the same sex the least important. Being from the same area was rated more important by British respondents – who gave it a score of 5.7, placing it second and a long way ahead of the third most important criterion – than by Irish respondents, who gave it a score of 4.7 and rated it only third. This may seem surprising, given the frequency of comment about the importance of the local connection in Irish politics. The explanation may be not that British voters are more locally oriented than Irish ones but that the phrase 'is from the same area' has different connotations in the two countries. In Britain, MPs are not necessarily local people; they may be ministerial special advisers or others with good connections with the party's centre who secure selection as a candidate in a constituency with which they have no previous connection. Thus, being 'from the same area' may be interpreted simply as 'being from this constituency'. In Ireland, in contrast, voters can take it for granted that their TDs will have strong local roots in the constituency. The great majority were local county councillors before becoming TDs (this was true of 82 per cent of those TDs elected in 2016 (Gallagher, 2016: 153)) and so 'the local area' may be understood as meaning 'this part of the constituency', which would be especially important in geographically large rural constituencies. Consistent with that interpretation, respondents in Dublin attached significantly less importance to this criterion than did voters elsewhere, and respondents in rural areas attached a significantly higher score to it (5.3) than did those living in the suburbs (4.1).[4]

We turn now from the examination of what personal characteristics voters want their TDs to possess to the question of what voters want their parliamentary representatives to do. In the third section of this chapter we will examine voters' evaluations of politicians' honesty and integrity, but first we will consider voters' expectations about the proper role of a politician. Should TDs be focusing mainly on national aspects of their role such as working on legislation, or should their focus be mainly on the local area? And what characteristics of voters are associated with prioritizing a local or a national role for their parliamentary representatives?

Over time the INES series provides some valuable trend data on citizen attitudes to the role of TDs. In their examination of the data for the 2002–2011 period, Gallagher and Suiter found that the importance attached to the constituency role of TDs has been consistently high, even in 2011 when national as opposed to local factors appeared more important than usual. In principle, there are reasons to expect some change in this regard, since 2016 was arguably an even bigger electoral earthquake, given the unprecedentedly weak showing of the traditional parties, than 2011 had been (Farrell and Suiter, 2016). In a context of such significant vote shifts, there could be grounds for anticipating some evidence of attitudinal shifts – at least among some categories of voters – relating to the role of TDs. As we shall see, though, the Irish attachment to constituency representation remained as strong as ever in 2016.

As was shown in chapter 7, at most elections many voters explain their vote primarily in terms of candidate factors, and 2016 was no exception. When asked whether the party or the candidate had been more important in deciding how they cast their vote, a majority (54 per cent) said it was the candidate with 46 per cent saying it was the party. Forty per cent of the former said that they would have voted for the same candidate even if he or she had been standing for a different party, and a further 43 per cent said that they might have done so depending on the other party. All of these figures are similar to those at past elections. Moreover, a long-standing poll question giving voters four criteria and asking which was most important in making up their mind how to vote has consistently found that around 40 per cent identify 'choosing a candidate to look after the needs of the constituency' as the main criterion. This too was no different in 2016: excluding the don't knows, 43 per cent stated that this was the most important factor, well ahead of the second most important, 'choosing between the policies as set out by the parties', which was given by 34 per cent (for more, see Marsh and McElroy, 2016: 179–80).

Respondents were asked to evaluate the importance of six aspects of the role of a TD, and as Table 10.2 shows, the four that could be seen as primarily national were all rated as more important than the two that relate to work for the constituency or for individual constituents. This appears to conflict with the situation found in 2011, when respondents expressed the view that TDs were currently spending too much time on national matters and not enough on constituency ones (Gallagher and Suiter, 2017: 160–61). The two pictures can be reconciled, though. In 2011, respondents did not say that they regarded

Table 10.2 Importance of various aspects of the role of parliamentary representative

Role	Average score
Raising awareness of important social needs and interests	3.98
Working on legislation	3.98
Developing policies	3.89
Balancing different interests in society	3.72
Getting as much for their constituency from the government as possible	3.33
Representing the individual interests of individual citizens	2.86

Source: INES3 2016.

Note: Minimum score is 1 (little importance) and maximum is 5 (great importance).
N = 1,000.

the local role as being more important than the national one, and in fact on average they felt that around 50–55 per cent of TDs' time should be spent on national matters; they simply felt that at present TDs were spending more time than this on national issues and thus wanted them to increase the proportion of their time they spent on constituency matters. One question that allows direct comparison between 2011 and 2016 asks whether respondents agree or disagree that 'The assumption that TDs should provide a local service is a strength of the Irish political system', and responses suggest a strengthening of interest in the local role; in 2011, 52 per cent agreed with the statement, whereas in 2016, 62 per cent agreed.

Unsurprisingly, there is considerable sub-group variation in attitudes to the roles that TDs should play, with the localist–cosmopolitan dimension being strongly related to most aspects of perceptions of TDs' roles, as Table 10.3 shows. Generally speaking, those closer to the cosmopolitan end of the spectrum regard TDs' legislative and scrutiny roles as the most important and are unenthusiastic about TDs focusing heavily on constituency work. In contrast, those with a localist outlook attach greater importance to the TD's role in getting resources for the constituency and in helping resolve the problems of individual constituents. Among those with a more cosmopolitan outlook, 63 per cent regard the legislative role as more important than getting resources

Table 10.3 Impact of local versus cosmopolitan orientation on perceptions of role of parliamentary representative

Statement	All	Localists	Equal	Cosmopolitans
Important that TDs work on legislation[a]	3.98	3.82	4.02	4.08
Important that TDs work on developing policies[a]	3.89	3.77	3.82	3.99
Important that TDs get resources for constituency from government[a]	3.33	3.88	3.39	2.94
Important that TDs represent interests of individual citizens[a]	2.86	3.36	2.77	2.56
Important that TD is from your area[a]	2.88	3.35	2.82	2.60
Agree that assumption that TDs should provide a local service is strength of Irish political system[b]	2.67	2.27	2.65	2.94

Source: INES3 2016.

Note: All differences across rows are significant at 0.01 level.
a: 1 = lowest importance, 5 = highest importance; b: 1 = strongly agree, 5 = strongly disagree.
Responses to 'Important that TD is from your area' recalculated for 1–5 scale (original question employed 0–10 scale).
N = 1,000.

for the constituency while 15 per cent took the opposite view; among localists the respective percentages are 28 and 33. By extension, the characteristics associated with a less localist outlook are also associated with attaching relatively less importance to TDs' constituency roles: those with more education, Dublin residents and middle-class respondents typically rate this as less important than do those with the opposite characteristics. In response to the further question asking whether respondents agree that 'The assumption that TDs should provide a local service is a strength of the Irish political system', the same pattern emerges, with localists, and those with associated characteristics, the most likely to agree. We should note, though, the broad consensus in favour of this proposition, with 62 per cent of all respondents agreeing and only 29 per cent disagreeing. Evidently, the expectation that TDs will keep in close contact with the local area remains deeply rooted in Irish political culture.

Contact with parliamentary representatives

Having established variation in voters' attitudes towards their parliamentary representatives, we now turn to examine variation in their behaviour. How many people contact their TD, about what subjects and by what methods? In their analysis of the evidence over the three elections of the 2002–2011 period, Gallagher and Suiter (2017) reported an apparently declining trend in contact over time, as shown in Table 10.4, but they cautioned against reading too much into this trend given changes in question wording and sampling frame across the three surveys. The proportion in 2016 was 16 per cent, which, being pretty much the average figure over the four elections for which we have such data, can stand as the current best estimate of the proportion of people who contact a politician in a twelve-month period. As in earlier years, those who make contact with a TD are, in most demographic respects, a fairly typical cross-section of the electorate, with such factors as class, education and gender not being significantly related to probability of contacting a TD. For the period 2002–2011 there was a consistent relationship with age, with the youngest and oldest age groups being the least likely to make such contact, but that does not hold

Table 10.4 Extent of contact between citizens and TDs, 2002–2016

	2002	2006	2011	2016
All	21.4	15.6	12.0	15.8
N	2,642	1,061	1,818	1,000

Source: For 2002–2011, Gallagher and Suiter 2017: 154; for 2016, INES3.

Note: In 2002, figures refer to those contacting a TD in the previous five years, while in 2006, 2011 and 2016 they refer to a one-year period.

true in 2016. Age is not significantly related to contact with a TD, and in fact, the youngest age group had the highest rate of contact at 19 per cent, possibly a result of the availability of email and social media. Regional differences were statistically significant in 2016, in line with the belief in an earlier literature (for details see Gallagher and Suiter, 2017: 148–49, 153) that contacting TDs was an essentially rural phenomenon, though the differences are not dramatic (11 per cent in Dublin had contacted a TD compared with 18 per cent in the rest of Ireland) and there was little sign of such a pattern in the 2002–2011 period (Gallagher and Suiter, 2017: 153).

It remains the case that those who display activity on other indicators of political engagement are the most likely to have contacted a TD. Those who reported having voted in 2016 were much more likely to have contacted a TD than those who say they did not vote (Table 10.5). Respondents were asked how much they knew about how the Dáil works and the more they felt they knew, the more likely they were to have contacted a TD: 26 per cent of those who claimed they knew a lot about the Dáil had contacted a TD compared with only 5 per cent among those who admitted knowing nothing about it. Those who were contacted by candidates during the campaign were much more likely to have themselves contacted a TD than those who were not contacted by a candidate (19 per cent as opposed to 8 per cent). This may in part reflect TDs' determination to remind constituents of any service rendered, and to request due reward in the polling booth (of those respondents who had contacted a TD, 87 per cent reported being contacted during the campaign, though we do not have data on whether the contact was made by the TD whom they had contacted). There is no significant relationship with voting behaviour.

Respondents were asked how they had made contact with their parliamentarians. In previous surveys they had been asked to specify one

Table 10.5 Contact and political engagement: percentage who have contacted a TD in preceding period 2002–2016

	2002	*2006*	*2011*	*2016*
All	21.4	15.6	12.0	15.8
Voted at previous election				
Yes	23.0	17.9	12.7	16.8
No	16.1	4.1	5.5	7.1
Significance level of chi-square	*0.001*	*0.001*	*0.004*	*0.012*
N	2,642	1,061	1,818	999

Source: For 2002–2011, Gallagher and Suiter 2017: 154; for 2016, INES3.

Note: In 2002, figures refer to those contacting a TD in the previous five years, while in 2006–2016, they refer to a one-year period. In 2006, 'voted at previous election' refers to the 2002 election.

means of contact but in the 2016 survey they were asked sequentially whether they had used each of a number of methods, meaning that some respondents stated that they had used more than one method. Of those reporting having made such contact, 11 per cent had made this by two different methods and 4 per cent (seven respondents), leaving nothing to chance, had utilized three different means. (These have been excluded from the subsequent analysis.) As noted in an earlier analysis, it may be that 'the modalities and even the meaning of contacting a TD' are changing over time (Gallagher and Suiter, 2017: 151). This is not just because TDs' offices are now better resourced and because changing cultural norms have made it less acceptable to call to TDs' homes at any time of day but also because of communication improvements over time. The option of sending an email to a TD, or to every TD, makes it easier than ever before to 'contact a TD', though, unlike a message delivered face to face, the sender cannot be confident that the recipient even reads the communication, let alone feels obliged to respond. In whatever way 'contacting a TD' is interpreted by respondents, by 2016 email had become the most common mode of contact (see Table 10.6). The proportion making contact by letter has declined greatly since 2002, reflecting the general decline in surface mail since then, but the traditional TD's clinic, while it has lost its previous top position, is proving more resilient. Even so, nearly half of those contacting a TD now do not meet or directly speak to the TD in question, a major change from the predominantly face-to-face interaction of earlier decades, something that used to be identified frequently as a cultural underpinning of several aspects of Irish politics.

Different individuals use different methods of contacting TDs, and the pattern that emerges is strongly underpinned by the local–cosmopolitan cleavage that was shown above to explain much of the variation in respondents' attitudes regarding the proper role of politicians. This local–cosmopolitan fault line is strongly related to making contact by email, with those who regard

Table 10.6 Modes of contact with TDs in 2002 and 2016

Mode	2002 (%)	2016 (%)
Visit to a clinic/in person	39.3	24.4
Phone	30.9	31.1
Letter	23.5	5.0
Through another person	6.3	n.a.
Email	n.a.	36.1
Social media	n.a.	3.4

Source: For 2002, Gallagher and Suiter 2017: 156; for 2016, INES3.

Note: Question wording varied across both surveys. Figures for 2016 exclude those who made contact by 'other means' or by multiple methods.

national matters as more interesting much more likely to make contact this way than were localists (50 per cent compared with 20 per cent). Not surprisingly, those making contact by email were particularly likely to be doing so about a matter of national policy (41 per cent of them said this). Likewise, email is disproportionately favoured by middle-class respondents, those with more education, younger respondents and those who have the standard elements of a non-localist political culture: those who do not regard it as important that TDs get resources for the constituency from the government and that TDs represent the interests of individual citizens, and who do not agree that the assumption that TDs should provide a local service is a strength of the Irish political system. As was found before (Gallagher and Suiter, 2017: 156), those living in local authority housing are particularly likely to make contact by presenting at a TD's clinic.

Turning to the reasons why TDs were contacted, again the question was asked in such a way that respondents could give more than one reason; for example, one respondent's explanation was recorded as 'Issue with Palestine and structural problems with the house where he lives'. Some gave other, miscellaneous reasons such as 'Just to chat' or 'To wish them good luck in the election'. Table 10.7 shows that compared with 2011, more people had made contact in 2016 about a matter of national policy and fewer had done so about a personal or family matter. Those at the local end of the local–cosmopolitan spectrum are the most likely to have made contact regarding personal matters, while those at the cosmopolitan end are the most likely to have done so about a matter of national policy. Urban–rural differences are again apparent: in Dublin, 42 per cent had made contact on a matter of national policy and 35 per cent regarding a personal matter, while in Connacht–Ulster the respective figures were 13 per cent and 47 per cent. In 2011, too, Dublin was distinct, but then it was for generating an exceptionally high proportion of contacts about community matters, an aspect where it does not stand out in 2016. The data do not carry information about exactly what topics contact was made about, but the relatively high degree of mobilization over water charges in Dublin, and the fact that supporters of parties opposed to water charges (Sinn Féin and AAA–PBP) who contacted a TD had an above-average tendency to contact them about a national policy matter, may partly account for the high proportion of contacts in the capital that concerned a national policy matter. Given the fluctuation from one election to the next and the fairly small number of respondents in each sub-group, though, we should hesitate before drawing sweeping conclusions about any urban–rural cleavage.

Unusually, there is a significant gender difference: 46 per cent of women, but only 27 per cent of men, had made contact about a personal or family matter. Also unusually, there is a relationship with party affiliation: supporters of the largest two parties at the election, Fine Gael and Fianna Fáil, were particularly

Table 10.7 On what subject were TDs contacted, 2011 and 2016

	2011 (%)	2016 (%)
A matter personal to you or your family	52.7	37.9
A matter that concerns the community where you live	38.9	37.1
A matter of national policy	8.4	25.0
Total	100.0	100.0
N	217	124

Source: For 2011, Gallagher and Suiter 2017: 157; for 2016, INES3.

Note: 2016 figures omit those who had made contact for 'other' reasons or for more than one reason.

unlikely to make contact about a matter of national policy, while supporters of minor parties – which, of course, were particularly strong in Dublin – were especially likely to have been exercised by such concerns, with supporters of Sinn Féin, Labour and Independents in a median position. Surprisingly, voters in the youngest age band are the most likely to have been making contact about a personal matter, and while we should not exaggerate the importance of this given the small number of respondents in the 18–24 category, it is notable that this youngest set of voters also have the most localist outlook, and they attach less importance to the legislative role of TDs and more importance to the role of getting resources for the constituency than any other age group does.

Do Irish voters trust their politicians?

The previous two sections paint a striking picture of how Irish citizens view the representative role of politicians, and the forms and degrees of contact large portions of citizens have with politicians. But what do Irish citizens think of their politicians? In this age of rising populism, it is timely to assess the degree to which Irish voters trust their politicians. At the heart of the populist challenge (whether from the hard left or the hard right) is an accusation that the established political class no longer represents the interests of citizens, that it is out of touch, even corrupt (e.g. Mudde, 2007) – perhaps best personified in US President Donald Trump's campaign promise to 'drain the swamp'. Module 5 of the Comparative Study of Electoral Systems project developed a battery of questions designed to tap this dimension, which was included in our INES2 survey. While Irish politics has (to date at any rate) seemed largely immune from the populist challenge (though not entirely: for discussion, see Tinney and Quinlan, 2017), there is no doubt that the traditional party system (ranged around Fianna Fáil, Fine Gael and Labour) faced its strongest challenge in 2016: this election saw more parties (and Independents) fielding candidates and being elected than ever before in the history of the state (Farrell and Suiter, 2016;

chapter 1 of this volume). Included in the mix were parties (notably Sinn Féin and AAA–PBP) and a number of the Independents expressing strong criticisms of the established political elite. And yet this crisis election – much like the one before it (Marsh, Farrell and McElroy, 2017) – did not result in a major breakthrough by a new populist force on the left or the right, although there is some evidence that populist attitudes towards politicians (although not towards immigration) are growing in Ireland (Tinney and Quinlan, 2017). The evident electoral losses by the traditional parties were distributed across a kaleidoscope of minor parties and Independents; once again the new-party dog did not bark (Bowler and Farrell, 2017).

The INES2 provides a good opportunity to explore the potential for a populist challenge to the traditional party system. This module of questions provides, to our knowledge, the first ever test of Irish voter attitudes to politicians: whether voters see them as trustworthy, whether they think they care about people generally or only the rich, whether they think the Irish political system is corrupt or not.[5] We start with the last of these themes. Ireland has not been immune from political corruption over the years as shown by the findings of a spate of expensive political tribunals (Byrne, 2012), though by any objective standards it remains one of the world's least corrupt countries, ranking nineteenth of 176 globally for levels of corruption (Transparency International, 2016). In the INES2, respondents were asked 'How widespread do you think corruption such as bribe taking is among politicians in Ireland?' On a four-point scale, views were pretty evenly divided with 49 per cent feeling corruption was quite or very widespread and 51 per cent feeling the opposite: the mean was 2.42. This varied on demographic and party grounds. Only 40 per cent of respondents with university degrees felt that corruption was very or quite widespread, while 54 per cent of those without degrees thought this. There were also striking differences among party supporters. A full 70 per cent of Sinn Féin and 80 per cent of AAA–PBP voters felt that corruption was quite or very widespread, while only 38 per cent of Labour voters and 33 per cent of Fine Gael thought the same.

Similar trends are revealed regarding attitudes to politicians. The respondents were asked whether they agreed or disagreed with a series of statements about politicians in Ireland, four of which are particularly pertinent to the theme of trust in politics: 'most politicians do not care about the people', 'most politicians are trustworthy', 'politicians are the main problem in Ireland' and 'most politicians only care about the interests of the rich and powerful'. The first column of Table 10.8 reports the mean positions of respondents on the four items, where the higher the number the more the average respondent disagreed with the statement, on a scale of one to five. In general, the mean position among all categories is fairly near the centre for every statement, revealing once again quite evenly divided views: slightly more than half of respondents feel

Table 10.8 What do Irish voters think of their politicians?

Statement	All Respondents	Fine Gael	Sinn Féin	Degree	No degree
Most politicians don't care about the people	3.13	3.56	2.51	3.54	2.92
Most politicians are trustworthy	3.14	2.77	3.41	2.90	3.26
Politicians are the main problem in Ireland	3.22	3.65	2.58	3.60	3.03
Most politicians only care about the rich and powerful	2.86	3.47	2.09	3.31	2.64

Source: INES2 2016.
Note: Minimum score is 1 (completely agree); maximum is 5 (completely disagree).
N = 1,000.

that politicians do care about the people and that politicians are not the main problem in society; however, slightly more than half think that politicians are not trustworthy and that politicians only think about the rich. There are quite distinct differences across the parties. Supporters of Fianna Fáil, Fine Gael, and Labour were all generally more likely to disagree with statements that implied a lack of trust in politicians. Labour and Fine Gael voters in particular disagreed very strongly with the idea that politicians don't care about the people, with scores of 3.77 and 3.56 respectively, but Fianna Fáil voters were not far behind with 3.24. These parties tended to mirror each other, as we might expect, perhaps reflecting a general 'establishment' pattern of parties. Fianna Fáil, Fine Gael and Labour supporters all agreed with the proposition that politicians are trustworthy with means of 2.91, 2.77 and 2.75 respectively. They disagreed that politicians are the main problem in society with scores of 3.36, 3.65 and 3.62. The only issue where there was a noticeable breach between them was whether politicians only care about the rich and powerful, with Fine Gael and Labour supporters disagreeing (3.48 and 3.41) more so than those of Fianna Fáil (2.93).

By contrast, other groups are much less positive about politics. Sinn Féin supporters were more inclined to believe that politicians do not care about the people and that they only care about the rich, and they were less inclined to feel that politicians were trustworthy (Table 10.8). Sinn Féin supporters were, at best, ambivalent about whether politicians were the main problem in society (a score of 2.58). On every one of these issues, supporters of AAA–PBP were more critical than those of Sinn Féin, while supporters of Independent politicians also expressed similar sentiments about every statement on these issues.

This suggests that there may be a divide between supporters of the 'traditional' parties (Fianna Fáil, Fine Gael and Labour) and supporters of parties that might be categorized as 'left-populist': Sinn Féin and AAA–PBP. On average, there is at least a 0.90 difference between the supporters of both kinds of party. The divide is sharpest on whether politicians care only about the rich, with supporters of the traditional parties on the whole thinking that politicians do not (3.93) while supporters of Sinn Féin and AAA–PBP are more inclined to think that they do (2.74). There are also quite distinct divisions on the issue of whether politicians are 'the main problem in society', with traditional party voters on the whole believing they are not (2.46) and left populists tending to believe that they are (3.45). On the remaining items, the means were similar for both sets of party supporters. Independents are somewhat between the two. They are a little closer to the left populists on whether politicians only care about the rich (2.43) and almost exactly between the two for whether politicians are the main problem in society (2.91). The gap is similarly even on other issues. Independents in Ireland are quite a diverse group politically (Bowler and Farrell, 2017) so it would not be advisable to extrapolate too much from this.

The demographics produce less distinct variations. The factor related most strongly to differences is whether or not the respondent had a university degree or not. Those with degrees were significantly happier with politicians than those without. This was true for every statement. Those with degrees disagreed that politicians don't care about people much more strongly than those without (3.54 versus 2.92). This was also true for politicians being the main problem in society (3.60 and 3.03), and politicians only caring about the rich (3.31 and 2.64). They are also more likely to feel that politicians were trustworthy (2.90 versus 3.26). This was easily the most significant demographic difference, and tallies somewhat with the discussion in earlier sections about the local–cosmopolitan cleavage. Those with more education are more likely to trust their TDs, even as they are less likely to look approvingly on their constituency service role.

Neither geography nor gender revealed notable variation on the different measures of attitudes about politicians. Age exhibited a consistent, although slight, pattern. In general, younger voters were happier with politicians than their parents and grandparents. For instance, those aged between 18 and 35 were most likely to disagree that politicians are the main problem in society (3.28). This falls to 3.23 among 35–50 year-olds, 3.22 among 50–65 year-olds and to 3.08 among those older than 65. The differences, though consistent, are quite minor, however, and they are less distinctive than the differences across education. Nevertheless, the finding that younger voters across all the statements took the least cynical position is an interesting, counter-intuitive finding, and one that is statistically significant across all measures of attitudes to politicians.

Taken together, the demographics and party preferences are suggestive. They hint at a pattern of approaches to politics that is not uniform. Just as age and (in particular) education are related to differing expectations of what politicians will do once they are in office, they are also related to how individuals think of politicians and politics in and of themselves. While locality is not significant, otherwise the same pattern of voters holds here. Better educated, younger voters have noticeably more trust in politicians than their older and less well-educated counterparts. When party is also taken into account, the pattern becomes even more stark. Supporters of the parties that the less educated voters prefer – Sinn Féin and AAA–PBP – are likewise more cynical of politicians, a pattern that exists for supporters of these parties in spite of the general pattern of these parties being especially supported by younger voters. These are the parties that might be considered putative populist parties (O'Malley, 2008).

In order to test for this more systematically, we factor-analysed the five items we have been examining in this section (the question on corruption and the four items relating to politicians): these all loaded onto one common dimension, which might be termed 'political trust'. All loaded with the expected sign, supporting the conclusion pointed to by the bivariate analysis, namely that support for the three established parties, and higher levels of education, are associated with higher levels of trust in politicians and in the political system. This is consistent with trends in other countries.[6]

Conclusion

There are certain features of Irish political culture that remain steadfast and unchanged. For the most part, Irish citizens still expect their TDs to retain a strong local presence, and citizen contact with TDs remains at the same level as before. At the same time, however, there were some important shifts in how Irish citizens related to their politicians in 2016 compared with previous elections. Newer, more impersonal, forms of contact with TDs have started to supersede the traditional modes – notably letters, but also to a degree the 'weekly clinics'. This would suggest that while the amount of contact remains as before, perhaps its intensity – or certainly its personal nature – is in decline.

There are notable patterns of variation based on some key demographics. In this election younger citizens were more likely than in previous elections to have contact with TDs. Perhaps again this reflects the growing use of newer modes of contact (especially social media), but it might also be a consequence of prominent online campaigns before and during the election campaign – notably on water charges – or perhaps of the experience of social media use during the 2015 marriage equality referendum (Elkink et al., 2017). There were variations also in the focus of citizen contact with TDs. Dublin and middle-class citizens were more inclined to focus their contact on policy issues than on personal or community issues. Similarly, those of a more 'cosmopolitan' tendency were more likely to focus on policy issues.

On the whole, many Irish voters have a relatively positive attitude towards their politicians, which reflects a benign disposition towards Irish political institutions among citizens generally.[7] In part, this may simply reflect a more general finding that the purported legitimacy crisis in representative democracy is rather more myth than reality (Van Ham et al., 2017), but, more specific to the Irish case, it may have something to do with the still fairly high degree of contact between citizens and politicians in Ireland that we have reported on in this chapter. Having said that, however, there are important variations depending on whether the respondent was a supporter of one of the traditional parties (Fianna Fáil, Fine Gael or Labour) or of a political party that in this election was presenting itself in a more populist hue (Sinn Féin or AAA–PBP): this indicates pockets of dissatisfaction with politicians that may be ripe for the picking in the future.

Notes

1 This might be said to correspond with wider debates over the distinction between globali-zation 'winners' and 'losers' lying at the heart of a new 'integration–demarcation' cleavage (e.g. Kriesi et al., 2008), which may in part help explain the emergence of populist parties. We return to this theme in section 3 below.
2 We cannot be sure whether it is the perception that the area is doing worse that leads to a more localist attitude, or whether the causal relation is in the other direction, or indeed what other factors might be producing these differing views. Nevertheless, as we show below, this localist–cosmopolitan distinction does manifest some striking variations in attitudes towards TDs and their role.
3 This set of questions was also asked in the 2011 INES survey. The results were very similar, with 'same political viewpoint' highest at 5.7 and 'same sex' least important at 2.6. The only difference was that in 2011 'same level of education' was ranked fourth most important, behind same area and same class, whereas in 2016 it overtook these two to become second most important; otherwise the ordering of the criteria was identical.
4 In 2011, in contrast, attitudes in Dublin were much the same as those in Ireland as a whole, with few signs of urban–rural differences on any item.
5 These survey questions were asked in the INES2 telephone poll, whereas the material cov-ered in the previous sections of this chapter used the INES3 telephone poll. This unfortu-nately limits our ability to tease out potential linkages between the themes covered in this section and those in the previous two.
6 For preliminary analysis of international trends on these populism measures in Module 5 of the CSES, see http://cses.org/plancom/2016Philadelphia/CSES_2016Philadelphia_Pretest.pdf
7 Eurobarometer data from November 2016 (reported here: https://ec.europa.eu/COMMFrontOffice/publicopinion/index.cfm/Chart/index) shows that 40 per cent of Irish voters have trust in the government (against an average of 31 per cent among the member states of the EU), 40 per cent trust the parliament (compared with a 32 per cent average among the EU), and 22 per cent trust political parties (compared with the EU average of 16 per cent).

References

Bowler, Shaun and David Farrell. 2017. 'The lack of party system change in Ireland', in Michael Marsh, David M. Farrell and Gail McElroy (eds), *A Conservative Revolution? Electoral Change in Twenty-First-Century Ireland.* Oxford: Oxford University Press, pp. 83–101.

Buckley, Fiona, Yvonne Galligan and Claire McGing. 2016. 'Women and the election: Assessing the impact of gender quotas', in Michael Gallagher and Michael Marsh (eds), *How Ireland Voted 2016: The Election that Nobody Won.* London: Palgrave Macmillan, pp. 185–206.

Buckley, Fiona, Yvonne Galligan. 2018. 'Women in politics', in John Coakley and Michael Gallagher (eds), *Politics in the Republic of Ireland,* 6th ed. Abingdon: Routledge and PSAI Press, pp. 216–39.

Byrne, Elaine. 2012. *Political Corruption in Ireland, 1922–2010: A Crooked Harp?* Manchester: Manchester University Press.

Cowley, Philip. 2013. 'Why not ask the audience? Understanding the public's representational priorities', *British Politics.* 8: 138–63.

Elkink, Johan, David Farrell, Theresa Reidy and Jane Suiter. 2017. 'Understanding the 2015 marriage equality referendum in Ireland: Context, campaign and conservative Ireland', *Irish Political Studies.* 32(3): 361–81.

Farrell, David, and Jane Suiter. 2016. 'The election in context', in Michael Gallagher and Michael Marsh (eds), *How Ireland Voted 2016: The Election that Nobody Won.* London: Palgrave Macmillan, pp. 277–92.

Gallagher, Michael. 2014. 'Politics in Mayo 1922–2013', in Gerard Moran and Nollaig Ó Muráile (eds), *Mayo: History and Society.* Dublin: Geography Publications, pp. 757–80.

Gallagher, Michael. 2016. 'The results analysed: The aftershocks continue', in Michael Gallagher and Michael Marsh (eds), *How Ireland Voted 2016: The Election that Nobody Won.* London: Palgrave Macmillan, pp. 125–57.

Gallagher, Michael, and Jane Suiter. 2017. 'Pathological parochialism or a valuable service? Attitudes to the constituency role of Irish parliamentarians', in Michael Marsh, David M. Farrell and Gail McElroy (eds), *A Conservative Revolution? Electoral Change in Twenty-First-Century Ireland.* Oxford: Oxford University Press, pp. 143–71.

Keenan, Lisa, and Gail McElroy. 2017. 'Who supports gender quotas in Ireland?', *Irish Political Studies.* 32(3): 382–403.

Kriesi, Hanspeter, Edgar Grande, Romain Lachat, Martin Dolezal, Simon Bornschier and Timotheos Frey. 2008, 'Globalization and its impact on national spaces of competition', in Hanspeter Kriesi, Edgar Grande, Romain Lachat, Martin Dolezal, Simon Bornschier and Timotheos Frey (eds), *West European Politics in the Age of Globalization.* Cambridge: Cambridge University Press, pp. 1–22.

Marsh, Michael, and Gail McElroy. 2016. 'Voting behaviour: Continuing de-alignment', in Michael Gallagher and Michael Marsh (eds), *How Ireland Voted 2016: The Election that Nobody Won*. London: Palgrave Macmillan, pp. 159–84.

Marsh, Michael, David M. Farrell and Gail McElroy (eds). 2017. *A Conservative Revolution? Electoral Change in Twenty-First-Century Ireland*. Oxford: Oxford University Press.

Mudde, Cas. 2007. *Populist Radical Right Parties in Europe*. Cambridge: Cambridge University Press.

O'Malley, Eoin. 2008. 'Why is there no radical right party in Ireland?' *West European Politics*. 31: 960–77.

Sacks, Paul M. 1970. 'Bailiwicks, locality and religion: Three elements in an Irish Dáil constituency election', *Economic and Social Review*. 1: 531–54.

Tinney, Deirdre, and Stephen Quinlan. 2017. 'A populist vote in the 2016 general election in Ireland?' Available at https://politicalreform.ie/2017/01/17/a-populist-vote-in-the-2016-general-election-in-ireland/ (accessed 2 June 2017).

Transparency International, 'Corruption Perception Index 2016'. Available at http://issuu.com/transparencyinternational/docs/2016_cpireport_en?e= 2496456/43483458 (accessed 28 March 2018).

Van Ham, Carolien, Jacques Thomassen, Kees Aarts and Rudy Andeweg (eds). 2017. *Myth and Reality of the Legitimacy Crisis: Explaining Trends and Cross-National Differences in Established Democracies*. Oxford: Oxford University Press.

11

Popularity and performance? Leader effects in the 2016 election

Stephen Quinlan and Eoin O'Malley

Introduction: What role for leaders in shaping the vote?

Understanding what motivated Irish voters to vote the way they did in 2016 requires us to go beyond the traditional determinants of voting behaviour and to look at alternative stimuli. In this chapter, we focus on one of these, namely the impact of party leaders on vote choice. A prominent strand of research in political science suggests that party leaders have grown in importance in recent decades, with 'leader centeredness' (Webb and Poguntke, 2013) permeating executive and electoral politics, as well as the media's coverage of it (see also Karvonen, 2010). Electoral scholars were quick to pick up on this noticeable shift in the saliency of leaders. In a seminal article two decades ago focusing on leaders and voting behaviour, Hayes and McAllister (1997: 3) argued that 'election outcomes are now, more than at any time in the past, determined by voters' assessments of party leaders'. To some, this observation might be regarded as blindingly obvious if one thinks of the many leaders worldwide who have at face value, translated their popularity into electoral success: Bob Hawke in Australia, Tony Blair in the United Kingdom and Pierre Trudeau in Canada. Certainly, the authority and responsibility that prime ministers are imbued with increases the likelihood that they influence voters' choices. This has led to the conventional wisdom that party leaders are an essential ingredient, if not the crucial feature, in explaining a party's success or failure at the polls. This account is something which recent comparative research seems to support (e.g. Bittner, 2011; Garzia, 2014; Costa-Lobo and Curtice, 2015).

Ireland has not been immune from expectations that leaders influence voters. Indeed, many of the political dynamics in Ireland lend themselves to leaders being important. Aside from the weakening of the traditional pillars of voting, the STV voting system encourages a personality dimension, allowing for a personal following to develop (see chapter 7 in this volume). Governments of the day can also be identified in the mould of the leader

(Marsh et al., 2008: chapter 6). Television debates during the campaign, which highlight the leader, have become more plentiful in recent elections, playing into the Irish media's tendency towards and interest in personalizing election campaigns (McMenamin et al., 2019).

However, buying into the prevailing narrative that leaders shape the vote overlooks two important things. First, a popular leader does not guarantee electoral success, nor does an unpopular leader prevent a party from winning. For example, Des O'Malley failed to translate his personal popularity into an avalanche of support for the Progressive Democrats in 1987. Conversely, Enda Kenny, a man whom many had ridiculed as personally wooden and professionally inept (Sheehan, 2009), and whose own party had tried to remove for this reason just months earlier, led Fine Gael to its best election performance in 2011. Second, the evidence for leader effects on the vote is mixed. While a recent profusion of studies has highlighted the importance of leaders, the more dominant view in the academic literature has been 'the personality of leaders and candidates matters a lot less, and less often, in elections than is usually supposed' (King, 2002: 220; also see Brettschneider et al., 2006; Gidengil and Blais, 2007). A volume exploring leader effects on voting in eight countries rejected the idea that 'leader centeredness' had permeated voting, finding little evidence of a growing importance of the leader on vote choice over time. The study found the influence of leaders on the vote was, at best, modest (Aarts et al., 2011). Even if we overlook the evidence of limited effects, we also need to consider that pre-existing opinions about parties might contaminate attitudes towards leaders (LeDuc and Price, 1985; Anderson and Evans, 2003). If this is the case, then individual attitudes about leaders may simply be a function of party likeability – i.e. leader effects are driven by attitudes to the party, with attitudes towards leaders simply a by-product of partisanship (Laver, Mair and Sinnott, 1987; Harrison and Marsh, 1994).

Our chapter teases out the impact of the four main party leaders (Enda Kenny of Fine Gael, Micheál Martin of Fianna Fáil, Gerry Adams of Sinn Féin and Joan Burton of Labour) on vote choice in the 2016 election. In doing so, we develop the study of leader effects in Irish elections, which is, for the most part, under-researched (an exception is Marsh et al., 2008). Our goal is three-fold. First, we show who was the most popular leader in the 2016 election. Second, we test whether leader popularity and leader performance in the television debates impact vote choice in a meaningful way. Third, to the extent possible, we try to separate leader effects on vote choice from party effects. In doing so, we make two contributions: to provide an updated and comprehensive account of the impact of leaders on the Irish voter today; and to contribute to the wider debate on leaders and thus offer some views on whether parties are wasting their effort in trying to pick the 'right' leader or not.

Leaders and vote choice: State of the art

There are three key things to bear in mind when taking stock of the academic research on leaders and the vote, namely: the different types of effects leaders can have, the conflicting evidence about such effects and the measurement challenges associated with quantifying leaders' influence. We deal with each of these in turn.

There are two different types of leader effects: indirect and direct (King, 2002). Indirect effects occur where the leader's shaping of his or her party or administration has knock-on impacts. For example, Tony Blair's repositioning of the Labour Party in the centre ground of British politics before the 1997 general election could be classified as an indirect effect. It was not solely Blair himself, but rather his influence in redirecting the party that contributed to its electoral success. While it is undeniable that leaders have potential to shape vote choice indirectly, most of the analysis of leader effects on the vote has concentrated on direct effects. Direct effects imply it is the leader themselves that motivates vote choice with no mediating influence. These influences come in the form of the leader's popularity, their personality traits, their perceived competency on the issues and their performance in television debates and set-piece campaign events.

There is no consensus on the extent of leader effects. The minimalist school of thought assumes that while leaders' personalities provide much colour for the media and may dominate election campaigns, leader effects are secondary to partisanship, opinions of economic performance, and social identities. In an influential study exploring the direct influence of leaders on the vote cross-nationally, King (2002: 216) inferred that of the near fifty elections studied by him and his colleagues that: 'it is possible to say in the cases of scarcely more than a handful that their outcomes probably turned on voters' differing perceptions of the personal qualities and traits of the principal party leaders and candidates'. A collection of chapters edited by Aarts et al. (2011) reached similar cautious conclusions. Evidence from single-country studies has also cast doubt on the leader-vote function (Brettschneider et al., 2006; Gidengil and Blais, 2007).

Conversely, there is the 'leaders matter' school of thought, which proposes that leaders have a substantial impact on voters. Bean and Mughan's (1989) pivotal study of Bob Hawke and Margaret Thatcher's influence on the vote of their respective parties championed the idea that leaders do influence vote choice. Support for this proposition gained traction among some (Wattenberg, 1991; Hayes and McAllister, 1997), and given the decline in the traditional determinant of the vote, there was a revival in the idea that leaders matter. Bittner (2011) focusing on Australia, Britain, Canada, Germany, New Zealand, Sweden and the US, resolved that perceptions of leader character influenced vote choice. Garzia (2014) reached similar conclusions from his analysis of leader influences in Britain, Germany and the Netherlands, noting that their sway is in part dependent on the alternative leaders on offer. More recent work exploring the issue from a comparative and longitudinal perspective concludes there is 'very strong support for the importance of leader evaluations in the vote choices of electorates today' (Costa-Lobo and Curtice, 2015: 247; also see Mughan, 2015). Concurrently, valence models of vote choice (as opposed to either class-based or spatial models of voting) have become more in vogue with their reference to the competence or capacity of those objects to deliver commonly held goals, such as low unemployment or economic growth. The emphasis is less on 'what would you do?' but rather on 'will it work?' or 'has it worked?' The model thus highlights competence, which leads to the focus being put on the parties and leaders best able to deliver commonly agreed goals. The valence model has been successful in accounting for electoral behaviour in various contexts (Clarke et al., 2004; 2016).

Another crucial aspect of leader effects on the vote is how their impact is measured. Direct leader effects may come in varying forms, which might explain some of the divergence in findings in the leader-vote literature: studies are measuring different facets of leadership, and some might matter more than others. For example, studies that have measured voters' perception of character traits of leaders have been the most optimistic about their impact on the vote (Bittner, 2011). Thus, there is a need to be mindful of what dimension of leadership we are measuring and for studies to distinguish clearly. However, even recognizing that there are different facets of leadership does not negate the main methodological challenge that bedevils leader effects – endogeneity. There is a not-unreasonable assumption that partisanship contaminates voters' assessments of party leaders. For example, a Fianna Fáil partisan's attitude towards Micheál Martin is likely to be positive not necessarily because of his assessment of Martin but because of his attachment to Fianna Fáil. Given the high stability in the support levels of the Irish parties up to 2011, it was reasonable to assume that people's assessments of party leaders are more affected by their assessments of the parties, rather than the assessment of the parties being affected by the leader assessments. If this is the case, as some scholars suggest, leader assessments may merely reflect attitudes towards the party, questioning whether leaders, in fact, have an independent effect on their own. However, the volatility of party support since 2011 might leave open the possibility of increased leader effects. Teasing out this relationship is challenging, especially in cross-sectional surveys. Holmberg and Oscarsson (2011: 45) point to this complexity, noting that measuring leader effects on their own probably overestimates their influence, but controlling simultaneously for party might underestimate their impact. Garzia (2014: 21) argues persuasively that the model specifications tend to underestimate the impact of leaders because they misattribute to partisan loyalties that which may be leaders' direct effects. Thus, it is crucial for studies to be clear about what element of leadership they are measuring and also, as far as is possible, to disentangle the impact of leaders from party evaluations.

Leaders and vote choice: The Irish case

Ireland is a country that boasts characteristics that might be conducive to leaders influencing voters: the decline of traditional determinants of vote choice – as evidenced by the growing volatility of elections – and a growing number of television debates during election campaigns. Also, vote choice in Ireland is more nuanced because it is not only first preference votes at stake but lower preferences too. The bigger parties especially have made a conscious effort to attract more transfers, and leaders are sometimes marketed to help them achieve this. For example, Murphy (2014) reflecting on his time as an adviser to former Fianna Fáil leader, Bertie Ahern, recalls that Ahern's popularity was leveraged by the party to attract lower preferences. All in all, the circumstances would seem to be ripe for leader effects to prosper in Ireland.

While a plethora of studies have explored the impact of candidates on the vote in Ireland (Marsh, 2007; Marsh et al., 2008; Marsh and Schwirz, 2016; chapter 7 in this volume), relatively few studies have examined the impact of leaders. Those that exist suggest modest effects at best. In their study of the 1987 general election Laver et al. (1987) found that Charles Haughey was a leader disliked by many outside Fianna Fáil (and indeed some voters for the party), but his party won the election. Seven years later, Harrison and Marsh (1994) concluded that leader effects on party popularity were relatively small. In his review of Irish voting behaviour over an 80-year period, Sinnott (1995) noted that leader effects were especially prominent in the 1982 elections when Charles Haughey and Fine Gael leader Garret FitzGerald went head to head. However, he acknowledged the difficulty in isolating the impact of leaders in other elections and noted that beyond 1982, the effects were likely to have been small (Marsh and Sinnott, 1993: 103–05).

The most authoritative analysis of leader effects in Irish elections was conducted by Marsh et al. (2008) in *The Irish Voter*. In an extensive multivariate analysis of the electorate in the 2002 election, they concluded that leaders were important but were 'far from being the dominant factor' (Marsh et al., 2008: 190). Instead, the impact of party was greater, highlighting that 'where the popularity of leaders and of their parties diverge ... voters follow parties rather than leaders. That is not to say that a popular leader is not an asset, but that the asset is one that makes only a marginal difference to vote totals' (2008: 221). But election campaigns are about marginal differences and if leaders can give a party a one or two-point advantage that could be the difference between governing or not.

The commentary in 2016 suggested that leaders were especially potent on this occasion. Reflecting on the election campaign, journalist Pat Leahy highlighted the central role of leaders, especially the saliency of Micheál Martin to Fianna Fáil. He remarked (2016: 93) 'its posters told the tale: big Micheál, small FF. A party leader hasn't been as influential in a campaign since 1997'. Similarly, there was a sense that Fine Gael's 2016 election setback stemmed from a leadership problem, with a view gaining traction that Enda Kenny's uninspiring election performance dented the party's fortunes (Leahy, 2016). Fears supposedly abounded among TDs, strategists and members, who were concerned that further electoral damage for Fine Gael would accrue were Kenny to remain in place (McConnell, 2016). This election campaign also saw party leaders go head to head on three occasions in television debates, increasing their saliency in the campaign. Could it be, then, that this election was characterized by strong leader effects, to an extent we have never seen before, and which might, in turn, explain in part the extent of electoral change in 2016?

Leader popularity in Election 2016

The first part of our analysis explores which leader was the most popular, our investigation is based on questions included in INES2. Respondents were asked to rate the main party leaders on a 0–10 scale, with 0 meaning they did not at all like the leader in question, and 10 meaning they liked the leader a lot.[1] We collapse these scores into three categories. We classify respondents who scored a leader '0–3' as 'disliking' that leader, those rating them '4–6' as having a 'neutral' view and those rating them '7–10' as having a 'positive' view. To put popularity in 2016 in context, we compare the 2016 likeability scores with the popularity score each leader earned in the 2011 election.

Figure 11.1 displays the leadership ratings given to the four main party leaders in both 2011 and 2016. Looking at Enda Kenny, the story of this election was a huge increase in the proportion of voters disliking the Taoiseach. Forty-two per cent said they 'disliked' Enda Kenny, up 26 points on the proportion saying likewise in 2011. Conversely, his likeability numbers fell by 21 points – with only 24 per cent of voters saying they 'liked' him in 2016. The dislike of Kenny is more notable given that Fine Gael had decided to highlight its leader in this election more so than before. One Fine Gael strategist admitted that its strategy was in part predicated on the idea that voters had 'priced Kenny into the bargain, they knew what they were getting'.[2] The evidence suggests this may have been a miscalculation given Kenny's lack of popularity vis-a-vis 2011. This was recognized by a Fine Gael TD, who remarked post-election that running

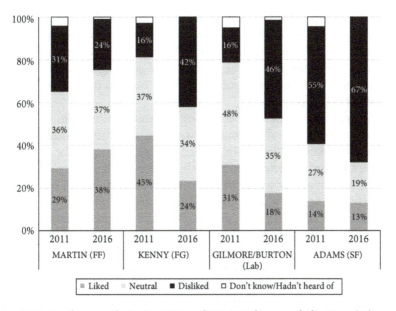

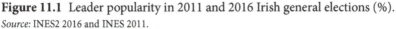

Figure 11.1 Leader popularity in 2011 and 2016 Irish general elections (%).

Source: INES2 2016 and INES 2011.

Note: Voters only. Leaders listed in descending order popularity in the 2016 election. Popularity scores based on an 11-point index. Leaders scored by voters 0–3 are classified as 'disliked'. Leaders scored 7–10 are classified as 'liked'. Leaders scored 4–6 are classified as 'neutral'.

a 'presidential-style campaign when Enda Kenny was the leader was incredibly stupid'.[3]

In contrast to Kenny, the Fianna Fáil leader Micheál Martin was comparatively popular. Thirty-nine per cent of voters 'liked' him, a nine-point increase on the proportion saying this in 2011, while only a quarter 'disliked' him. However, as Figure 11.1 shows, Martin was never that unpopular, even when his party was. In 2011, 29 per cent of voters said they 'liked' him, an impressive score considering the lows Fianna Fáil would fall to in that election, and remarkable as only 6 per cent said likewise about his predecessor, the outgoing Taoiseach Brian Cowen.

The Sinn Féin leader, Gerry Adams, had been a household name for over thirty years and was leading his party into a fourth national campaign.[4] If social media were a barometer of popularity, his status in 2016 was high, for Adams had a following much larger than any other party leader. However, as Figure 11.1 shows, Gerry Adams is deeply unpopular and has been for some time. In 2016, only 13 per cent of voters said they 'liked' him, much the same as 2011. Two-thirds of voters in 2016 expressed a 'dislike' of him, an increase of 12 points on 2011. No other party leader prompts such hostility, and he is the most unpopular leader we have seen since we started measuring leader popularity in this way in 2002. The reasons for this hostility towards Adams are most likely due to his past involvement in the conflict in Northern Ireland and his denials of membership of the IRA. Adams' campaign performances were also criticized, with detractors focusing on his obvious lack of substance and grasp of detail (Minihan, 2016)

Joan Burton was a new leader, having replaced Éamon Gilmore as Labour leader after the party's disastrous showings in the 2014 midterm elections (Quinlan and Okolikj, 2016). Gilmore had been relatively popular in 2011, with 31 per cent saying they 'liked' him and only 15 per cent saying they 'disliked' him. However, his popularity waned in government, with Labour perceived to have rowed back on several policy proposals. Burton's accession to the leadership had been expected to help the party as she was ranked by voters as the most popular cabinet minister in a 2013 survey (Collins, 2013). But as Figure 11.1 shows, the Tánaiste (deputy prime minister) was not all that popular as leader of her party. The ratio of 'dislikes' to 'likes' is 2.5:1 as nearly half of voters (46 per cent) disliked Burton, slightly more than disliked Kenny. Only 18 per cent said they 'liked' her, marginally above the likeability of Adams.

Separating leader popularity from that of the party they lead is a critical element of establishing the true extent of any leader effect. Therefore, there is a need to explore the esteem to which the electorate holds each leader's party and see how this ranks vis-à-vis the likeability of the leader. We do this by comparing the average likeability of the leaders in 2016 with the mean likeability of the parties they lead. We also compare it against the scores achieved in 2011 for

Table 11.1 Average popularity of leaders among voters in the 2016 general election and change in mean rating since the 2011 election

Party	Leader and party	Mean popularity rating among voters in 2016	Change in mean popularity rating since among voters since 2011 election
Fine Gael	Enda Kenny	4.12	−1.78
	Party	5.10	−0.79
Fianna Fáil	Micheál Martin	5.45	+0.65
	Party	5.02	+1.62
Sinn Féin	Gerry Adams	2.59	−0.76
	Party	2.96	−0.40
Labour	Joan Burton	3.77	−1.72*
	Party	4.02	−1.32

Source: INES2 2016 and INES 2011.

Base: Voters only. *=Comparison is with Eamon Gilmore, leader of Labour in 2011.

both the leader and the party, and display the mean change between the two elections. What emerges from this comparison (Table 11.1) is that Enda Kenny lagged his party in popularity. Kenny's popularity dropped much more than that of his party – his mean score was down 1.78 in 2016 compared with 2011, while the Fine Gael drop is 0.79. The analysis confirms that Micheál Martin was the most popular leader, but it shows the gap in popularity between him and his party is lower than expected. The gap between his popularity and that of his party decreased. Thus, the real popularity gain for Fianna Fáil in 2016 was for the party brand rather than the leader himself. For Joan Burton and Gerry Adams, Table 11.1 shows their popularity was relatively close to that of their parties. The story for Burton and Labour is that not only was her party less popular in 2016 compared to 2011 (–1.32), the Tánaiste was much less popular than her party. For Sinn Féin, both its mean party rating and Adams' popularity had fallen back a bit in 2016.

Leaders and vote choice in Election 2016

The real test of the leader-vote function is to establish what direct effect if any, assessments of leaders have on vote choice. As the office of Taoiseach is nearly always held by a party leader, leaders are, in effect, the candidate for Taoiseach. The office of Taoiseach is a powerful one within its own system, and as such, voters might make their choice on this basis. In the past three general elections, exit polls have asked voters *'Which of these was most important to you in making up your mind how to vote in this election?'* with four potential answers including *'Choosing who will be Taoiseach'*. In 2016, only 9 per cent of voters said it was the most important factor, well behind choosing a candidate for the constituency (43 per cent) or choosing between parties' policies (35 per cent). At face value, we might deduce that leaders are in fact not all that important to voters.

Yet media coverage focuses on leaders to a great extent (McMenamin et al., 2019). Leader debates are the set-piece events of modern election campaigns and reinforce voters' focus on leaders. A feature of campaigns in Ireland since 1982, they allow voters to assess the temperament and the policies of party leaders. They are eagerly covered by the media and produce hundreds of column-inches as pundits anticipate a knockout blow or the delivery of a killer line. Such incidents are rare, perhaps because leaders put ever more preparation into them. Despite this, television debates typically gain large television audiences.[5]

The research on the impact of television debates on voters is ambiguous. Evidence from Britain (Pattie and Johnston, 2011), Canada (Blais and Perrella, 2008) and the United States (Druckman, 2003) suggests that they can influence voters decisively. But sceptics argue that debates simply reinforce partisan leanings, with attitudes towards leaders contaminated by pre-existing views which, if anything, debates reinforce (LeDuc and Price, 1985; Warner, 2011). Some highlight cases when strong debate performances from participants failed to translate into support for that candidate, such as Michael Noonan's robust performance in 2002 against Bertie Ahern. While Noonan was judged by most to be the victor (McGee, 2011) he went on to lead Fine Gael to one of its worst performances ever. Detailed research however on the impact of TV debates in Ireland is scant.

There were three leader debates in 2016: two involving Martin, Kenny, Adams and Burton; a third saw the leaders of the small parties, Richard Boyd Barrett for the People Before Profit Alliance, Lucinda Creighton of Renua and Stephen Donnelly of the Social Democrats join the four main leaders.[6] To investigate the impact of the television debates on voters, we turn to INES1 which included two questions on the debates. If television debates are to have a strong impact on the vote, we would expect to see positive performances from leaders result in increased support for their party. We might expect this effect to be particularly potent among non-partisans: their view might be coloured less by existing political inclinations.

We begin by exploring the bivariate relationship between vote and leader performance in the debate.[7] Voters who watched debates were asked who they thought had performed best.[8] Table 11.2 details the behaviour of three different groups – all voters (columns 1 and 2), partisan voters (those close to the leader's party) (columns 3 and 4) and non-partisan voters (columns 5 and 6) – and, for each leader, tells us the proportion of voters in each group who thought that that leader had performed best in the debate and the proportion who voted for that leader's party.[9]

Among all groups, Micheál Martin was judged to have performed best. Overall, 39 per cent of voters ranked his performance top while 38 per cent of non-partisans did too. Not surprisingly, huge swathes of Fianna Fáil partisans also thought he performed well (74 per cent of them judged him best). However, even 25 per cent of Fine Gael identifiers and 27 per cent of Labour partisans judged Martin best. Martin was way out in front of his nearest competitor, Sinn Féin leader, Gerry Adams, whom 10 per cent of voters thought performed best.

Table 11.3 shows, as expected, that partisanship colours attitudes to debate performance: Fianna Fáil, Fine Gael and Sinn Féin identifiers all tended to feel that their party's leader had performed best. But the most important point to emerge from the analysis is how debate performances translate into support at the ballot box. Despite being judged to have performed best, Micheál Martin did not translate all that positivity about his performance into support for Fianna Fáil. Among all voters who felt he performed best, only 43 per cent voted for Fianna Fáil. His capacity to attract the support of non-partisans who rated his performance best was lower, with only 33 per cent voting for Fianna Fáil. Labour's Joan Burton found it equally difficult to translate opinions of a

Table 11.2 Assessments of leader performance in television debates among all voters, partisans and non-partisans and impact on vote choice in 2016 Irish general election (%)

	All voters		Own-party partisans		Non-partisans	
	1	2	3	4	5	6
	Leader that performed best in TV debates	Proportion that thought leader performed best and voted for leader's party	Leader that performed best in TV debates	Proportion of own-party partisans that thought leader performed best and voted for leader's party	Leader that performed best in TV debates	Proportion of non-partisans that thought leader performed best and voted for leader's party
Martin	39	43	74	87	38	33
Adams	10	62	53	93	9	49
Kenny	8	61	30	88	6	46
Burton	5	26	16	100	5	29

Source: INES1 2016.

Base: Voters who reported watching some/either of the debates.

positive debate performance into votes for Labour. Few voters thought she had performed well, but even among those who had, only 26 per cent voted for Labour. Conversely, Gerry Adams and Enda Kenny were far more successful in turning their popularity into votes for their party. Among all voters, 62 per cent who thought Adams performed best voted for Sinn Féin while 61 per cent, feeling Kenny performed best, voted Fine Gael. Martin's apparent lack of success in converting popularity into votes must be balanced by the fact that his broad popularity had an impact on far more voters.

Next, we estimate a series of regression models to discover whether a good debate performance increases the likelihood of a voter voting for the leader's party. We use reported vote in INES1 as our dependent variable.[10] Figure 11.2 plots the impact of good debate performances on voting for the four top parties individually. The symbols represent the likelihood of supporting that party depending on positive evaluations of the leader. The lines around the symbol represent the level of uncertainty for these estimates (the confidence interval). Figure 11.2 shows that even when considering other factors (including partisanship), a good performance in the debate does increase the likelihood of voting for the leader's party. In Micheál Martin's case, it increased the chances of voting Fianna Fáil by 21 points. For Kenny, there was an 18 point increase in the probability of voting Fine Gael, while for Adams and Burton it was 27 and 18 points respectively, though again we should be careful not to assign causality, not to mention a direction to any causality.

In sum, there is evidence to suggest the debates mattered: a good debate performance does have potential to increase support for a leader's party, though it is no guarantee of support. However, there are limits to how much the debates mattered. While Micheál Martin's performance was judged to be the best by almost two in five voters and this increased the chances of these people voting for him, it was no guarantee. In absolute terms, he had great difficulty in ensuring this was a definite vote for Fianna Fáil. Enda Kenny and Gerry Adams, on the other hand, were more adroit at translating perceptions of a good debate performance into support.

Voters vote for the parties of leaders they like, but this appears to be weakest among the most popular leaders. This pattern is confirmed when we probe the impact of a leader being a voter's favourite on vote choice. Table 11.3 shows that Fine Gael and Sinn Féin harvest more votes when their leader is judged as favourite. They gain the support of 82 per cent and 94 per cent of votes from those who rank Enda Kenny and Gerry Adams as their sole favourite leader. Fianna Fáil and Labour do less well, however. Among those rating Micheál Martin as their favourite leader, 62 per cent vote for Fianna Fáil, a good return given that he was the most popular, but less of a return than Fine Gael and Sinn

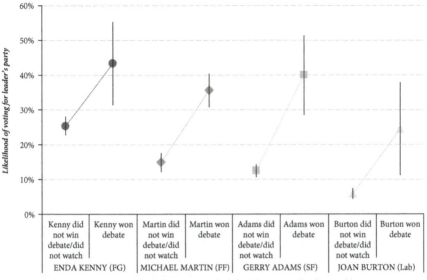

Assessments of the four main party leader's performances in the television debates

Figure 11.2 Average predicted effect of voting for the four main parties dependent on the leader's performance in the television debates.

Source: INES1 2016.

Base: Voters only.

Note: Marginal effects based on logistic regression coefficients and their standard errors. The symbols represent the likelihood of supporting each party dependent on the evaluation of the leader in the debate. The lines around the symbol reflect the 95 per cent confidence intervals.

Féin received. A similar pattern is seen for Joan Burton, with only 56 per cent of voters rating her best voting for Labour, which seems somewhat surprising, but given the small numbers involved these estimates are less robust.

Meanwhile, there is little difference in the likelihood of voting for Fine Gael dependent on whether Enda Kenny was the sole or joint favourite. Kenny delivered votes no matter whether he was the sole or joint favourite. Fine Gael's problem was that few voters ranked him as either. However, this distinction mattered for the other three parties. Much fewer voters voted for Fianna Fáil, Sinn Féin, and Labour when their leader was jointly favoured. The difference is stark for Micheál Martin, who only attracted 36 per cent of support to Fianna Fáil among those who rated him jointly as their favourite. There is a clear message emanating from these analyses: being favourite or classified as the most popular leader is far from a guarantee of a vote, which suggests that something besides leader assessment is at play.

If leaders are the crucial determinant of the vote, we need to separate out feelings towards leaders and the parties which they lead. We will do this in

Table 11.3 Proportion of voters voting for each party dependent on leader popularity

Popularity of each party leader and proportion of respondents voting for the party in 2016 Irish general election	FG	FF	Lab	SF
Voting for party when its leader is the most favoured	82	62	56	94
Voting for party when its leader is jointly favoured	79	36	44	60
Voting for party when its leader is not most favoured	19	13	7	9

Source: INES2 2016.

Base: Voters only.

FF = Fianna Fáil; FG = Fine Gael; Lab = Labour; SF = Sinn Féin.

several ways. Figure 11.3 does this by exploring the behaviour of four different groups of voters: voters who ranked neither the leader nor the party as their favourite, voters who ranked the leader of a party solely as their favourite, voters who rated the party only as their favourite and voters who classified the leader and the party as their favourite (for a similar analysis see Marsh et al., 2008). Bars 2 and 3 are the most interesting in Figure 11.3 as they provide a direct test of voting for a party whose leader you preferred but whose party was not preferred (Bar 2) and voting for the party that was preferred over others, but whose leader was not (Bar 3). Among all four parties, favouring the party yielded more votes (Bar 3 for each party). Among those who ranked Sinn Féin as the most popular party 67 per cent voted for the party, for Fine Gael it was 65 per cent, for Fianna Fáil it was 60 per cent and for the Labour Party, it was 56 per cent. However, among those who favoured solely the leader, the return was far less. Among voters who preferred Gerry Adams or Enda Kenny, 40 per cent and 38 per cent respectively voted Sinn Féin and Fine Gael. The return was much less, however, for Fianna Fáil and Labour. Of those who solely had Martin as their favourite, only 19 per cent voted for his party while for Burton it was only 15 per cent. It reaffirms the pattern that Kenny and Adams were better at translating their personal support into votes, but equally we could say that only those who are strong partisans approve of the leaders. However, more importantly, it strongly suggests that party evaluations are more important than leader assessments for the vote. That is not to discount the impact of leader popularity. It has an impact, even if it is a small impact on its own. Nonetheless, taken together with party popularity (the fourth bars in Figure 11.3) we see that it adds to the votes of parties. Among those who rated both the party and its leader as best, overwhelming majorities voted for the respective parties – for Sinn Féin 97 per cent, for Fine Gael 90 per cent, for Labour 83 per cent and – somewhat less impressive – for Fianna Fáil 73 per cent.

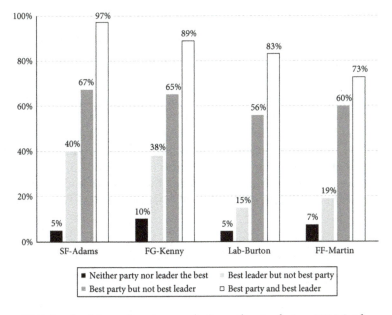

Figure 11.3 Leadership and party popularity and vote choice: 2016 Irish general election (%).

Source: INES2 2016.

Base: Voters only.

Note: Leaders listed in descending order of proportion of the vote won among both leader and party favourite.

We next estimate logit models with reported vote for each party as the dependent variable. This allows us to test leader popularity simultaneously with other factors that influence voting including attitudes to the economy, partisanship, ideology, age, education and region of residence.[11] For completeness, we measure leader effects in three different ways (Mughan, 2015): a *leader favourite* model, which tests the effect of the leader in question being judged the voter's sole favourite (versus not the sole favourite, including if there are ties); a *leader compared* model, which takes into account that leader judgments are likely to be influenced by assessments of the other leaders (Nadeau et al., 1996; Mughan, 2015);[12] and a *leader versus party* model, which is perhaps the toughest test. It specifically tests the impact of leader popularity over party popularity. If leader effects are strong, we would expect that leaders who are more popular than their party will lead to an increased likelihood of the voter opting for that party. This model is tested by subtracting each party's popularity score from the popularity rating of its own leader. Then, the outcomes are dichotomized into a preference for the leader versus the party.

Figures 11.4 to 11.7 plot the impact of these different leader evaluations on voting for the four main parties. The grey bars in each plot represent the number of voters who held this view and are a means of giving us an idea of how potent the impact is in absolute terms. When a leader is judged to be the favourite, it increases the likelihood of voting for his or her party in all four cases. The results were particularly robust for Enda Kenny and Micheál Martin, although stronger for Kenny. Figure 11.4 shows that when Kenny is favoured, the likelihood of voting Fine Gael increases by 27 points. For Martin, the effect is also positive, but more modest: him being judged the favourite leader increases the chances of voting Fianna Fáil by 12 points (see Figure 11.5). The effects are also positive for Adams: when he is judged the favourite leader, the chances of voting for Sinn Féin increase by 54 percentage points (see Figure 11.6). For

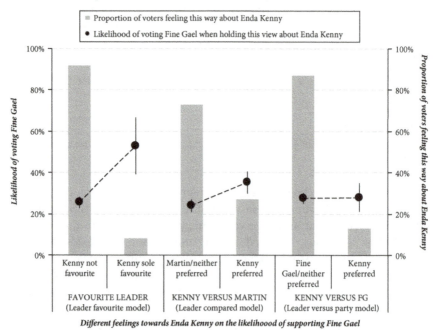

Different feelings towards Enda Kenny on the likelihood of supporting Fine Gael

Figure 11.4 Average predicted effect of voting for Fine Gael, dependent on feelings towards Enda Kenny.

Source: INES2 2016.

Base: Voters only.

Note: Marginal effects based on logistic regression coefficients and their standard errors. The circle symbol represents the likelihood of supporting the party, dependent on the evaluation of the leader. The lines around the symbol reflect the 95 per cent confidence intervals. The grey bars represent the distribution of the variable.

Joan Burton, the effect is smaller: a 16-point increase in the likelihood of voting Labour when voters saw her as their favourite leader (see Figure 11.7). However, the robustness is weaker because few people named either Adams or Burton as their favourites. In sum, being the favourite leader increases the likelihood of voting for the leader's party, but there are clear differences between how much benefit each party receives from this.

Leader comparisons also matter, but primarily it is the comparisons between the Taoiseach and the leader of the opposition that impact on vote choice. Preferring Martin to Kenny increased the likelihood of voting Fianna Fáil by 15 points (see Figure 11.5). Preferring Kenny to Martin worked in Fine Gael's favour, increasing the likelihood of voting for the party by 11 percentage

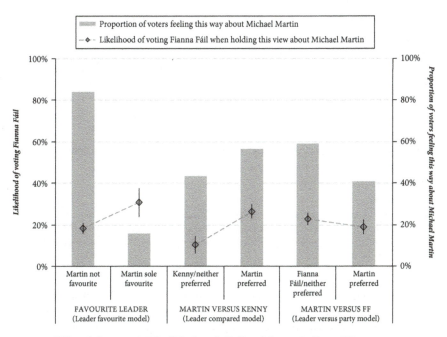

Different feelings towards Michael Martin on the likelihoood of supporting Fianna Fáil

Figure 11.5 Average predicted effect of voting for Fianna Fáil, dependent on feelings towards Micheál Martin.

Source: INES2 2016.

Base: Voters only.

Note: Marginal effects based on logistic regression coefficients and their standard errors. The diamond symbol represents the likelihood of supporting the party dependent on the evaluation of the leader. The lines around the symbol reflect the 95 percent confidence intervals. The grey bars represent the distribution of the variable.

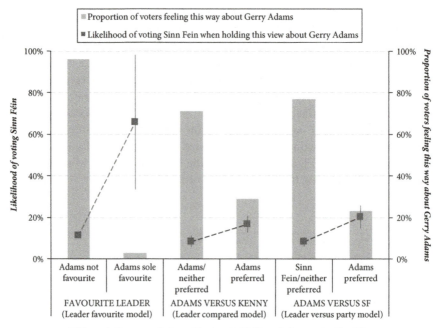

Different feelings towards Gerry Adamson the likelihoood of supporting Sinn Féin

Figure 11.6 Average predicted effect of voting for Sinn Féin, dependent on feelings towards Gerry Adams.

Source: INES2 2016.

Base: Voters only.

Note: Marginal effects based on logistic regression coefficients and their standard errors. The square symbol represents the likelihood of supporting the party dependent on the evaluation of the leader. The lines around the symbol reflect the 95 percent confidence intervals. The grey bars represent the distribution of the variable.

points. However, the effect was more potent for Fianna Fáil in absolute terms, given that more voters preferred Martin to Kenny. The comparative effects for Adams and Burton are much less convincing and robust. While there is some evidence that preferring Burton over Martin increased the chances of voting Labour and preferring Adams over Kenny did likewise for Sinn Féin, the effects are, at best, limited.

When it comes to party favourability compared to leader favourability, it seems preferring the leader as opposed to preferring the party has little impact on the likelihood of voting Fine Gael, Fianna Fáil or Labour. In other words, preferring the leader but not the party did not increase the probability of voting for these parties, which would seem to confirm that leader effects are secondary to party. Only for Sinn Féin do we see a positive effect, with a preference for

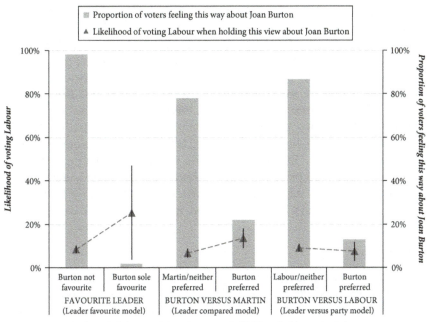

Different feelings towards Joan Burton on the likelihoood of supporting Labour

Figure 11.7 Average predicted effect of voting for Labour, dependent on feelings towards Joan Burton.

Source: INES2 2016.

Base: Voters only.

Note: Marginal effects based on logistic regression coefficients and their standard errors. The triangle symbol represents the likelihood of supporting the party dependent on the evaluation of the leader. The lines around the symbol reflect the 95 percent confidence intervals. The grey bars represent the distribution of the variable.

Gerry Adams over Sinn Féin increasing the likelihood of voting for the party by 12 points. These findings are an important warning: leader effects, while clearly in existence, are muted when we include party ratings.

Leader popularity and vote totals

Leader popularity can influence vote choice but might have little impact on the overall outcome of an election. What is key, therefore, to understand, is how much leaders on their own contributed to the vote totals of each party? Answering this question is not straightforward and there are several ways it can be estimated. We follow the Marsh et al. (2008: chapter 6) strategy of estimating the percentage of the vote that accrues to a party because its leader is ranked as the favourite but not the party. This is a conservative estimate but given the evidence that we have that leader assessments are influenced by party evaluations, we suggest it is warranted. This suggests that about six per cent of Fianna Fáil voters voted for the party based solely on Micheál Martin – about 1.5 percentage points. While not insignificant, it is a small proportion and is much smaller than the proportion of the Fianna Fáil vote attributed to the party brand, which we estimate added five points to the Fianna Fáil vote. The effects of the other three party leaders on their vote are even smaller: Kenny added about 0.9 points, Adams 0.3 points and Burton 0.2 points. This may be an overestimate, as we have no real way of telling who didn't vote for a party because of the leader. This, of course, does not factor in the proportions of voters who voted for a party when they ranked both the leader and party their favourite, and this was substantial for all parties. But evaluating the leader effect in isolation reveals that while they mattered, it was not to a massive extent.

Conclusion

Our study shows that leader evaluations did influence vote choice in the 2016 election. Even controlling for other classic correlates of the vote including partisanship, ideology, perceptions of economic performance and socio-demographics, voters who preferred a leader were more likely to vote for that leader's party. Leader performances in the television debates also mattered: a good performance in the debates increased the likelihood that a voter opted for the leader's party. On this basis, it is tempting to conclude leaders are influential to the vote. However, the story is more nuanced. We should not lose sight of the fact that Micheál Martin was by far the most popular leader in 2016 and he was judged to have performed best in the debates. However, his party came second in votes and seats and failed to form a government. Enda Kenny's popularity slipped back substantially on what it had been in 2011. Nonetheless, his party won the most votes, seats, and formed a government, although in both cases narrowly. Two observations help explain this.

First, while leader effects exist and increase the chances of an individual voting for that leader's party, turning this popularity into a vote is challenging. Micheál Martin had particular difficulty in doing this. Many people who thought he had performed best in the debate voted for another party, and although his popularity was widespread, fewer voters who had this view voted for Fianna Fáil. Thus, his performance in the television debates and his popularity made it more likely a voter would opt for Fianna Fáil, but it was by no means a guarantee. Conversely, Enda Kenny and Gerry Adams were better at translating their popularity into votes, yet neither was that popular in 2016 and so may just have been speaking to a 'base'.

Second, and perhaps more crucially, the attitudes of voters to the party that the leader heads influence their perceptions of the leader. It is a strong sign that partisan bias contaminates attitudes towards leaders. While separating these effects from one another is challenging with cross-sectional data, we have tried to isolate the impact of leader only effects (i.e. as distinct from party assessments). The analysis suggests that leader effects are modest indeed. For example, there were no distinct differences in the likelihood of voting for Fianna Fáil, Fine Gael or Labour when the leader was preferred over the party they lead. Only for Sinn Féin did the effect exist, and this only influenced a small slice of the electorate. Further, when we isolate the impact of leader only effects on vote totals, we also see weak effects. The most popular leader, Micheál Martin, probably contributed less than two percentage points to the Fianna Fáil vote in 2016: notable, but hardly system shattering. Nevertheless, we recognize that small percentage gains for a party can, and did, influence the choices for government formation in 2016, so it would be unwise to infer that these effects are insignificant. Thus, the leaders' impact probably matters enough to make parties' leadership selection and campaign strategies relevant.

Data availability restricted us from exploring the impact of personality traits on the vote, which has been shown to be the most interesting element of leader effects. While future research should examine this in the Irish context, we argue that the popularity measure we use encompasses some of these personality dynamics that voters judge leaders on. In sum, leaders did shape the vote in 2016, and therefore they do matter. However, their impact is much smaller than the extent of media coverage on personality, popularity and performance warrants. The evidence that they were the decisive reason or that they can solely account for the seismic changes in the election or the evolution of the Irish voter remains underwhelming.

Notes

1 The question posed to respondents read: '*After I read the name of party leader, please rate them on a scale from 0 to 10, where 0 means you strongly dislike that candidate and 10 means that you strongly like that candidate*'.
2 Private interview with Eoin O'Malley, 12 June 2016.
3 Private interview with Eoin O'Malley, 30 November 2016.
4 Gerry Adams has been president of Sinn Féin since 1986 but his prominence in election campaigns in the Republic prior to the 2002 breakthrough his party made was minimal.
5 Over 1.1 million watched the final debate on RTÉ, equivalent to a 47 per cent audience share on the evening. People from 66 countries worldwide logged on to the RTÉ Player to watch the programme, which generated over 21,000 live streams (RTÉ, 2016).
6 Stephen Donnelly was co-leader of the Social Democratic party while Richard Boyd Barrett was the nominated person to represent the People Before Profit Alliance in the debate.
7 Sixty-five per cent of voters said they watched some or all of the debates in the 2016 elections.
8 The question posed to respondents read: '*Did you watch any of the televised leaders' debates or not? Who do you feel came out best overall?*'

9 Partisan voters are classified as those who said they felt close to a political party.
10 We estimate four separate logit regression models. Our models control for the impact
    of the respondent's age, education and region of residency; ascribed importance by the
    respondent of the issues of economy, health and water; and partisanship on the prob-
    ability of voting for each party. For specific details of the models, contact the authors.
11 For specific details of the models, contact the authors.
12 To test this, we subtract the leader popularity scores of the opposition leaders (Martin
    and Adams) from Enda Kenny's popularity score and then dichotomize the outcomes as a
    preference for one leader over another. We do the same for Enda Kenny and Joan Burton
    except we compare their scores against Micheál Martin, the main opposition leader.

References

Aarts, Kees, André Blais and Hermann Schmitt. 2011. *Political Leaders and Democratic Elections*. Oxford: Oxford University Press.

Anderson, R., and G. Evans. 2003. 'Who Blairs wins? Leadership and voting in the 2001 election', *British Elections & Parties Review*. 13: 229–47.

Bean, C., and A. Mughan. 1989. 'Leadership effects in parliamentary elections in Australia and Britain', *American Political Science Review*. 83: 1165–79.

Bittner, A., 2011. *Platform or Personality? The Role of Party Leaders in Elections*. New York: Oxford University Press.

Blais, A., and A. M. L. Perrella. 2008. 'Systematic effects of televised candidates' debates', *International Journal of Press/Politics*. 13: 451–64.

Brettschneider, F., K. Neller and C. Anderson. 2006. 'Candidate images in the 2005 German national election', *German Politics*. 15: 481–99.

Clarke, H. D., P. Kellner, M. Stewart and P. Whiteley. 2016. *Austerity and Political Choice in Britain*. London: Palgrave.

Clarke, H. D., D. Sanders, M. Stewart and P. Whiteley. 2004. *Political Choice in Britain*. New York: Oxford University Press.

Collins, S. 2013. 'Joan Burton is the most popular Minister, James Reilly the least', *The Irish Times*, 17 June.

Costa-Lobo, M., and J. Curtice (eds). 2015. *Personality Politics? The Role of Leader Evaluations in Democratic Elections*. Oxford: Oxford University Press.

Druckman, J. N. 2003. 'The power of television images: The first Kennedy-Nixon debate revisited', *Journal of Politics*. 65: 559–71.

Garzia, D. 2014. *Personalization of Politics and Electoral Change*. Basingstoke: Palgrave.

Gidengil, E., and A. Blais. 2007. 'Are party leaders becoming more important to vote choice in Canada', in Hans J. Michelmann, Jeffrey S. Steeves and Donald Clarke Story (eds), *Political Leadership and Representation in Canada: Essays in Honour of John Courtney*. Toronto: University of Toronto Press, pp. 39–59.

Harrison, M. J., and M. Marsh. 1994. 'What can he do for us? Leader effects on party fortunes in Ireland', *Electoral Studies*. 13: 289–312.

Hayes, B., and I. McAllister. 1997. 'Gender, party leaders, and election outcomes in Australia, Britain, and the United States', *Comparative Political Studies*. 30: 3–26.

Holmberg, S., and H. Oscarsson. 2011. 'Party leader effects on the vote', in K. Aarts, A. Blais and H. Schmitt (eds), *Political Leaders and Democratic Elections*. Oxford: Oxford University Press, pp. 35–51.

Karvonen, L. 2010. *The Personalisation of Politics: A Study of Parliamentary Democracies*. Colchester: ECPR Press.

King, A. (ed.). 2002. *Leaders' Personalities and the Outcomes of Democratic Elections*. Oxford: Oxford University Press.

Laver, M., P. Mair and R. Sinnott (eds). 1987. *How Ireland Voted: The Irish General Election 1987*. Dublin: Poolbeg Press.

Laver, Michael, Richard Sinnott and Michael Marsh. 1987. 'Patterns of party support', in M. Laver, P. Mair and R. Sinnott (eds), *How Ireland Voted: The Irish General Election 1987*. Dublin: Poolbeg Press, pp. 99–140,

Leahy, P. 2016. 'Campaign Strategies: How the Campaign was won and lost?' in M. Gallagher and M. Marsh (eds), *How Ireland Voted 2016: The Election that Nobody Won*. London: Palgrave Macmillan, pp. 75–97.

LeDuc, L., and R. Price. 1985. 'Great debates: The televised leadership dates of 1979', *Canadian Journal of Political Science*. 18: 135–53.

Marsh, M. 2007. 'Candidates or parties? Objects of electoral choice in Ireland', *Party Politics*. 13: 500–27.

Marsh, M., and L. Schwirz. 2016. 'Exploring the non-alignment of party and candidate assessments in Ireland: do voters really follow candidates?', in J. A. Elkink and D. Farrell (eds), *The Act of Voting: Identities, Institutions, and Locale*. London: Routledge, pp. 178–91.

Marsh, M., and R. Sinnott. 1993. 'The voters: Stability and change', in M. Gallagher and M. Laver (eds), *How Ireland Voted 1992*. Dublin: Folens, pp. 93–114.

Marsh, M., R. Sinnott, J. Garry and F. Kennedy. 2008. *The Irish Voter*. Manchester: Manchester University Press.

McConnell, D. 2016. 'Fine Gael: A party with two political corpses left in charge', *Irish Examiner*, 8 July.

McGee, H. 2011. 'Leaders' debates: A television history', *The Irish Times*, 28 January.

McMenamin, I. Michael Breen, Michael Courtney, Eoin O'Malley and Kevin Rafter. 2019. *Resilient Reporting: Media Coverage of Irish Elections Since 1969*. Manchester: Manchester University Press.

Minihan, M. 2016. 'Election 2016: Opportunity missed despite success for Sinn Féin', *The Irish Times*, 28 February.

Mughan, A. 2015. 'Parties, conditionality and leader effects in parliamentary elections', *Party Politics*. 21: 28–39.

Murphy, B. 2014. 'The transfer Gospel, according to Bertie', in B. Murphy, M. O'Rourke, and N. Whelan (eds), *Brian Lenihan: In Calm and Crisis*. Dublin: Merrion Books, pp. 159–80.

Nadeau, R., R. Niemi and T. Amato. 1996. 'Prospective and comparative or retrospective and individual? Party leaders and party support in Great Britain', *British Journal of Political Science*. 26: 245–58.

Pattie, C., and R. Johnston. 2011. 'A tale of sound and fury, signifying something? The impact of the leaders' debates in the 2010 UK general election', *Journal of Elections, Public Opinion, and Parties*. 21: 147–77.

Quinlan, S. 2016. 'Identity formation and political generations: Age, cohort, and period effects in Irish elections', in D. Farrell and J. A. Elkink (eds), *The Act of Voting: Identities, Institutions, and Locale*. London: Routledge, pp. 255–75.

Quinlan, S., and M. Okolikj. 2016. 'This time it's different … but not really! The 2014 European Parliament Elections in Ireland', *Irish Political Studies*. 31: 300–14.

RTÉ. 2016. *Audiences for RTÉ's Prime Time Leaders' Debate*. Dublin, IE.

Sheehan, F. 2009. 'FG leader "wooden" in Dáil, admits Bruton', *The Irish Independent*.

Sinnott, R. 1995. *Irish Voters Decide: Voting Behaviour in Elections and Referendums since 1918*. Manchester: Manchester University Press.

Warner, B. 2011. 'Will the "Real" candidates for president and vice president please stand up? 2008 pre- and post-debate viewer perceptions of candidate image', *American Behavioural Scientist*. 55: 232–52.

Wattenberg, M.. 1991. *The Rise of Candidate-Centered Politics: Presidential Elections of the 1980s*. Cambridge, MA: Harvard University Press.

Webb, P., and T. Poguntke. 2013. 'The presidentialisation of politics thesis defended', *Parliamentary Affairs*. 66: 646–54.

Whyte, J. 1974. 'Ireland: Politics without social bases', in R. Rose (ed.), *Electoral Behavior: A Comparative Handbook*. New York, NY: The Free Press, pp. 619–51.

Winham, G. R., and R. B. Cunningham. 1970. 'Party leader images in the 1968 federal election', *Canadian Journal of Political Science*. 3: 37–55.

Appendix

The INES 2016 questionnaires

The Irish National Election Study (INES) 2016 was based on three separate surveys: INES1 2016, which was an exit poll commissioned in partnership with RTÉ (the Irish national broadcaster) and carried out by the market research agency Behaviour and Attitudes; and INES2 2016 and INES3 2016, which were post-election telephone polls carried out by the RED C market research agency.

INES 1 was conducted among a sample of 4,283 voters nationwide, interviewed immediately after they had voted in the general election on Friday, 26 February 2016. The sample was spread throughout all forty Dáil constituencies and undertaken at 223 polling stations, between four and seven per constituency, meaning typically around twenty interviews per polling statation. Interviews were conducted face-to-face with randomly selected individuals throughout the hours of polling from 7.00 am to 10.00 pm. In accordance with the 1992 Electoral Act, no interviews took place within 100 yards of a polling station. Interviewing was continuous throughout each time period. In the event of refusal at contact, the interviewer noted the person's gender, approximate age and social class, and sought to replace that person at the first available opportunity with a person sharing similar demographic characteristics. There were three variations of the questionnaire: version 1 was administered to 1,436 respondents, version 2 to 1,429 respondents and version 3 to 1,418 respondents.

INES2 was carried out by RED C by telephone in the week after the 2016 election: This is the survey that included the Comparative Study of Electoral Systems (CSES) questions. INES3 was carried out by RED C in the second week after the 2016 election. The methodology used in these recall polls was to conduct a quota-controlled sample of 1,000 among a random representative sample of voters who had been called across the twelve polls in the run up to the general election.

The pre-election polls were conducted as follows: A random digit dial (RDD) method was used to ensure a random selection process of households to be included – this also ensured that ex-directory households were covered. Half of the sample were interviewed using an RDD landline sample, with the other half of interviews conducted using an RDD mobile phone sample. This ensured 98 per cent coverage of the population, reaching landline-only households, mobile-only households and those with both a landline and a mobile. Interviews were conducted across the country and the results weighted to the profile of all adults, including age, gender, region, social class and education level. Twelve pre-election polls were conducted, with approximately 65 per cent of respondents agreeing to be re-contacted. This provided the sample pool of 8,000 people polled in the run up to the election, from which to undertake the recall polls. A random contact approach was conducted among the 8,000 leads, again using both mobile and landline approaches. Quotas were set to provide an accurate representation of the population in the final recall poll. Where it was necessary to reach these quotas, new interviews were conducted using the initial RDD approach where leads were not sufficient to complete from those that had taken part in the pre-election polls.

The survey questions and marginals for INES1, INES2 and INES3 are reported in this appendix. All responses are weighted to provide a sample representative in terms of age, class, gender and region. For reasons of space, no demographics are shown.

Behaviour and Attitudes/RTÉ Exit poll questionnaire
19 February 2016

Version 1	Timed:	8.5 mins

Good Morning/afternoon/evening. My name is .... from Behaviour and Attitudes, the independent market research company. We are carrying out a short survey about the general election, for RTÉ. The results of this survey will be broadcast on RTÉ's Election Special programmes.

The interview will be conducted in accordance with Irish and International Market Research Society guidelines, and any information you give will be treated in complete confidence.

INTERVIEWER: PLEASE HAND THE BALLOT PAPER TO THE RESPONDENT

Q.1 The candidates for election **in the general election** are listed on this ballot paper. Please mark the ballot paper giving your order of preference as you have just voted.

Q.2 Did you vote in the last general election in 2011?

Yes – I voted in 2011	87	– ASK Q.3
No – I was too young to vote in 2011	3	
No – I did not vote in 2011	8	} GO TO Q.4
Can't recall	2	

ALL VOTED IN 2011

Q.3 To which party or Independent candidate did you give your first preference vote in the 2011 general election? **DO NOT READ OUT**

Fine Gael	37
Labour Party	12
Fianna Fáil	19
Sinn Féin	11
Green Party	2
Socialist Party	*
People Before Profit Alliance	1
United Left Alliance	*
Independent	9
Other specify _____	1
Don't know	9

Q.4 Thinking about the economy as a whole, do you think that the country is better off, worse off, or about the same as last year?

Better off	46
The same	35
Worse off	19

Q.5 Do you yourself feel better off financially, worse off financially or about the same compared to last year?

Better off	26
The same	48
Worse off	26

IF RESPONDENT VOTED FOR A PARTY CANDIDATE IN Q.1, ASK Q.6 AND Q.7. IF AN INDEPENDENT OR INDEPENDENT/NON-PARTY CANDIDATE, ASK Q.6A AND Q.7A

Q.6 Which would you say was more important in deciding how you just cast your first preference vote – the party or the candidate him/herself?

The party	44
The candidate	53
Don't know	3

Q.7 If your first preference candidate had been running for any of the other parties or groupings, would you still have given a first preference vote to him/her?

Yes	40
No	42
Depends on the party	18

SKIP TO Q.8 IF RESPONDENT DID NOT VOTE FOR AN INDEPENDENT/NON-PARTY CANDIDATE IN Q.1

Q.6A Which would you say was more important in deciding how you just cast your first preference vote – the candidate him/herself or the fact that the candidate was Independent/Non-Party?

The candidate	69
The fact that the candidate was Independent/Non-Party	26
Don't know	5

Q.7A If your first preference candidate had been RUNNING FOR A PARTY, would you still have given a first preference vote to him/her?

Yes	56
No	25
Depends on the party	19

ASK ALL

Q.8 In politics, people sometimes talk of left and right. Where would you place yourself on a scale from 0 to 10 where 0 means the left and 10 means the right?

LEFT								RIGHT			DON'T KNOW (DK)
0 0	1	2	3	4	5	6	7	8	9	10	X
2	4	6	8	10	34	10	9	6	2	3	6

Q.9 Candidate gender quotas for political parties were introduced for these elections to the Dáil. How much do you support the use of gender quotas for national elections on a scale from 0 to 10, where 0 means strongly oppose and 10 means strongly support?

	Strongly oppose								Strongly support			DK
	0 0	1	2	3	4	5	6	7	8	9	10	X
	6	2	3	4	6	25	8	12	10	5	15	4

Q.10 Do you usually think of yourself as close to any political party?

Yes	27	ASK Q.10
No	73	GO TO CLASSIFICATION

IF YES ASK

Q.11 Which party is that? **DO NOT PROMPT. SINGLE CODE ONLY.**

Fianna Fáil	35
Fine Gael	33
Labour	7
Green Party	2
Sinn Féin	19
Independent Candidate	*
Workers Party	*
Socialist Party	1
Anti-Austerity Alliance – People Before Profit Alliance	*
RENUA Ireland	*
Social Democrats	1
Independent Alliance	*
Other (specify)	*
Can't remember/refused	1

Version 2	Timed:	8.5 mins

Q.1–Q.3 asked of entire sample. See above for results.

Q.4 On a scale from 0 to 10, where 0 means you strongly believe that *there should be a total ban on abortion in Ireland* and 10 means that you strongly believe that *Abortion should be freely available in Ireland to any woman who wants to have one*, where would you place your view? **SINGLE CODE ONLY**

There should be a total ban on abortion in Ireland							*Abortion should be freely available in Ireland to any woman who wants to have one*				DK
0 0	1	2	3	4	5	6	7	8	9	10	
8	4	3	5	4	19	7	9	11	4	22	4

Q.5 In terms of the long-term future of Northern Ireland, which would you prefer: Northern Ireland should: **READ OUT. SINGLE CODE.**

Remain in the UK with a direct and strong link to Britain	15
Remain in the UK and have a strong Assembly and Government in Northern Ireland	32
Unify with the Republic of Ireland	36
Other	3
Don't know	14

Q.6 On a scale of 0 to 10, '0' means the government should CUT TAXES A LOT and SPEND MUCH LESS on health and social services, and '10' means the government should INCREASE TAXES A LOT and SPEND MUCH MORE on health and social services. Where would you place yourself in terms of this scale?

SINGLE CODE ONLY

Government should CUT TAXES A LOT and SPEND MUCH LESS on health and social services								*Government should INCREASE TAXES A LOT and SPEND MUCH MORE on health and social services*			DK
0 0	1	2	3	4	5	6	7	8	9	10	11
3	2	2	4	6	31	11	13	11	5	8	5

Q.7 On a scale from 0 to 10, where 0 means you strongly believe that the government SHOULD ACT to reduce differences in income and wealth, and 10 means that you strongly believe that the government SHOULD NOT ACT to reduce differences in income and wealth, where would you place your view?

SINGLE CODE ONLY

The Government SHOULD ACT to reduce differences in income and wealth								The Government SHOULD NOT ACT to reduce the differences in income and wealth			DK
0 0	1	2	3	4	5	6	7	8	9	10	
13	10	8	7	6	21	8	7	8	3	6	3

Q.8 Which of these religious denominations/faiths, if any, do you adhere to?

SHOW CARD

Catholic Church	79
Church of Ireland/Anglican/Episcopal	2
Methodist	*
Presbyterian Church	*
Free Presbyterian	*
Other Protestant (write in _____)	1
Jewish	0
Muslim	*
Agnostic	1
Atheist	4
I'm not religious, although I do consider myself a spiritual person	9
Would rather not say	4

Q.9 How often nowadays do you attend religious services? **SHOW CARD**

Several times a week	5
Once a week	29
Once a month	15
A few times a year	27
Never/hardly ever	24

Q.10 and Q.11 from version one asked of entire sample. See above for results.

Version 3	Timed:	9.5 mins

Q.1–3 asked of entire sample. See above for results.

Q.4 What was the **one issue** or problem that **most influenced** your decision as to how you voted? **PROBE TO PRE-CODES. SINGLE CODE ONLY.**

Q.5 And what issue or problem was the **second most influential** in your decision as to how you voted? **SINGLE CODE ONLY.**

	Q.4 Most Influence	Q.5 Second Most Influence
Crime/law and order	4	6
Management of the economy	18	13
Health services/hospitals	20	16
Mortgage repayment rates/house prices/ cost of rent	1	3
The homeless situation/lack of local authority housing	6	8
Unemployment/jobs	6	9
Water charges	8	9
Childcare	1	2
Abortion	2	2
Issues within my own constituency	6	4
Education	3	4
Taxation/structure of taxation/universal social charge	5	7
Stable government	9	6
Other specify _____	6	5
Don't know	2	7

Q.6 Can you remember exactly when you finally made up your mind about which party or Independent candidate you would give your first preference vote to in this election?

Today/yesterday	15
During the past week	20
2–3 weeks ago/since the election was called	23
Sometime before the election was called	23
Always vote for that party/the same way	18
Can't remember	1

Q.7 There are various ways in which a government might be formed after this election. Which one of these would you prefer? **SHOW CARD – ORDER ROTATED. SINGLE CODE.**

Fine Gael single-party Government	5
Fine Gael and Labour	21
Fine Gael and Fianna Fáil	13
Fianna Fáil and Sinn Féin	5
Fianna Fáil and other parties or Independents	14
Fine Gael, Labour and other parties or Independents	9
Sinn Féin and other parties or Independents	15
Other specify _____	5
Don't know	13

Q.8 Do you think there is likely to be another election in the next twelve months, or not?

Election likely	50
Election not likely	33
Don't know	17

Q.9 Which of these was most important to you in making up your mind how to vote in this election? SINGLE CODE.

READ OUT – ORDER ROTATED	
Choosing who will be Taoiseach	9
Choosing the set of Ministers who will form the Government	13
Choosing between the policies as set out by the parties	33
Choosing a candidate to look after the needs of the constituency	41
Don't know (DO NOT READ OUT)	5

Q.10 Did you watch any of the televised leaders' debates or not?

Yes – watched any TV debate	66
No – did not watch any TV debate	34

IF YES

Q.11   Who do you feel came out best overall? DO NOT PROMPT.

Gerry Adams	10
Joan Burton	5
Lucinda Creighton	3
Enda Kenny	8
Micheál Martin	39
Richard Boyd Barrett	5
Stephen Donnelly	7
No one came out best	23

Q.12 and Q.13, as Q.10 and Q.11 in version 1, asked of all respondents. See above for results.

INES2 2016 questionnaire (RED C)

SECTION A
VOTING INTENTIONS
ASK ALL AGED 18+
Good morning/afternoon/evening. My name is … and I'm calling on behalf of RED C Research, the independent Irish research organization. Today we would like to ask you a few questions about the recent general election, held on Friday 26 February. I am not trying to sell you anything and all your answers will be completely confidential.

Q.1   How interested would you say you are in politics? Are you very interested, somewhat interested, not very interested or not at all interested?

1. Very interested	43
2. Somewhat interested	43
3. Not very interested	9
4. Not at all interested	5

Q.2   And how closely do you follow politics on TV, radio, newspapers or the Internet? Very closely, fairly closely, not very closely or not at all?

1. Very closely	32
2. Fairly closely	49
3. Not very closely	13
4. Not at all	6

Q.3   Please tell me whether you strongly agree, somewhat agree, neither agree nor disagree, somewhat disagree or strongly disagree with each of the following statements:

You feel you understand the most important political issues of this country.

1. Strongly agree	45
2. Somewhat agree	42
3. Neither agree nor disagree	3
4. Somewhat disagree	5
5. Strongly disagree	4

Q.4   Do you strongly agree, somewhat agree, neither agree nor disagree or strongly disagree with the following statements?

In a democracy it is important to seek compromise among different viewpoints

1. Strongly agree	72
2. Somewhat agree	24
3. Neither agree nor disagree	2
4. Somewhat disagree	1
5. Strongly disagree	*

Most politicians do not care about the people.

1. Strongly agree	19
2. Somewhat agree	23
3. Neither agree nor disagree	9
4. Somewhat disagree	26
5. Strongly disagree	24

Most politicians are trustworthy

1. Strongly agree	6
2. Somewhat agree	37
3. Neither agree nor disagree	13
4. Somewhat disagree	23
5. Strongly disagree	21

Politicians are the main problem in Ireland

1. Strongly agree	16
2. Somewhat agree	22
3. Neither agree nor disagree	10
4. Somewhat disagree	28
5. Strongly disagree	24

Having a strong leader in government is good for Ireland, even if the leader bends the rules to get things done.

1. Strongly agree	19
2. Somewhat agree	29
3. Neither agree nor disagree	7
4. Somewhat disagree	18
5. Strongly disagree	27

The people, and not politicians, should make our most important policy decisions.

1. Strongly agree	28
2. Somewhat agree	27
3. Neither agree nor disagree	8
4. Somewhat disagree	23
5. Strongly disagree	15

Most politicians care only about the interests of the rich and powerful.

1. Strongly agree	24
2. Somewhat agree	26
3. Neither agree nor disagree	8
4. Somewhat disagree	26
5. Strongly disagree	17

Poor people should have a greater voice in politics.

1. Strongly agree	43
2. Somewhat agree	28
3. Neither agree nor disagree	13
4. Somewhat disagree	8
5. Strongly disagree	7

Q.5a Now thinking about ethnic minorities: Do you strongly agree, somewhat agree, neither agree nor disagree or strongly disagree with the following statement? Ethnic minorities should adapt to Ireland's way of life.

1. Strongly agree	41
2. Somewhat agree	39
3. Neither agree nor disagree	8
4. Somewhat disagree	8
5. Strongly disagree	4

Q.5b And now thinking specifically about immigrants: Do you strongly agree, somewhat agree, neither agree nor disagree or strongly disagree with the following statements?
B) Immigrants are generally good for Ireland's economy.

1. Strongly agree	25
2. Somewhat agree	46
3. Neither agree nor disagree	12
4. Somewhat disagree	8
5. Strongly disagree	8

C) Ireland's culture is generally harmed by immigrants.

1. Strongly agree	7
2. Somewhat agree	12
3. Neither agree nor disagree	10
4. Somewhat disagree	29
5. Strongly disagree	43

Q.6 Now changing the topic … Some people say that the following things are important for being truly Irish. Others say they are not important.
How important do you think each of the following is: very important, fairly important, not very important or not important at all?
To have been born in Ireland.

1. Very important	22
2. Fairly important	28
3. Not very important	33
4. Not important	16

To have lived in Ireland for most of one's life.

1. Very important	24
2. Fairly important	36
3. Not very important	29
4. Not important	11

To be able to speak Irish

1. Very important	11
2. Fairly important	20
3. Not very important	42
4. Not important	27

To be Roman Catholic

1. Very important	6
2. Fairly important	9
3. Not very important	37
4. Not important	48

To respect Ireland's political institutions and laws.

1. Very important	62
2. Fairly important	29
3. Not very important	5
4. Not important	3

To feel Irish

1. Very important	46
2. Fairly important	37
3. Not very important	12
4. Not important	4
8. Volunteered: don't know	*

To have Irish ancestry.

1. Very important	23
2. Fairly important	28
3. Not very important	31
4. Not important	18

Q.7 Now, onto another topic. How widespread do you think corruption such as bribe-taking is among politicians in Ireland: very widespread, quite widespread, not very widespread or it hardly happens at all?

1. Very widespread	16
2. Quite widespread	33
3. Not very widespread	43
4. It hardly happens at all	8

Q.8 Some people think that the government should cut taxes even if it means spending less on social services such as health and education. Other people feel that the government should spend more on social services such as health and education even if it means raising taxes. Where would you place yourself on this scale, where 0 is 'Governments should decrease taxes and spend less on services' and 10 is 'Governments should increase taxes and spend more on services'?

00. Governments should decrease taxes and spend less on services	3
01.	1
02.	2
03.	2
04.	4
05.	19
06.	11
07.	18
08.	20
09.	6
10. Governments should increase taxes and spend more on services	16

Q.9 Now thinking about the performance of the government in general, how good or bad a job do you think the government did over the past five years? Have they done a very good job? A good job? A bad job? A very bad job?

1. Very good job	10
2. Good job	55
3. Bad job	24
4. Very bad job	11

Q.10a   Would you say that any of the parties in Ireland represent your views reasonably well?

| 1. Yes | 68 |
| 5. No → go to Q.11 | 31 |

Q.10b   <IF YES AT Q.9a>   Which party represents your views best? DO NOT READ OUT. PROBE TO PRE-CODE.

Fianna Fáil	23
Fine Gael	33
Labour	7
Sinn Féin	13
The Green Party	4
Independent Candidate	2
Anti-Water Tax Socialist Party	*
People Before Profit	1
Direct Democracy Ireland	*
Anti-Austerity Alliance	2
Independent Alliance	1
Renua	2
Social Democrats	10
Workers Party	*
Other Party	*

Q.11a   Would you say that over the past twelve months, the state of the economy in Ireland has gotten much better, gotten somewhat better, stayed about the same, gotten somewhat worse or gotten much worse?

1. Gotten much better	13
2. Gotten somewhat better	55
3. Stayed the same	25
4. Gotten somewhat worse	5
5. Gotten much worse	3

Q.11b   Would you say that over the past twelve months, the financial situation of your household has gotten much better, gotten somewhat better, stayed about the same, gotten somewhat worse or gotten much worse?

1. Gotten much better	3
2. Gotten somewhat better	23
3. Stayed the same	54
4. Gotten somewhat worse	14
5. Gotten much worse	5

Q.12P1-a Talking to people about the recent general election on Friday 26 February, we have found that a lot of people *didn't* manage to vote. What about you, did you vote?

1. Respondent voted	90
5. Respondent did not vote	10

ASK ALL THAT VOTED – CODE 1 AT Q.12P1-a. Thinking about how you voted in the general election on 26 February, what party or Independent candidate did you give your first preference vote to?

Fianna Fáil	21
Fine Gael	26
Labour	8
Sinn Féin	12
The Green Party	6
Independent Candidate	14
Anti-Water Tax Socialist Party	*
People Before Profit	1
Direct Democracy Ireland	*
Anti-Austerity Alliance	1
Independent Alliance	*
Renua	2
Social Democrats	5
Respondent cast invalid ballot	*
Volunteered: refused	2
Volunteered: don't know	*

Q.12P3-b Thinking again about how you voted at the general election on 26 February, can you tell me the name of the candidate you gave your first preference vote to? WRITE IN.

Q.12P4 ASK ALL THAT VOTED (CODE 1 AT Q.12P1-a). Can you tell me when you finally made up your mind about who you would vote for? PROBE TO PRE-CODES.

Within 24 hours of voting	21
Within a few days of voting	10
A week before voting	14
2–3 weeks before the election	18
When the election was called	10
Sometime before the election was called	19
I always vote for the same party	8

Q.12P9 ASK ALL. If there was another election in next few weeks/months, to what party or Independent candidate would you give your first preference vote to this time around?

Fianna Fáil	20
Fine Gael	24
Labour	6
Sinn Féin	12
The Green Party	4
Independent Candidate	12
Anti-Water Tax Socialist Party	*
People Before Profit	1
Direct Democracy Ireland	*
Anti-Austerity Alliance	2
Independent Alliance	*
Renua	1
Social Democrats	5
Other party (STATE _____ & CODE)	*
I will not vote if another election is held	3
Refused	1
Don't know	7

Q.13a　I would now like you to think back, very carefully, to elections in the past, specifically the general election held five years ago in February 2011 we have found that a lot of people *didn't* manage to vote. What about you, did you vote?

1. Respondent voted	84
5. Respondent did not vote	10
6. Ineligible to vote	6
8. Don't know	*

ASK ALL THAT VOTED – CODE 1 AT Q.13-a. Thinking again about the general election held five years ago in February 2011: Can you tell me the party or Independent candidate you actually gave your first preference to at the polling station?
PROMPT IF NECESSARY; Was it Fianna Fáil, Fine Gael, Labour, Sinn Féin, the Green Party, an Independent candidate or some other party?

Fianna Fáil	14
Fine Gael	44
Labour	16
Sinn Féin	8
The Green Party	3
Independent candidate	9
Other Party (STATE _____ & CODE)	1
Volunteered: refused	*
Volunteered: don't know	5

Q.14　Some people say that, no matter who people vote for, it won't make any difference to what happens. Others say that who people vote for can make a big difference to what happens. Using a scale where ONE means that voting won't make any difference to what happens and FIVE means that voting can make a big difference to what happens, where would you place yourself?

1. Who people vote for won't make any difference	4
2.	5
3.	13
4.	23
5. Who people vote for can make a big difference	55

Q.15 I'd like to know what you think about each of our political parties. After I read the name of a political party, please rate it on a scale from 0 to 10, where 0 means you strongly dislike that party and 10 means that you strongly like that party. If I come to a party you haven't heard of or you feel you do not know enough about, just say so.

The first party is Fine Gael.

Using the same scale, where would you place Fianna Fáil?

Using the same scale, where would you place Sinn Féin?

Using the same scale, where would you place Labour?

Using the same scale, where would you place Green?

Using the same scale, where would you place Social Democrats?

Using the same scale, where would you place Anti-Austerity Alliance – People Before Profit?

	FG	FF	SF	LAB	GRN	SD	AAA/PBP
00. Strongly dislike	11	11	34	14	10	7	17
01.	5	4	10	7	6	5	12
02.	8	7	10	11	8	8	9
03.	8	11	8	11	9	9	9
04.	11	10	7	11	11	9	12
05.	13	15	8	16	20	14	8
06.	9	12	5	10	11	10	6
07.	11	11	5	9	10	9	5
08.	13	10	5	6	7	8	1
09.	4	4	3	2	3	5	2
10. Strongly like	8	6	5	2	3	3	3
96. Haven't heard of party	*	*	*	*	1	3	3
97. Volunteered: refused	*	*	*	*	*	1	*
98. Don't know enough about/don't know where to rate	*	*	1	1	4	11	5

Q.16 And what do you think of the party leaders? After I read the name of the party leader, please rate them on a scale from 0 to 10, where 0 means you strongly dislike that candidate and 10 means that you strongly like that candidate. If I come to a presidential candidate/party leader you haven't heard of or you feel you do not know enough about, just say so.

The first is Enda Kenny.
Using the same scale, where would you place Micheal Martin?
Using the same scale, where would you place Joan Burton?
Using the same scale, where would you place Gerry Adams?
Using the same scale, where would you place Eamon Ryan?
Using the same scale, where would you place Stephen Donnelly?
Using the same scale, where would you place Richard Boyd Barrett?

	KENNY	MARTIN	BURTON	ADAMS	RYAN	DONNELLY	BARRETT
00. Strongly dislike	18	7	18	35	7	5	14
01.	7	4	7	12	4	2	7
02.	11	6	11	12	8	4	10
03.	7	7	10	7	8	6	9
04.	11	9	11	7	9	7	8
05.	12	15	12	9	15	9	11
06.	12	13	11	4	11	8	8
07.	10	13	10	5	9	8	5
08.	8	12	4	3	7	10	7
09.	2	5	1	2	1	6	3
10. Strongly like	3	7	1	4	3	4	2
96. Haven't heard of party	*	1	2	*	9	17	8
98. Don't know enough about/ don't know where to rate	*	1	1	1	10	15	9

Q.17 In politics, people sometimes talk of left and right. Where would you place Fine Gael on a scale from 0 to 10 where 0 means the left and 10 means the right?
Using the same scale, where would you place Fianna Fáil?
Where would you place Sinn Féin?
Where would you place Labour?
Where would you place the Green Party?

Where would you place the Social Democrats?
Where would you place the Anti-Austerity Alliance – People Before Profit?

	FG	FF	SF	LB	GRN	SD	AAA/PBP
00. Left	4	4	14	6	5	7	21
01.	1	1	9	2	3	4	19
02.	2	2	14	6	6	11	15
03.	3	2	16	12	11	16	11
04.	3	5	14	19	17	16	5
05.	11	15	12	24	28	15	7
06.	14	16	3	9	10	7	3
07.	18	19	3	5	5	5	2
08.	17	15	1	3	3	2	3
09.	8	6	1	1	*	*	*
10. Right	11	8	2	2	2	1	2
95. Volunteered: haven't heard of left–right	7	7	7	8	7	7	8
96. Volunteered: haven't heard of party	*	*	*	*	*	1	1
97. Volunteered: refused	1	1	2	1	3	5	3

Q.18 Where would you place yourself on this scale?

00. Left	2
01.	1
02.	3
03.	8
04.	10
05.	23
06.	14
07.	15
08.	8
09.	1
10. Right	5
95. Volunteered: haven't heard of left–right	7
97. Volunteered: refused	1

Q.21 On the whole, are you very satisfied, fairly satisfied, not very satisfied or not at all satisfied with the way democracy works in Ireland?

1. Very satisfied	13
2. Fairly satisfied	51
4. Not very satisfied	25
5. Not at all satisfied	11

Q.22a Do you usually think of yourself as close to any particular party?

1. Yes → GO TO Q.22c	30
5. No	69

Q.22b Do you feel yourself a little closer to one of the political parties than the others?

1. Yes	52
5. No → GO TO QUESTION AFTER Q.22d	47

Only ask respondents who answered 'YES' in Q.22a or Q.22b

Q.22c Which party do you feel closest to?

	Yes to Q.22A	Yes to Q.22B
Fianna Fáil	28	25
Fine Gael	33	31
Labour	9	8
Sinn Féin	16	13
The Green Party	5	5
Independent Candidate	1	1
People Before Profit	2	1
Anti-Austerity Alliance	1	3
Renua	1	1
Social Democrats	4	12

Only ask respondents who mentioned a party in Q.22c

Q.22d   Do you feel very close to this party, somewhat close, or not very close?

1. Very close	19
2. Somewhat close	66
3. Not very close	15

INES3 2016 questionnaire (RED C)

SECTION A
VOTING INTENTIONS
ASK ALL AGED 18+
Good morning/afternoon/evening. My name is ... and I'm calling on behalf of
RED C Research, the independent Irish research organization. Today we would
like to ask you a few questions about the recent general election, held on Friday
26 February. I am not trying to sell you anything and all your answers will be
completely confidential.

Q.1P1-a Talking to people about the recent general election on Friday 26 February,
we have found that a lot of people *didn't* manage to vote. What about you,
did you vote?

1. Respondent voted	90
5. Respondent did not vote	10
6. Volunteered: respondent not registered to vote	*

ASK ALL THAT VOTED – CODE 1 AT Q.1P1-a.

Q.1P2-b Thinking about how you voted at the general election on 26 February, what
party or Independent candidate did you give your first preference vote to?

Fianna Fáil	21
Fine Gael	26
Labour	8
Sinn Féin	10
The Green Party	5
Independent Candidate	17
Anti-Water Tax Socialist Party	*
People Before Profit	1

Direct Democracy Ireland	*
Anti-Austerity Alliance	2
Independent Alliance	*
Renua	1
Social Democrats	4
Workers Party	*
Other Party (**STATE** _____ **&** **CODE**)	1
Volunteered: invalid ballot	*
Refused	1
Don't know	1

Q.1P3-b Thinking again about how you voted at the general election on 26 February, can you tell me the name of the candidate you gave your first preference vote to?

Q.2a Did you contact any TDs from your constituency in the 12 months before the election?

Yes	16
No	84

(If Yes at Q.2a) Q.2b. Did you contact them about a matter of national policy, about a matter that concerns the community where you live or about a matter personal to you or your family? MULTICODE.

National policy	29
Community where you live	41
A matter personal to you or your family	40

(If Yes at Q.2): Q.2c. How was this contact made? Probe to Pre-Codes

Letter	7
Phone	35
Visit to a TDs' constituency office	24
Email	37
Social media	12
Other (specify) _____	0

Q.3. To what extent would you agree or disagree with the following statement? Please use a scale of strongly agree / agree / neither / disagree / strongly disagree. I find the things that happen directly in my local area more interesting than news about national and international developments.

Strongly agree	10
Somewhat agree	24
Neither	14
Somewhat disagree	37
Strongly disagree	15

Q.4 When thinking about the work of a TD, how important, if at all, are the following aspects of their work? Please use a 5-point scale where 1 = of little importance and 5 = of great importance. ROTATE. ALLOW DK.

	Mean importance score (out of 5)
Working on legislation	4.0
Raising awareness of important social needs and interests	4.0
Developing policies	3.9
Getting as much for their constituency from the government as possible	3.3
Balancing different interests in society	3.7
Representing the individual interests of individual citizens	2.8

Q.5 How much do you feel that you know about the way in which the Dáil works and operates on a daily basis? Would you say you know a lot, a fair amount, some, very little or nothing? SINGLE CODE.

A lot	16
A fair amount	38
Some	26
Very little	16
Nothing	4

Q.6a Which of the following, if any, would be your preferred way of receiving information about the Houses of the Oireachtas? SINGLE CODE. READ OUT.

Newspapers	22
TV	28
Radio	15
Oireachtas TV	4
Oireactas.ie	3
Social media	23
None of the above	5

Q.6b And which of the following, if any, would be other ways you might like to receive information? MULTICODE. READ OUT. ONLY SHOW THOSE NOT MENTIONED IN Q.6A.

Newspapers	40
TV	39
Radio	38
Oireachtas TV	12
Oireactas.ie	12
Social media	23
None of the above	5

Q.7a Candidate gender quotas for political parties were introduced for these elections to the Dáil. How much do you support the use of gender quotas for national elections on a scale from 0 to 10, where 0 means strongly oppose and 10 means strongly support?

Strongly oppose								Strongly support			DK
0	1	2	3	4	5	6	7	8	9	10	X
13	2	4	5	4	19	8	10	11	3	20	1

Q.7b And using the same scale, how much would oppose or support a strengthening of these measures?

Strongly oppose								Strongly support			DK
0	1	2	3	4	5	6	7	8	9	10	X
14	3	6	7	5	21	8	9	9	2	17	1

Q.8 In politics, people sometimes talk of left and right. Where would you place yourself on a scale from 0 to 10, where 0 means the left and 10 means the right?

Left								Right			DK
0	1	2	3	4	5	6	7	8	9	10	
6	1	3	8	12	30	9	12	7	2	6	1

Volunteered: haven't heard of left–right: 3.

Q.9 Do you think the difference in income between rich and poor people in Ireland today is larger, smaller or about the same as fifteen years ago, around the year 2000?

Much larger	38
Somewhat larger	32
About the same	22
Somewhat	5
Much smaller	3
DK	1

Q.10 The unemployment rate in Ireland has varied between 4 per cent and 17 per cent between the early 1980s and today. The average unemployment rate during that time was 11 per cent. As far as you know, what is the current rate of unemployment? That is, of the adults in the Republic who wanted to work during the last week of February, what percent of them would you guess were unemployed and looking for a job?

Record % answer.

AVERAGE 13%

Q.11 Suppose a rich person has a Euro, and a poor person has a Euro. How many cents in that Euro should be taken out in tax?

Rich person, 70 cents; poor person, 25	17
Rich person, 55 cents; poor person, 25	38
Rich person, 40 cents; poor person, 25	36
Rich person, 25 cents; poor person, 25	9

Q.12 Now, please can you indicate, using a 0 to 10 scale, how important each of the following is, where 0 means not at all important and 10 means very important. All other things being equal, how important do you think it is that your TD ...

	Mean importance score (out of 10)
Has the same political viewpoint as you?	6.1
Is of the same sex as you?	1.7
Is from the same area as you?	4.7
Is from the same social class as you?	4.0
Has the same religious views that you have?	2.3
Is of approximately the same age as you?	2.4
Has the same level of education that you have?	4.8

Q.13a During the campaign, did a party, candidate or political organization contact you about voting for a particular party or candidate?

Yes	73
No	26
Don't know/can't recall	*

IF YES AT Q.13a, ANSWER Q.13b; OTHERS GO TO Q.14.

Q.13b How did they contact you? MULTICODE. PROBE TO PRE-CODE.

In person	81
By mail or phone	54
By text	3
By email, or through a social networking site	8
Other specify	7

Q.14 During the campaign, did you see information about any TD or political party via any of the following online means?

	Yes
Search engines (Google, Yahoo, Bing etc.)	29
On a social networking site (Facebook, myspace etc.)	48
Online video platforms (youtube, Vimeo, etc.)	24
Online news sources (irishtimes.ie, RTE.ie, Independent.ie etc.)	65

Q.15 I am now going to read out a number of statements covering a range of different areas and topics. Thinking about each, can you please use a scale of strongly agree / agree / neither / disagree / strongly disagree.

	SA	A	Neither	D	SD
I would be willing to pay much higher taxes in order to protect the environment	7	36	14	30	12
Ordinary working people get their fair share of the nation's wealth	8	22	8	40	21
People with disabilities should receive financial support directly, rather than payments being given to non-government organizations and service providers	35	41	12	10	2
I would be willing to pay much higher taxes in order to provide the money for better public services	13	43	9	25	10
Members of the Travelling community should be formally recognized as having a distinct ethnicity	13	34	13	24	14
Introducing supervised injection centres in Ireland would help to tackle the problem of drug addiction	21	45	13	14	6
Racial and cultural diversity in Ireland now makes it a better place to live	23	50	11	12	3

* UP to 1% DK on each item.

Q.16 I will now read out some more statements. Thinking about each, can you again please use a scale of strongly agree / agree / neither / disagree / strongly disagree.

	SA	A	Neither	D	SD
There is nothing wrong with some people being a lot richer than others	13	54	9	17	7
In general, things would improve if there were more women in politics	16	40	24	17	3
People should not have to put up with Travellers' halting sites in their neighbourhood	13	30	18	31	9
The assumption that TDs should provide a local service is a strength of the Irish political system	11	51	9	20	9
There should be very strict limits on the number of non-EU immigrants coming to live in Ireland	19	37	11	25	8
The presence of large international companies is good for the Irish economy	36	54	5	4	1

Q.17 We have a number of political parties in Ireland, each of which would like to get your vote. How probable is it that you will ever give your first preference vote to the following parties? Please use the numbers on this scale to indicate your views, where 1 means not at all probable and 10 means very probable. ALLOW DK. READ OUT. ROTATE ORDER.

	Mean score (out of 10)
Fianna Fáil	5.3
Fine Gael	5.4
Labour	4.5
Sinn Féin	3.2
Independent candidate	6.2

Q.18 Thinking back over the last five years – the lifetime of the 2011–2016 Fine Gael/Labour government – would you say that the economy in Ireland over that period of time got a lot better, a little better, stayed the same, got a little worse or got a lot worse? SINGLE CODE.

Got a lot better	30
Got a little better	51
Stayed the same	7
Got a little worse	5
Got a lot worse	6
DK	0

ASK ALL CODE 1–5 AT Q.18. IF DON'T KNOW AT Q.18 – SKIP TO Q.20.

Q.19 Do you think this was MAINLY due to the policies of that government or NOT MAINLY DUE to the policies of that government? SINGLE CODE.

Mainly due to the policies of that government	60
Not mainly due to the policies of that government	38
DK	2

Q.20 I would like you to think about changes in the economy in the area around here since the general election five years ago. Do you think your area has been doing better than the rest of the country, the same as the rest of the country or worse than the rest of the country?

Better	21	51
About the same	46	7
Worse	33	5
DK	1	6

Q.21 And how about the financial situation of your household over the last five years? Has that gotten got a lot better, a little better, stayed the same, got a little worse or got a lot worse? ALLOW DK.

Got a lot better	4
Got a little better	26
Stayed the same	35
Got a little worse	22
Got a lot worse	12
DK	*

Q.22 Before the 2011 GE, promises were made by each of the parties who afterwards formed the government. On the whole, how far did each party do what it had promised?
A. So, Fine Gael, did they…
B. And Labour, did they…

	Fine Gael	Labour
Do more or less as promised	10	8
Do some of what they promised	48	30
Do very little of what was promised	34	42
Do none of what was promised	6	18
DK	2	2

Q.23 I am going to read some statements that describe people. Please indicate whether you completely agree, somewhat agree, somewhat disagree or completely disagree with each of the statements. I…

	CA	SA	SD	CD
1 … am reserved	19	41	22	17
2 … am generally trusting, believe in the good in people	48	44	6	2
3 … tend to be lazy	5	17	24	54
4 … am relaxed, handle stress well	31	44	18	7
5 … have few artistic interests	19	30	24	26
6 … am outgoing, sociable	52	37	8	3
7 … tend to find fault with others	7	31	37	24
8 … do a thorough job	61	32	4	2
9 … get nervous easily	11	24	29	36
10 … have an active imagination	34	44	14	8

- Up to 1% DK on each answer

Index